Macroeconomic Policy in the European Monetary Union

This book collects contributions of distinguished researchers from different European countries and institutions which offer the reader a multifaceted assessment of the implementation of macroeconomic policies in the Euro zone five years after the launch of the common currency. Albeit this volume has a larger scope – how economic policy works inside a monetary union – it is very much focused on the functioning of fiscal policy under the Stability and Growth Pact (SGP).

The book begins by sketching a unified conceptual framework, providing the reader with a benchmark with which the conclusions of the individual chapters can be evaluated. The overall assessment is mixed. The SGP is considered both as an opportunity to strengthen macroeconomic stability across the countries belonging to the Euro area, and as an ill-designed institutional device to combine fiscal discipline with effective stabilization at the national level. The critical elements that emerge from the analyses presented here concern the monetary and fiscal policy-mix, the evolution and control of fiscal aggregates over the business cycle and their implications for the SGP rules, the accountability of debt evolution, the financial spill-over of national fiscal policies, and the measurement and assessment of automatic stabilizers. Through stressing country heterogeneity and considering how the size of the country impinges on the effectiveness of fiscal policy, these essays go some way in broadening the interpretative focus of the pros and cons of the SGP.

This book will be of great interest to students and researchers engaged with macroeconomic stabilization and monetary and fiscal policy interactions, as well as professionals in the public sector and the financial institutions of the EU.

Francesco Farina is a Professor of Economics at the University of Siena.

Roberto Tamborini is Head of the Department of Economics at the University of Trento.

Routledge Studies in the European Economy

Macroeconomic Policy in the European Monetary Union

From the old to the new Stability
and Growth Pact

Edited by
Francesco Farina and
Roberto Tamborini

LONDON AND NEW YORK

First published 2008
by Routledge
2 Park Square, Milton Park, Abingdon, Oxon OX14 4RN

Simultaneously published in the USA and Canada
by Routledge
270 Madison Ave, New York, NY 10016

*Routledge is an imprint of the Taylor & Francis Group,
an informa business*

© 2008 Selection and editorial matter, Francesco Farina and
Roberto Tamborini; individual chapters, the contributors

Typeset in Times New Roman by
Newgen Imaging Systems (P) Ltd, Chennai, India
Printed and bound in Great Britain by
Biddles Digital, King's Lynn

British Library Cataloguing in Publication Data
A catalogue record for this book is available from the British Library

Library of Congress Cataloging in Publication Data
A catalog record for this book has been requested

ISBN10: 0–415–42900–5 (hbk)
ISBN10: 0–203–93453–9 (ebk)

ISBN13: 978–0–415–42900–9 (hbk)
ISBN13: 978–0–203–93453–1 (ebk)

Contents

Figures

x   *Figures*

Tables

Contributors

M. Catenaro, *European Central Bank*

J. Creel, *OFCE*, *Paris*

F. Farina, *Univeristy of Siena*, *Italy*

E. Gaffeo, *University of Trento*, *Italy*

J. Le Cacheux, *OFCE*, *Paris*

J. Mélitz, *University of Strathclyde*, CREST-INSEE, and CEPR

R. Morris, *European Central Bank*

A. Muscatelli, *University of Glasgow*, *UK*

G. Passmani, *University of Trento*, *Italy*

R. Ricciuti, *University of Florence*, *Italy*

T. Ropele, *University of Milan – Bicocca*, *Italy*

F. Saraceno, *OFCE*, *Paris*

S. Schiavo, *University of Trento*, *Italy*

R. Tamborini, *University of Trento*, *Italy*

P. Tirelli, *University of Milan – Bicocca*, *Italy*

1 Introduction

F. Farina and R. Tamborini

On 1 January 2007, the euro celebrated its fifth anniversary of circulation as the single currency of twelve countries of the European Union (EU). On the same day, the euro club welcomed the thirteenth country, Slovenia. The protracted and sometimes confused debate on the costs and benefits of a single currency, on Europe as an optimum currency area, and on the accession parameters has become a matter for the historians. The task now is to understand the extent to which the common monetary house is robust, well-designed and in line with the aspirations of the citizens who inhabit it.

This book collects contributions of distinguished researchers from different European countries and institutions who met at the conference series organized by the Jean Monnet Chair in 'European Macroeconomics' at the University of Siena (Italy) in 2004–6. The contributions selected for this book focus on economic policy in the context of macroeconomic stabilization goals in the European Monetary Union (EMU). Taking stock of the long-lasting debate about the pros and cons of the design of the EMU, the general aim of the book is to provide the reader with a multifaceted assessment of the *implementation* of macroeconomic policies in the euro zone and of their effects five years after the inception of the euro.

The state of affairs

On the fifth anniversary, the press has given prominence to opinion polls about the citizens' sentiments towards the euro. An example, drawn from the Eurobarometer survey, is provided by Table 1.1, reporting on the perceived cost-benefit balance after adoption of the euro.

The picture is not particularly rosy, both in absolute terms (only 48% of the EMU citizens strike a positive cost-benefit balance) and in terms of trend over time (the percentage was 51 one year earlier). The most significant item on the cost side of the balance is the rise in the general price level (81% of respondents); at some distance followed by difficulties in adaptation and use (19%), higher unemployment (7%) and loss of sovereignty (5%).

The opinion of academics is well represented by Charles Wyplosz (2006), who sees some 'dark sides' in a 'major success'. Interestingly, the academic ranking of discontent is almost the reverse of that of the general public: low and stable inflation

Table 1.1 Percentage of respondents for whom the benefits of
the euro are greater than the costs

	2006	2005
Ireland	75.4	72.0
Finland	64.7	67.0
Luxemburg	63.8	77.0
Austria	62.3	54.0
Belgium	58.4	68.0
Spain	54.6	61.0
France	51.0	57.0
EURO 12	48.0	51.0
Germany	46.0	47.0
Portugal	42.7	45.0
Italy	41.4	43.0
Netherlands	38.4	38.0
Greece	38.0	39.0

Source: Eurobarometer.

is ranked high on the positive side of the balance sheet; problems of acquaintance with the new currency are not even mentioned. The poor performance of the euro area in terms of growth and job creation is not charged to the single currency. On the other hand, prominent on the negative side of the balance sheet are some flaws in the institutional design of the area. These concern the transparency and accountability of the European Central Bank (ECB), and the trembling Stability and Growth Pact (SGP). As a matter of fact, the only major setback in the general functioning of the euro area in these five years has occurred at this junction, namely the suspension of the SGP excess deficit procedure obtained by Germany and France in November 2004 in opposition to the Commission's recommendation.

This event reminds us that, eventually, the most important opinions remain those of the political forces that alternate in power in the EMU sovereign states. These opinions, however, are not easily intelligible, and may be revealed more by deeds than words. In this respect we can only say that the SGP crisis is a representation of a more general tension in the EU among the three key actors on the stage of democracy: elected governments, public opinion and technocrats (Fitoussi, 2002). This tension has been tangible throughout the entire history of the EMU, from the Delors Report and the Maastricht Treaty, to the adoption of the SGP and the choice of the first group of euro countries (Wyplosz, 2006; Tamborini and Targetti, 2005). This complex triangle cannot be reduced to the caricature of 'good guys' (economists and technocrats) vs. 'bad guys' (governments) as is often perceived from economic analyses and prescriptions. Whatever the economists' opinion may be, the dissatisfaction of the majority of the public opinion with the euro, and with the EU more generally (as witnessed by the rejections of the 'constitutional' draft in different countries) can hardly be overemphasized when assessing finer institutional and operational aspects of the EMU. And if economists may, with some reason, wish to refrain from being involved in these matters, they should be aware that 'politics' amounts to much more than a white noise in models and forecasts.

Hence, introductorily we wish to remind the broader scenario where this epoch-making *political* creature should be framed, though what the reader will find in this book is a collection of self-contained, mostly empirical, economic analyses of the first five years of EMU and its prospects.

First and foremost, the EMU represents a major change in the 'political-economic regime' for its member countries.[1]

[1]By 'political-economic regime' we mean the set of constraints, goals and opportunities that face private and public agents in a given economic system. The liberalization of the circulation of goods, capitals and individuals, the adoption of a single currency and the devolution of monetary sovereignty to an independent supranational institution, the introduction of a common 'economic constitution' in the form of the Treaty of Maastricht, and self-imposed fiscal rules through the SGP, all have yielded profound consequences not only on economic magnitudes and structures but also on the economic institutions.

Following these changes, the EMU countries are shifting from a well-defined and consolidated political-economic regime – what we may call the *international regime* – to one still incipient, uncertain in shape, and with difficult to predict outcomes. The *ancien régime* was founded on the following premises: 1) The sovereignty of the policy makers – the monetary authorities (MAs) and the fiscal authorities (FAs) – had the same geographical extension as the state. 2) Geo-politics coincided with geo-economics, or, in other words, the geographical boundaries of the states and their organisms coincided with economic areas which were internally homogeneous, and mutually heterogeneous, as regards a) national identity and definition of national interests, and b) economic-social structures.

The time-honoured international regime in Europe was eroded over the last twenty years by numerous factors determining the collapse of both its premises. First, the experience of the European Monetary System of fixed exchange rates – and more in general the effects of the globalization of markets – has shown that substantial political-economic sovereignty, both in terms of independence and of effectiveness, has been lost, despite the formal sovereignty of the state (Padoa Schioppa, 1992). Second, the geo-economic map of Europe no longer exactly coincides with its geo-political map. Economically homogeneous areas (the 'macro-regions', in EU vocabulary) have boundaries which often cross two or more states, and this tends to disrupt the coincidence between nationality and economic interests, and the consistency of government actions defined solely by the geographical domain of the state.

In the presence of these phenomena, public economics suggests that policy-making should be articulated into 'levels of government' hierarchically arranged according to their ability to regulate and control the interdependences and spatial externalities of public and private economic choices. This suggestion has been followed in the past by those numerous nation-states that have devolved powers to their regions, as well as obviously by the federal states. At least from a normative point of view, the process ongoing in Europe is towards rearranging the national policy authorities into what we may call an *interregional regime*: that is, a system characterized by 1) a common currency, 2) the close integration of cross-border geo-economic areas which are internally homogeneous (but not necessarily homogeneous among each other), 3) the hierarchical organization of territorial economic policy competences, and therefore of policy agencies. The first manifest step in this direction has been taken with the single currency and the creation of the ECB. To a large extent, in the EMU the national MAs and the ECB are already operating in an interregional regime which may not yet be thoroughly defined as regards the allocation of functions between centre and periphery, but is nevertheless solidly established.

The framework in which the national FAs operate is much more uncertain. As yet, this framework is not even remotely interregional in nature; nor does it look like becoming so in the near future. In its present form it is a hybrid between the old and the new, one that might be called a *constrained international regime*. This institutional mismatch between MAs and FAs has caused much concern for scholars and politicians. It has led to the proposal of a complete interregional regime (to use our terminology) with the creation of a central FA to parallel the ECB. This view is by no means universally shared, however. Some argue that a 'monetary giant' surrounded by 'fiscal dwarves' is a better guarantee of the independence of the central bank, of monetary and financial stability, of restricted growth of the public sector, and of fiscal discipline. Yet, it cannot be overlooked that, so far, it is governments themselves that have resisted to a larger devolution of fiscal prerogatives to a supranational authority (Buti and Franco, 2005; Wyplosz, 2006). Hence, it comes as no surprise that the SGP, and fiscal policy more generally, appear as the weakest pillar of the EMU. It also seems reasonable to predict that improvements cannot only come from better economic engineering, and that they may take a long and troubled road to come.

Thus, albeit this volume has a larger scope – how economic policy works inside a monetary union – it is very much focused on the functioning of fiscal policy under the SGP. Particular emphasis is given to the constraints of the SGP on the one hand, and the presence of a single monetary policy on the other. In this respect, the focus is on the most recent advances in the literature, namely how the *fiscal-monetary policy mix* is actually working within the peculiar institutional setup of the EMU. The critical elements that emerge from the analyses presented here concern the evolution and control of fiscal aggregates over the business cycle and their implications for the SGP rules, the accountability of debt evolution, the financial *spillovers* of national fiscal policies, the measurement and assessment of automatic stabilizers, the relationship between fiscal performance and country size.

The overall assessment is mixed. In particular, the SGP is considered both as an opportunity to strengthen macroeconomic stability across the countries belonging to the euro area, and as an ill-designed institutional device to combine fiscal discipline with effective stabilization at the national level. Though the positive design of the EMU institutions and policy instruments is beyond the scope of the book, we are confident that the results presented here may allow for an informed judgement on the SGP reform introduced in March 2005 and on the prospective evolution of economic policy in the EMU. A more detailed presentation of the contributions to the volume follows in the next section.

Looking forward

We wish now to draw the reader's attention to three main prospective issues that we distil from this assessment of the first five years of EMU.

The first is that the new SGP remains silent about the problem of monetary and fiscal policy co-ordination, thus showing a difficulty to recognize the central role of monetary and fiscal interactions in the euro area (see also Wyplosz, 2006).

The 'consensus view' is that monetary and fiscal policy co-ordination can be waived as the ECB and national FAs are committed to the same inflation and output objectives (Dixit and Lambertini, 2003). There results the 'division of labour' between the ECB taking care of EMU-wide shocks and national FAs taking care of domestic asymmetric shocks. Yet the problem of the complex monetary and fiscal interactions which develop in a monetary union should not be downplayed. The recognition of this problem will probably have to go beyond the role of the SGP rules as a substitute for open co-ordination (Beetsma *et al.*, 2001). The role, if any, is in fact limited to the well known 'common pool problem'. Each government in a monetary union might free-ride on the common pool of financial resources and fail to endogenize the negative *spillovers* (higher interest rates) towards the other members stemming from its fiscal stance. Yet, the quest for a co-ordination of national fiscal policies in the EMU does not arise only from this problem. The real question is not just a possible co-ordination failure among the FAs, but, more importantly, the overall co-ordination between a single monetary stance and a plurality of fiscal stances.

First of all, the EMU countries differ both as for growth differentials and for persistent differences across business cycles. Symmetric shocks, or asymmetric shocks originating in one country and generating *spillover* effects throughout the euro area, may cause different weights put by the ECB and by the FAs in their respective loss functions become relevant (Tamborini, 2004: 154–5). One or more governments might then indulge in discretionary fiscal policies which are mutually compatible with the common inflation and output objectives, but possibly not compatible with overall macroeconomic conditions as shaped by the ECB and the other FAs. The ECB and the national FAs should therefore co-ordinate in order to avoid that the impulse on the euro interest rate resulting from the governments' fiscal stances clashes with the conduct of monetary policy.

There are reasons to think that the debate on policy co-ordination should be resumed soon. The substantial demise of co-ordinated macroeconomic policies of stabilization might not be unrelated to the large current account imbalances recently observed among EMU economies, following widening divergences across real effective exchange rates (Tamborini, 2001; De Grauwe, 2006), as well as to the structural current account surplus of the euro area as a whole vis-à-vis the rest of the world. The limitation of (unco-ordinated) fiscal policies to domestic fiscal shocks can also be questioned from a welfare point of view. As shown by Muscatelli *et al.* (this volume), the euro area displays conditions whereby welfare gains, in terms of consumption smoothing, can be obtained by combining monetary and fiscal stabilization in the area as a whole.

The new Pact has allowed the European Commission more room for discretionality in the evaluation of public budgets. This improved relevance of the specific state of public finances and of the overall macroeconomic conditions is probably a step forward in the direction of removing the stringencies created by a monetary and fiscal tightening during a recession, but not a clear recognition of policy co-ordination as a central question.

The second issue for the future that it is worth considering is that the shift of focus of the new SGP from current deficits to debt brings into light a new possible conflict between the two fiscal policy objectives of output stabilization and the stabilization or the decumulation of debt (depending on whether or not a country is presently respecting the 60% limit for the debt/GDP ratio). During Stage II of the pre-EMU procedures (1993–7), the credible threat of exclusion from the single currency was an effective enforcement device for the Maastricht criteria. In most EMU countries, both the deficit/GDP and the debt/GDP ratios were successfully reduced. The savings on interest expenditure helped in the consolidation of public finances, and compliance at least with the deficit/GDP Maastricht limit admission was successfully accomplished also by 'high debt' countries such as Italy and Belgium. Starting from Stage III, however, the sanction of exclusion from the monetary union has no longer been in place. After the inception of the EMU, public deficit and debts over GDP have begun to increase again.

The common wisdom in the debate on monetary integration in Europe is that the accumulation of public debt in the past decades was mainly the consequence of fiscal profligacy. The view has been put forward that the establishment of a 'monetary dominance' regime, whereby fiscal authorities abide by the restrictive monetary stance of the central bank, is hampered in Europe by the FAs' lack of compliance with the SGP (Buti and Franco, 2005). The 'fiscal indiscipline' which impaired the monetary and fiscal policy mix of the European countries throughout the 1980s was not completely dismissed in the 1990s and after, also considering that the fiscal retrenchment has then been conducted by raising tax pressure more than by cutting public expenditures. The Pact just relies on a penalty for 'excessive deficit' which is much lower than the threat of the pre-EMU period (the exclusion from the EMU). The end of the enforcement represented by the Maastricht clauses for admission to the monetary union has favoured the resurgence of large public deficits and provoked a sort of 'consolidation fatigue' (Huges-Hallett *et al.*, 2003).

In this view, the empirical evidence witnessing a long story of pro-cyclical fiscal policies should not be traced back to the ill-conceived design of the SGP. Quite the contrary, the accumulation of public debt was the direct consequence of continuously expanding public expenditures, as 'pro-cyclical behaviour seems to pertain mostly to good times' (European Commission, 2006: 187). After the recourse, during bad times, to discretional fiscal policies in addition to automatic stabilizers, many governments in the good times failed to engineer the fiscal retrenchment which was needed for the budget to stay 'close to balance or in surplus' (Buti and Franco, 2005). In this perspective, the constraints put on the fiscal stance – first by the Maastricht Treaty, and then by the SGP – did not represent an obstruction to the goal of output stabilization in the EMU. Econometric estimates of fiscal stances conducted by Galì and Perotti (2004) support this view. By using the cyclically adjusted public budget balance (CAPB) – the value that the public budget would have assumed 'if the output level would have not changed' – as a proxy of dis- cretionary fiscal policy, they found for the EMU countries 'a clear trend towards a smaller value' of the co-efficient linking the cyclically adjusted primary deficit- GDP ratio to the output gap (*ibidem*: 547). Galì and Perotti interpret their estimates as indicating the FAs' switch from a pro-cyclical to an a-cyclical variation of fiscal stances and as a proof of lack of evidence that the 3% limit has impeded the full operation of automatic stabilizers during downswings.

However, the exclusive reliance of most empirical research on the CAPB obscures the problem of the possible conflict between output stabilization and debt reduction. In fact, the CAPB and the growth rate of the debt/GDP ratio respond to different variables. Whereas the former just cancels out the effect of the *cyclical* component of GDP on the *total* budget, the latter depends on the evolution of the *primary* balance in connection with the gap between the real interest on debt and the GDP growth rate.[2]

On the one hand, the alleged a-cyclicity of fiscal policy from Maastricht onwards could also stem from the strengthening of the consolidation effort, which obliged fiscal authorities to renounce to expansionary interventions during upswings and turn excess fiscal revenues to the reduction of the debt/GDP ratio. On the other hand, it may well happen that an upward leap in the interest rate (and then in interest payments) and/or a lower growth rate causes the rise of the deficit and debt above the planned figures for reasons different from deliberate expansionary interventions by the FAs. Since it measures the variation of the fiscal stance just as a *residual*, the CAPB is unable to indicate whether a violation of the SGP is due to a lack of 'fiscal discipline' or to a lack of 'room for manoeuvre' caused to the FAs by a non-expected squeeze of the fiscal revenues, following a slowdown in the growth rate of income, and/or an excessive absorption by interest payments after a rise in the interest rate provoked by international financial markets or by the ECB monetary stance. Whatever the origin of a deficit/GDP above the 3% limit, the SGP imposes on the FAs the obligation to compensate for any exogenous shock to the public budget. The fiscal retrenchment, which is needed in order to abide by the 3% limit and/or to impede the further accumulation of public debt, may come at the cost of suspending the operation of automatic stabilizers. Thus, the SGP requirements are potentially conducive to a deflationary bias in the overall macroeconomic governance. Disappointingly, this is not detected by the current method of evaluating the variation of fiscal stances by the EMU governments (Farina and Tamborini, 2001 and 2004).

The difficulty to reconcile the objectives of output stabilization and debt decu- mulation has to be traced back to the incompleteness of the institutional design of the Pact. The *Tax Smoothing* principle, to which the SGP is inspired, dictates that cyclical fluctuations in the primary budget should be averaged out in order to stick to a balanced budget in the medium term. Yet, no account is taken of exogenous shocks increasing the deficit/GDP ratio during bad times, which may cause the two objectives of output stabilization and debt decumulation to be in conflict.

Therefore, a weakness of the old and the new SGP is to be unable to differently evaluate and regulate the case in which a deviation from the CAPB in the medium term derives from excessive expenditure at the numerator of the public budget/GDP ratio, or from a sluggish growth at the denominator. The several failures manifested by the EMU governments in their attempts to abide by the public deficit and debt/GDP ratios not necessarily are a proof of a tendency to renege on the SGP commitments. The recent recession in the euro area has slowed down the formation of additional revenues, and the room for fiscal manoeuvre has narrowed accordingly. Some EMU governments proved unwilling to curb automatic stabilizers. FAs auto-absolved from the 'sin' of postponing debt decumulation and implementing the discretionary interventions needed for output stabilization through higher public expenditure and/or tax cuts. Some other EMU governments, instead, acknowledged that the SGP does not allow for a violation of the 3% limit due to an unexpected reduction in fiscal revenues. These FAs have been using fiscal revenues for debt consolidation in the rush to comply with the requirements for admission to the euro. Many 'high debt' EMU countries, however, even when refraining from discretionary fiscal policies during the recession following the 'Twin Towers', have been unable to reduce their public debt (Farina and Ricciuti, 2006).

Contrary to the presumption of the above-mentioned econometric estimates, Figure 1.1 shows that the average behaviour of the EMU governments' fiscal stances appears to be highly pro-cyclical, even using the CAPB, a method of measuring the FAs' behaviour we have questioned, as it might underestimate the width of fiscal restrictions. Furthermore, after that, pro-cyclical fiscal stances in bad times have been complemented by the turn to higher interest rates by the ECB. Figure 1.2 witnesses that the monetary *and* fiscal policy mix in the EMU have recently become restrictive.

The foregoing considerations lead us to the third question, only marginally tackled by the new SGP; that is, the lack of attention for the connections between fiscal policy and growth in the euro area. As stressed above (see also Gaffeo *et al.*, this volume), the growth rate is a major determinant of the room for fiscal manoeuvre within the SGP boundaries. As a matter of fact, it has been claimed that the lower-than-expected potential growth, which seems to have established in Europe after the deficit limit was set, calls for a corresponding adjustment from the 3% down to 1.8% (Gros, 2004). No doubt, fostering its poor growth is also imperative for Europe in order to relax the SGP constraint. In this perspective, the 'Frankfurt-Brussels consensus' subscribes to the view of 'the cycle around the trend' where the two phenomena are taken as independent. Stabilization policy (basically, aggregate demand management) is aimed at smoothing cyclical fluctuations but it is not

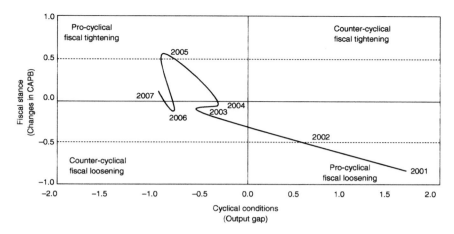

Figure 1.1 Euro-area fiscal stance and cyclical condition, 2001–7.

Source: European Commission Services, 2006.

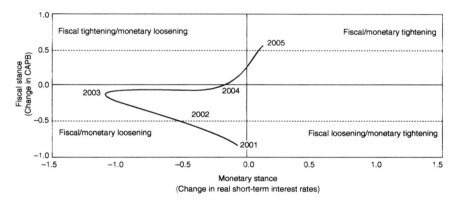

Figure 1.2 Euro-area policy-mix, 2001–5.

Source: European Commission Services, 2006.

(it should not be) regarded as a means to affect the trend. Fiscal policy is almost entirely confined within this dimension. After monetary unification, the tool-box of policy-makers has been left with fiscal policy as the sole instrument for adjustment, but under the constraint of the SGP, which discourages discretionary interventions.

This recommendation of the European Commission is also a consequence of (non-uncontroversial) empirical evidence showing so-called Non-Keynesian effects of fiscal policy (Giavazzi and Pagano, 1996), and a limited width of the fiscal multiplier (Blanchard and Perotti, 2002). As a result, the endogenous feedback of an expansionary fiscal policy on output is downplayed. Whatever the macroeconomic conditions, any deviation of the total balance from the condition of a zero structural total deficit/GDP ratio, different from the impact of the cycle on the primary balance/GDP ratio, should be compensated. Fiscal authorities are required to react by a fiscal retrenchment, disregarding that raising aggregate demand is an alternative source of improvement of public finances.

In order to raise the trend of output, the recommended strategy is to push the economic system towards the efficiency frontier by injecting more competition and flexibility into the economy. The EMU countries with a slow trend of total factor productivity are pressed to implement a wide range of supply-side policies. The objective is to sustain growth by eliminating rents and boosting the turnover of firms in order to prompt the adoption of new technologies. The competitive advantage conquered by the best performers as for liberalization is taken to act as incentive for reforms in the labour market and Welfare institutions by the more 'rigid' countries (Tabellini and Wyplosz, 2004).

On the other hand, it should not be overlooked that the recovery of potential growth in Europe is both a problem of market liberalization and of enhancement of the determinants of growth. In this perspective, the *composition* as well as the *extent* of the government budget do matter (e.g. Afonso *et al.*, 2005). It is now generally agreed that programmes of growth-friendly public expenditures (infrastructural investments, other expenses aimed at fostering innovation and improving human capital) should be resumed. True, a pro-growth *composition* of the government budget does not imply sustained deficits. Yet, there are at least three direct or indirect connections with deficits. The first is that, as a result of *hysteresis*, the extent and speed of stabilization may affect the average growth rate of output: unduly prolonged recessions that wear out physical and human capital displace the economy onto a lower growth path. A second and more specific one relates to capital market imperfections that prevent the private sector from keeping the economy on the efficient growth path after a shock: in some cases there are distinct gains from redistributing resources intertemporally by means of government's borrowing (Andersen and Dogonowsky, 1999). A third connection, widely discussed in the SGP debate, is that the so-called structural reforms may be quite costly in fiscal terms in the short run, whereas they produce social gains and fiscal revenues in the future: again, a welfare dimension of fiscal imbalances emerges that has no relation with the cycle but with the trend of GDP. The new Pact waives the obligation to consider expenditures in public investment in the computation of the public balance only for the EMU countries with sound finances. Yet, the economies which may be more in need of pro-growth public investments are those with a deficit/GDP ratio burdened by a sluggish growth. To this aim, the new methods of economic integration in Europe, in particular the Method of Enhanced Co-operation, could be fruitfully exploited. Joint ventures in R&D projects and networks among the European governments, oriented to boost the diffusion of the Information and communication technologies, should be soon organized in order to fuel convergence across the EMU economies.

Overview of the book

Vis-à-vis the enormous literature available, the major features of this book are that

- in the general assessment of the macroeconomic performance of the euro area, and in particular of fiscal policy under the SGP, the focus is on the most recent advance in the literature, namely how the *fiscal-monetary policy mix* is actually working within the peculiar institutional setup of the EMU;
- the book covers in an organized and compact manner the main issues and questions concerning fiscal and monetary policy, the SGP and macroeconomic performances in the EMU, that have proliferated in a vast and heterogeneous literature, such as: structural analyses of fiscal-monetary interactions, the evolution and control of fiscal aggregates over the business cycle and their implications for the SGP rules, the controllability of debt evolution, the financial *spillovers* of national fiscal policies, the measurement and assessment of automatic stabilizers, the relationship between fiscal performance and country size;
- all contributions are essentially empirical in nature, though firmly rooted in theoretical analyses that are aptly expounded and discussed; all the issues are examined and tested with a variety of up-to-date techniques and from multifaceted points of view.

The contributions are organized in three parts covering, respectively, macroeconomic governance in the EMU, empirical analyses of national fiscal stances, and other fiscal policy issues such as heterogeneity, interdependence and divergence.

Part I opens with an introductory, broad assessment of fiscal policy in the EMU provided by Marco Catenaro and Richard Morris ('Fiscal policy implementation in EMU: From Maastricht to the SGP reform and beyond'). Prior to EMU, fiscal policies in Europe exhibited severe deficit and debt biases. The Maastricht Treaty and the SGP introduced a fiscal framework aimed at correcting such biases and ensuring sound budgetary positions in EMU. However, following significant consolidation efforts in the run-up to EMU, recent years have witnessed a re-emergence of fiscal imbalances, and the SGP has come under increasing strain and criticism. Against this background, the authors examine the fiscal rules that have recently been revised, and conclude that they are now more tailored to economic and country-specific circumstances. This may not only enhance 'ownership' – that is, the political endorsement of the SGP – but also presents new implementation challenges. A rigorous implementation of these new rules will therefore be essential to restore credibility and ensure prudent fiscal policies.

In the subsequent chapter, 'Macroeconomic adjustment in the euro area: The role of fiscal policy', Anton Muscatelli, Tiziano Ropele and Patrizio Tirelli move from the 'Frankfurt-Brussels consensus', based on the view that the ECB alone should stabilize the union-wide economy, and address the question whether fiscal policy, modelled as feedback rules on output, that is, automatic stabilizers, adds value to the stabilization role played by monetary policy in the euro area as a whole. They perform this task by means of a small two-country model of EMU, estimated by using the synthetic euro-data collected over the period 1970–98. They find that the stabilizing effects of fiscal policy in response to EMU-wide shocks carry over to the case of asymmetric disturbances only if a significant home bias characterizes national consumption bundles. Thus, results suggest a novel approach to the philosophy of EMU macroeconomic policymaking. At the euro area level, the action of automatic stabilizers should be regarded as a useful complement to the ECB actions. The usual case for fiscal stabilization of within-EMU asymmetric shocks is confirmed only if the composition of national aggregate demand functions is sufficiently biased towards domestic production.

Part II presents three chapters devoted to the more specific issue of the correct measurement of fiscal stances, which is notoriously problematic in view of the correct implementation and assessment of fiscal rules. Jacques Melitz ('Measuring and assessing fiscal automatic stabilizers') compellingly argues that not just unemployment compensation, but many more categories of government spending (payments for pensions, sickness, subsistence, invalidity, childcare and subsidies of all sorts to firms), respond automatically and significantly to the cycle. In addition, if potential output is not deterministic but subject to supply shocks, the current practice that divides the official figures for cyclically adjusted budget balances by potential output produces inefficient estimates of discretionary fiscal policy. Accordingly, the paper provides separate estimates of the impact of the cycle on the levels of budget balances and the ratios of budget balances to output. The author concludes that the cyclical adjustments depend more on inertia in government spending on goods and services than they do on taxes (which are largely proportional to output), and still more on transfer payments. Besides calling for different series for discretionary fiscal policy, these results also raise questions about the general policy advice to 'let the automatic stabilizers work'.

'Getting measures of fiscal stance right for the new SGP', by Edoardo Gaffeo, Giuliana Passmani and Roberto Tamborini, casts the problem in a macroeconometric framework, their main point being that fiscal stances cannot be isolated from the concomitant evolution of the macroeconomic scenario, with particular regard to monetary policy, interest rates and the growth rate. The authors present an econometric estimate and simulations of a macroeconomic model of Italy and Germany which addresses three issues. First, interactions between monetary and fiscal rules are modelled and examined in a dynamic setting. Second, consistently with common perception and the new formulation of the SGP, the business cycle and the responses of policy variables are cast in terms of *growth gaps*, not gaps in levels, with respect to potential. Third, budgetary components (primary expenditure and total tax revenue) are examined as separate fiscal rules, which allows us to track the reaction of the fiscal stance to growth shocks more precisely. Then, simulations of negative growth shock highlight several pitfalls in current measures of fiscal ratios to GDP, and suggest more accurate assessment of fiscal stances.

Francesco Farina and Roberto Ricciuti ('Testing the fiscal theory of the price level for European countries: A cointegrated VAR approach') address the same issue from a different angle. They investigate the interaction, which took place in Europe during the last decades, between liabilities – the sum of public debt and monetary base – and budget surplus. Their econometric estimates confirm the hypothesis that the Ricardian Regime theorized by the Fiscal theory of the price level (FTPL) is even less likely to be found in the European countries than in the US case studied by Canzoneri *et al.* (2001). By analyzing the impulse part of the response functions through the estimate of cointegrated Vector auto-regression (VAR), this econometric investigation finds that in European countries an innovation in surplus is not consistently correlated with the subsequent surpluses. Especially in 'high debt' countries, compliance with the *Tax Smoothing* principle is not found. By turning to the new SGP, the European Commission has pointed to a lessening of the obligations for the 'low debt' countries, while it keeps exerting a tough pressure on the 'high debt' countries for a rapid reduction of the liabilities/GDP ratio. For these latter FAs, no improvement in the rules, aimed to reconcile output stabilization and debt decumulation, has been envisaged.

Finally, Part III broadens the scope of macro-policy analysis to the dimensions of heterogeneity, interdependence and divergence within the euro area. To begin with, Jacques Le Cacheux and Francesco Saraceno ('one size does not fit all country size and fiscal policy in a monetary union') analyze the heterogeneous nature of the euro zone from the vantage point of the co-existence of small and large countries. Each group faces different incentives and constraints, thus adopting divergent strategies in the occurrence of common macroeconomic shocks. In particular, large countries have not been able, or willing, to abide by the HSGP rule for 'excessive deficits'. The authors propose a simple two-country model of the macroeconomics of a monetary union, in order to shed light on the role of size in the determination of fiscal policy stances. Since the re-interpretation of the Pact has not taken the size criterion into account, a comprehensive discussion of the EMU rules, starting with the SGP, cannot be further postponed.

The role of interdependence across EMU members due to the so-called financial spillovers of fiscal policy, which figures prominently in the traditional justifications for the SGP, is carefully examined by Stefano Schiavo in his paper 'Assessing financial spillovers of national fiscal policies'. By blending historical surveys and econometric tests, the chapter offers a multifaceted approach to this issue: encompassing the correct measure of financial spillover of fiscal imbalances (flow vs. stock), the marginal impact of national fiscal imbalances on EU total wealth, how national interest rate spreads over the bund rate react to news about national deficits. Overall, despite the strong co-movements displayed by European interest rates, empirical evidence does not support the idea that fiscal variables are a key determinant of these interrelations.

Jean Creel and Jacques Le Cacheux ('Inflation divergence and public deficits in a monetary union') reconsider the link between, on the one hand, domestic public debts and, on the other hand, average and domestic inflation rates in a monetary union. Introducing three realistic assumptions in a model recently proposed by

Beetsma and Vermeylen (2005), they show that the causation between inflation dynamics and public finances may go from the former to the latter. They conclude that inflation divergence may have been responsible for the diverging patterns of public finances in Europe, some countries having had to let their public deficits go adrift to cope with high inflation pressures. Despite the constitution of the euro area, homogeneous fiscal rules, like the ones considered in the SGP, are not optimal in this respect, at least insofar as inflation convergence has not been achieved.

Notes

1 We have developed this approach in Farina and Tamborini (2001).
2 In fact, denoting with d_t, b_t and b'_t the GDP ratios of debt, total balance and primary balance, respectively, the usual approximation for the change in the debt/GDP ratio yields

$$\Delta d_t \approx d_{t-1}(r_t - g_t) - b'_t$$

where r_t is the real interest rate and g_t is the the GDP growth rate. A typical SGP plan requires the government to commit itself to a certain $\Delta d^* \leq 0$ per year upon the estimated trend values of $\bar{r}$ and $\bar{g}$. This implies a path for the primary balance such that

$$b'^*_t = -\Delta d^* + d_{t-1}(\bar{r} - \bar{g})$$

As a conseqence, along this path the total balance will evolve according to

$$b_t \approx b'_t - r_t d_{t-1}$$
$$b^*_t = -\Delta d^* - d_{t-1}\bar{g}$$

Clearly, in a debt-control perspective, the year by year commitment on the decifit/GDP ratio has no connection with the 3% ceiling, but it is determined by the debt/GDP target and the estimated growth trend of GDP. For instance, along a debt reduction path, the prescription that the medium-term total budget should be 'close to balance or in surplus' only applies if the GDP growth trend is lower than the planned year rate of change of the debt/GDP ratio ($\bar{g} \leq -\Delta d^*/d_{t-1}$). On the other hand, *ceteris paribus*, a low growth trend requires more ambitious primary and total budget *surpluses*. At the same time, random shocks to the real interest rate or to the growth rate will give rise to deviations of the debt and total balance GDP ratios from their planned paths. This will occur by pure accounting factors, even if the government does not change its planned primary balances in response to shocks, as shown by the following expressions of the *actual* evolution of Δd_t and b_t upon introducing the planned primary balance b'^*_t and assuming that $r_t = \bar{r} + \varepsilon_{rt}$ and $g_t = \bar{g} + \varepsilon_{gt}$:

$$\Delta d_t - \Delta d^*_t = d_{t-1}(\varepsilon_{rt} - \varepsilon_{gt})$$
$$b_t - b^*_t = -d_{t-1}\varepsilon_{rt}$$

In this framework, positive shocks to the real interest rate and negative shocks to the growth rate bear the main responsibility for debt and budget GDP ratios worse than planned. These ratios will deteriorate to a greater extent if the primary balance also displays a cyclical component.

References

Andersen, T. M. and Dogonowsky, R. R. (1999), 'Social insurance and the public budget', in Hughes-Hallett, A. J., Hutchinson, M. M., Hougaard Jensen, S. E. (eds), *Fiscal Aspects of European Monetary Integration*, Cambridge: Cambridge University Press.

Beetsma, R., Debrun, X. and Klaassen, F. (2001), 'Is fiscal policy coordination in EMU desirable?', *Swedish Economic Policy Review*, 8: 57–98.

Blanchard, O. and Giavazzi, F. (2003), 'Macroeconomic effects of regulation and deregulation in goods and labour markets', *Quarterly Journal of Economics*, 118: 879–907.

Blanchard, O. and Perotti, R. (2002), 'An empirical characterization of the dynamic effects of shocks to government spending and taxes on output', *Quarterly Journal of Economics*, 117: 1329–68.

Buti, M. and Franco, D. (2005), *Fiscal policy in Economic and Monetary Union*, Cheltenham: Edward Elgar.

Canzoneri, M., Cumby, R. and Diba, B. (2001), 'Is the price level determined by the needs of fiscal solvency?', *American Economic Review*, 91: 1221–36.

De Grauwe, P. (2006), 'What have we learnt about monetary integration since the Maastricht Treaty?', *Journal of Common Market Studies*, 44: 711–30.

Dixit, A. and Lambertini, L. (2003), 'Symbiosis of monetary and fiscal policies in a monetary union', *Journal of International Economics*, 60: 235–47.

European Commission (2006), 'Public finances in EMU 2006', *European Economic Reports and Studies*, 3.

Farina, F. and Tamborini, R. (2001), 'Macroeconomic stabilization policies in Europe under the new regime of monetary union', Quaderni del Dipartimento di Economia Politica, Università di Siena, n. 317. [Social Science Research Network (SSRN), Macroeconomics, http://papers.ssrn.com.]

—— (2004), ' "Set a sufficiently ambitious budget target and let the automatic stabilizers work." Can it really work in the European Monetary Union?', *Open Economies Review*, 15: 143–68.

Farina, F. and Ricciuti, R. (2006), 'Fiscal rules and the evaluation of fiscal stances in Europe', *Revue de l'OFCE*, 4: 275–301.

Fitoussi, J. P. (2002), *La régle et la choix*, Paris: Editions de Seuil.

Galí, J. (2005), 'Modern perspectives on fiscal stabilization policies', *CESifo Economic Studies*, 51: 587–99.

Galí, J. and Perotti, R. (2003), 'Fiscal policy and monetary integration in Europe', *Economic Policy*, n. 37: 535–72.

Giavazzi, F. and Pagano, M. (1996), 'Non Keynesian effects of fiscal policy changes: international evidence and Swedish experience', *Swedish Economic Policy Review*, 3: 67–103.

Gros, D. (2004), 'The nine lives of the Stability Pact', Special Report of the CEPS Macroeconomic Policy Group, Bruxelles.

Hughes-Hallett, A., Lewis, J., and von Hagen, J. (2003), *Fiscal Policy in Europe, 1991–2003. An Evidence-based Analysis*, London: CEPR.

Padoa Schioppa, T. (1992), *l'Europa verso l'unione monetaria. Dallo Sme al Trattato di Maastricht*, Turin: Einaudi.

Tabellini, G. and Wyplosz, C. (2004), 'Supply-side policy coordination in the European Union', *Swedish Economic Policy Review*, 13: 101–56.

Tamborini, R. (2001), 'Living in the EMU: Interest rates, prices and the adjustment of payments in a monetary union', *Journal of Common Market Studies*, 39: 123–46.

—— (2004) 'The "Brussels Consensus" on macroeconomic stabilization policies in the EMU: A critical assessment', in F. Torres, A. Verdun, C. Zilioli, H. Zimmermang (eds) *Governing EMU: Political, Economic, Historical and Legal Aspects*, Florence: European University Press.

Tamborini, R. and Targetti, F. (2005), 'The crisis of the Stability Pact and a proposal', in Arestis, P., McCombie, J. and Vickerman, R. (eds), *Growth and Economic Development. Essays in Honour of A. P. Tirwall*, Aldershot: Edward Elgar, forthcoming.

Wyplosz, C. (2006), 'European Monetary Union: The dark sides of a major success', Economic Policy, 46: 207–61.

Part I
Macroeconomic governance in the EMU

2 Fiscal policy and implementation in EMU

From Maastricht to the SGP reform and beyond[1]

M. Catenaro and R. Morris

2.1 Introduction

Prior to Economic and Monetary Union (EMU), fiscal policies in Europe exhibited severe deficit and debt biases. The Maastricht Treaty and the Stability and Growth Pact (SGP) introduced a fiscal framework aimed at correcting such biases and ensuring sound budgetary positions in EMU. However, following significant consolidation efforts in the run-up to EMU, the early years of the millennium witnessed a re-emergence of fiscal imbalances, and the SGP came under increasing strain and criticism. Against this background, the fiscal rules have recently been revised and are now more tailored to economic and country-specific circumstances. This may enhance ownership but also presents new implementation challenges.

In the light of the SGP reform, this chapter examines how the EU fiscal rules have evolved over time and how they have been implemented from the adoption of the Maastricht Treaty to the present day, including initial experiences with the implementation of the reformed Pact. Section 2.2 starts by providing an overview of the EU fiscal rules and their implementation since the adoption of the Maastricht Treaty up until the reform of the Pact. Section 2.3 explains and assesses the Pact reform. Section 2.4 then makes an attempt to interpret the first experiences with the implementation of the new framework. All in all, it is concluded that implementation has been smooth and consistent, but with consolidation requirements that are rather lenient while fiscal targets and projections point to only slow and back-loaded progress towards sound public finances in many countries. The assessment of the implementation of the revised rules is therefore mixed and it remains to be seen whether the new rules will be implemented in a manner that is sufficient to ensure fiscal sustainability in EMU.

2.2 The EU fiscal rules and their implementation

2.2.1 From Maastricht to the SGP

In the decade and a half before the signing of the Maastricht Treaty (in 1992) the aggregate debt/GDP ratio of the euro area effectively doubled from around

30% to almost 60%. Similarly, large increases in debt ratios also occurred in other (non-European) industrialized countries, such as the United States and Japan.

Over time, persistently high deficits and rising debt levels such as those experienced in the late 1970s and 1980s are likely to have a detrimental impact on economic stability and growth. Profligate fiscal policies can also impede the effective conduct of a stability-oriented monetary policy. Among other things, high deficit and debt levels may reduce the scope for governments to use fiscal policy as a tool for stabilizing domestic demand, since deficits that are increasing from already high levels could spark fears concerning the sustainability of public finances. Excessive government borrowing may contribute to inflationary pressures and put upward pressure on interest rates, which would crowd out private investment. Higher debt also increases the interest payment burden with the result that government spending tends to be diverted from more productive uses.

In EMU, the sharing of a single currency implies that the deficit bias is likely to be greater than would otherwise be the case (as at least one disciplining mechanism, the nominal exchange rate, has been removed). Moreover, given the combination of a single monetary policy with decentralized fiscal policies, some kind of implicit co-ordination mechanism is needed to ensure fiscal policies are mutually consistent and do not threaten macroeconomic stability and cohesion of the euro area.[2]

To address concerns that large deficits and rising debt could threaten the smooth functioning of EMU, the Maastricht Treaty introduced into the European Community Treaty (henceforth the 'Treaty') a number of rules aimed at disciplining EU Member States' fiscal policies. These include the prohibition of monetary financing of deficits by the European System of Central Banks (ESCB) (Article 101) and the so-called no-bail-out clause, which states that European institutions or Member States shall not be liable for or assume another Member State's financial obligations (Article 103). The former contributes to a clear separation between monetary policy and fiscal policy, which should ensure that a stability-oriented monetary policy is not directly compromised by excessive government borrowing. The latter makes clear that in EMU, Member States do not have to bear the cost of financing other Member States' debt. This should, in principle, encourage financial markets to distinguish between different euro area governments' debt instruments, thereby strengthening financial market discipline on fiscal policies.

In addition to these basic safeguards, the Treaty obliges Member States to avoid 'excessive deficits' assessed against 'reference values' of 3% of GDP for the deficit and 60% of GDP for debt (Article 104). The sustainability of a government's financial position, in the sense of not having a deficit that is 'excessive' as defined by Article 104 of the Treaty, is one of the convergence criteria for adoption of the euro. Moreover, breaches of the reference values result in the initiation of an Excessive Deficit Procedure (EDP) with the aim of examining and, if necessary, correcting the situation. For Member States that have adopted the single currency, this procedure can ultimately lead to financial sanctions. However, the procedure as laid down in the Treaty is in no sense mechanistic, and ultimately leaves it to the discretion of the EU Council of Ministers of Economic Affairs and Finance (henceforth the 'ECOFIN Council') to decide whether to take action.

In the years that followed the signing of the Maastricht Treaty, the 3% reference value served as a relatively simple yardstick of the success of fiscal policy and received considerable prominence in the public debate. It greatly facilitated monitoring of fiscal performance by the public and by financial markets, since in most countries the objective of qualifying for adoption of the euro attracted widespread support. A number of governments staked their reputations on bringing deficits below 3% in time to be among the first wave of countries to adopt the euro. As a consequence, fiscal balances in most EU Member States improved significantly in the run-up to EMU (see Table 2.1).[3] For the euro area as a whole, the general government deficit was reduced from 4.5% of GDP in 1991 to below 3% in 1997. The structural improvement in the budget balance was even more significant, amounting to more than 3 percentage points of GDP.

Nonetheless, concerns remained that the fiscal rules as set out in the Maastricht Treaty would not provide enough of a 'stick' to ensure fiscal discipline once the 'carrot' of participation in the single currency had been eaten. There were concerns that compliance with the 3% of GDP reference value may not be sufficient to maintain or reduce debt to reasonable levels. There were also fears that fiscal

Table 2.1 Fiscal consolidation in the run-up to EMU (as a % of GDP)

	1991	1992	1993	1994	1995	1996	1997
General government budget balance							
Belgium	−6.0	−6.8	−7.0	−4.7	−4.4	−3.8	−2.0
Germany	−3.2	−2.7	−3.4	−2.5	−3.2	−3.3	−2.6
Greece	−11.4	−12.6	−13.6	−9.9	−10.2	−7.4	−6.6
Spain	−4.2	−3.9	−6.6	−6.0	−6.5	−4.8	−3.3
France	−2.0	−3.8	−5.6	−5.6	−5.5	−4.1	−3.0
Ireland	−2.2	−2.4	−2.3	−1.5	−2.0	0.0	1.3
Italy	−9.7	−9.2	−9.1	−8.8	−7.4	−7.0	−2.7
Luxembourg	1.5	0.6	1.3	2.3	2.4	1.2	3.7
Netherlands	−2.7	−3.7	−3.1	−3.6	−4.3	−1.9	−1.2
Austria	−2.9	−1.9	−4.1	−4.8	−5.6	−3.9	−1.7
Portugal	−5.5	−2.7	−5.6	−5.6	−5.2	−4.5	−3.4
Finland	−1.4	−5.6	−7.8	−6.0	−6.2	−3.5	−1.2
Euro area	**−4.5**	**−4.7**	**−5.5**	**−5.0**	**−5.0**	**−4.2**	**−2.6**
Cyclically adjusted budget balance							
Euro area	**−5.5**	**−5.2**	**−4.7**	**−4.3**	**−4.5**	**−3.5**	**−2.1**
General government debt							
Euro area	**57.5**	**59.3**	**65.1**	**67.8**	**72.4**	**74.1**	**73.6**

Source: European Commission, AMECO database.

Notes
1 The figures presented in the table are those available under the ESA 95 accounting framework at the end of 2006. They show that in 1997, the government deficit stood above the 3% of GDP reference value in two countries that entered EMU in 1999 (Spain and Portugal). The figures available at the beginning of 1998, when the decision on the countries entering EMU was taken, were based on ESA 79. Those figures showed deficits that complied with the 3% of GDP limit.
2 Euro area refers to the composition until 31 December 2006, thus comprising the 12 Member States listed in the table.

policies would become pro-cyclical if Member States were forced to increase taxes or reduce spending during recessions in order to keep their deficits below 3% of GDP. Such concerns led to the negotiation and signing of the SGP, which sought to put more "flesh on the bones" of the fiscal framework of the Maastricht Treaty.[4]

2.2.2 The 'original' SGP

The SGP aims to prevent excessive deficits through policy surveillance and co-ordination, and to deter as well as correct excessive deficits by providing clear rules for the application of the EDP. It is primarily based on two Council Regulations, which in accordance with their aims and functions are often referred to as the 'preventive arm' and the 'corrective arm' (or 'deterrent arm') of the Pact.[5] These were backed by a solemn declaration of the European Heads of State or Government, which expressed Member States' political commitment to implementing the rules in a strict and timely manner.[6]

Under the preventive arm, Member States submit annual stability and convergence programmes, which present information regarding their economic and fiscal policies.[7] These programmes include in particular the 'medium-term objective' of fiscal policy and, where applicable, the adjustment path towards it. In its original form, the SGP specified that the medium-term objective (MTO) should be a budget that is 'close to balance or in surplus'. The rationale was both to ensure fiscal positions that would be sustainable in the long run while also creating sufficient room for fiscal policy to help smooth output fluctuations in the short run without breaching the 3% of GDP deficit ceiling.[8] The generic term 'close to balance or in surplus' reflected the fact that while close-to-balance budgets should be, as a rule, sufficient to ensure sustainable fiscal positions, some countries might wish to target surpluses with a view to reducing debt ratios more rapidly and so create room to accommodate the future fiscal burden of ageing populations. The Member States' stability programmes are assessed by the Commission and may be examined by the ECOFIN Council, which can choose to make public its opinion on each programme. The preventive arm also includes an early-warning device whereby the Council can issue recommendations to Member States to take corrective measures if budgetary developments point to the risk of an excessive deficit. Overall, however, the emphasis of the preventive arm is on 'soft' procedures which foster fiscal discipline and policy co-ordination through multilateral surveillance and peer pressure.

By contrast, the corrective arm relies on stricter and more formal procedures designed to enforce fiscal discipline in countries where deficits have become excessive and are therefore giving rise to greater concern. To this end, the EDP already outlined in the Treaty was clarified and 'speeded up', in particular with regard to the following:

- *Exceptional circumstances*: The conditions under which a deficit above 3% could be deemed exceptional and temporary (and therefore not excessive) were defined strictly as cases in which a country experiences an annual fall in real GDP of at least 2%. A fall in real GDP of between 0.75% and 2% could also be deemed exceptional in the light of supporting evidence submitted by the Member State in question regarding the accumulated output loss and the abruptness of the downturn.

- *The deadline for the correction of excessive deficits*: It was specified that the correction of an excessive deficit should be completed 'in the year following its identification unless there are special circumstances', although the nature of such special circumstances was not explicitly defined.
- *The timing of procedural steps*: A timetable with precise deadlines for the various steps of the procedure was laid out whereby, in the event of non-compliance by a Member State with the recommendations and decisions of the Council, the time between the reporting of a deficit above 3% of GDP and the imposition of sanctions should be no more than ten months.
- *The nature of sanctions*: It was clarified that, if the Council were to impose sanctions on a Member State, a non-interest-bearing deposit would be required which, in the event of a further two years of non-compliance, would, as a rule, be converted into a fine.

With these clarifications, the corrective arm of the SGP provided for a strict and timely application of all elements of the EDP. Nonetheless, it fell short of the original proposal of the German government, which had supported a fully automatic sanctioning mechanism outside the standard Treaty framework (Stark, 2001). Such automatism was considered inappropriate by some Member States. The SGP that was finally agreed instead took the form of EU secondary legislation with decisions to be taken within the standard legislative framework (i.e. Council recommendations or decisions, adopted by qualified majority, on the basis of recommendations by the Commission). The Commission therefore preserved its 'right of initiative', while the Council ultimately retained discretion in taking decisions within an overall rules-based framework.

2.2.3 Experience under the original Pact

Notwithstanding the gradual fiscal consolidation made during the mid-1990s, by the time the SGP entered into force shortly before the introduction of the single currency in January 1999, most euro area Member States were still some way from achieving medium-term budgetary positions that were close to balance or in surplus. Further consolidation was therefore necessary in order to create room for the operation of the automatic fiscal stabilizers while maintaining a safety margin with respect to the 3% deficit ceiling (Buti *et al.*, 1998).

In the early years of Stage Three of EMU, nominal budget balances generally continued to improve and, by 2000, the euro area budget deficit was reduced to just 1% of GDP. However, fiscal consolidation slowed down and, from 2001 onwards, the euro area budget balance ratio started to deteriorate, increasing to above 3% of GDP by 2003, with only a small decline back below this level in 2004 (see Table 2.2). This return to higher deficits in the euro area needs to be seen in the context of the slowdown in economic growth and, more importantly, consolidation fatigue, which started soon after the launch of the single currency. In some countries, structural budgetary positions started to deteriorate as early

Table 2.2 Fiscal developments under the Stability and Growth Pact (as a % of GDP)

	1998	1999	2000	2001	2002	2003	2004
General government budget balance							
Belgium	−0.8	−0.5	0.1	0.4	0.0	0.0	0.0
Germany	−2.2	−1.5	−1.1	−2.8	−3.7	−4.0	−3.7
Greece	−4.3	−3.4	−4.0	−5.4	−5.2	−6.1	−7.8
Spain	−3.1	−1.3	−0.9	−0.5	−0.3	−0.0	−0.2
France	−2.6	−1.7	−1.5	−1.6	−3.2	−4.2	−3.7
Ireland	2.4	2.7	4.6	0.8	−0.6	0.3	1.5
Italy	−2.8	−1.7	−2.0	−3.1	−2.9	−3.5	−3.4
Luxembourg	3.4	3.4	6.0	6.1	2.1	0.3	−1.1
Netherlands	−0.9	0.4	1.3	−0.2	−2.0	−3.1	−1.8
Austria	−2.3	−2.2	−1.8	0.0	−0.5	−1.6	−1.2
Portugal	−3.0	−2.7	−3.2	−4.3	−2.9	−2.9	−3.2
Finland	1.7	1.6	6.9	5.0	4.1	2.5	2.3
Euro area	**−2.2**	**−1.3**	**−1.0**	**−1.8**	**−2.5**	**−3.1**	**−2.8**
Cyclically adjusted budget balance							
Belgium	−0.4	−0.8	−1.0	0.2	−0.1	0.5	0.0
Germany	−1.8	−1.3	0.6	−3.4	−3.6	−3.4	−3.2
Greece	−3.4	−2.6	−3.4	−4.8	−5.1	−6.4	−8.4
Spain	−2.8	−1.6	−1.8	−1.4	−0.7	−0.1	0.0
France	−2.5	−2.1	−2.6	−2.5	−3.6	−4.1	−3.7
Ireland	1.9	1.1	2.3	−0.9	−1.8	−0.3	1.4
Italy	−2.5	−1.6	−1.7	−4.1	−3.4	−3.5	−3.3
Luxembourg	4.1	2.9	4.1	5.1	1.4	1.0	−0.2
Netherlands	−1.3	−0.9	0.2	−1.4	−1.9	−2.1	0.9
Austria	−2.5	−2.8	−2.5	0.3	−0.3	−0.9	−0.7
Portugal	−3.4	−3.5	−4.2	−5.5	−3.5	−2.4	−2.6
Finland	0.6	0.6	5.4	4.1	4.1	3.3	3.0
Euro area	**−2.0**	**−1.5**	**−0.9**	**−2.6**	**−2.8**	**−2.7**	**−2.5**
General government debt							
Euro area	**73.2**	**72.0**	**69.3**	**68.3**	**68.2**	**69.3**	**69.8**

Source: European Commission, AMECO database. Data exclude receipts from the sale of Universal Mobile Telecommunications System (UMTS) licenses.

Note
The figures presented in the table are those available under the ESA 95 accounting framework at the end of 2006. They therefore include all the statistical revisions that have taken place since 1998 in the euro area countries (in particular, in Greece and Portugal).

as 2000 since, in a context of favourable economic growth, tax cuts were not matched by equivalent expenditure reductions. While the fiscal consolidation that was achieved during the 1990s was largely attributable to an increase in the revenue/GDP ratio, which, for the euro area as a whole, rose from 44% in 1991 to 47% in 1999 (see Figure 2.1), after 1999 about two-thirds of the earlier increase in the revenue/GDP ratio was reversed.[9] Meanwhile, primary expenditure, which had been reduced by more than 1% of GDP in the run-up to EMU, started to increase again after 1999.

A key mistake that was made by many Member States in the early years following the adoption of the euro was to fail to take advantage of 'good times' to achieve

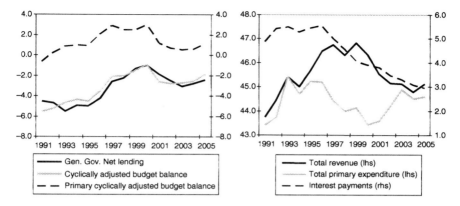

Figure 2.1 Euro area fiscal developments, 1991–2005: determinants and components (as a % of GDP).

Source: European Commission.

sound fiscal positions. This may have been partly because improving nominal budget balances in the early years of the Pact's implementation initially contributed to the false perception that fiscal positions were also getting better. In theory, the evolution of cyclically adjusted budget balances should have alerted policy-makers to the fiscal loosening that was taking place. In practice, however, estimates of the cyclically adjusted budget balance are prone to error due to the difficulty of measuring the cyclical position of the economy in real time and the sensitivity to the cycle of some budget items. This was especially true in the early years of the single currency when estimates of trend or potential output growth for many countries proved to be over-optimistic. In cases where potential growth is over-estimated, there is likely to be a bias towards estimating negative output gaps (i.e. concluding that actual output is below potential) and a corresponding tendency to underestimate (overestimate) the cyclically adjusted deficit (surplus). In addition, methods used for the cyclical adjustment of fiscal variables do not always capture all temporary influences on the budget balance. For example, the impact of asset prices on tax revenues is not well captured by current methods and hence there is a tendency for cyclically adjusted budget balances to paint an overly positive picture of the true state of the public finances during asset price booms such as that related to the 'dot.com bubble' of the late 1990s.

The deterioration of budget balances in many countries from 2001 onwards very quickly put the SGP to the test. Six euro area Member States have incurred excessive deficits since 1999: Portugal in 2001 (and again in 2005), Germany and France in 2002, the Netherlands and Greece in 2003, and Italy in 2004. Among these, only the Netherlands succeeded in correcting its excessive deficit in a timely and durable manner. Some Member States resorted to temporary measures to comply nominally with the rules. Moreover, owing to large statistical revisions, some excessive deficits were only identified several years after the 3% of GDP reference value was breached from an *ex post* perspective, after statistical corrections led to upward revisions of earlier deficit figures.[10] Typically, this took place when initially reported deficits coincided with significant adverse deficit-debt adjustments, notably in Greece, Italy and Portugal.

Faced with deteriorating fiscal positions in a number of countries, the ECOFIN Council appeared reluctant to implement the Pact in a strict manner. The first evidence of this came in early 2002, when the Council rejected Commission recommendations to issue 'early warnings' to Germany and Portugal to take action to prevent their deficits from exceeding the 3% reference value. Instead, the Council took the view that such a formal step was unnecessary in the light of commitments by these countries to take corrective measures.[11] In both cases, however, the 3% limit was breached and EDPs were subsequently launched.[12]

An even more significant deviation from the rules and procedures of the Pact came in November 2003, in the context of the EDPs against Germany and France. Having been given until 2004 to correct their excessive deficits, it became clear by autumn 2003 that the measures taken by both countries would not be sufficient to comply with the Council's recommendations. The Commission recommended that the Council should step up pressure on both countries by issuing 'notices' (i.e. one step in the EDP before sanctions), while also suggesting an extension of the 2004 deadline by one more year.[13] However, the Council failed to achieve the necessary qualified majority to adopt these decisions. Instead, it issued 'conclusions' in which it put the procedures in abeyance in the light of commitments expressed by Germany and France to take effective action to correct their excessive deficits by 2005.[14] These conclusions were subsequently challenged by the Commission and annulled by the European Court of Justice (ECJ) on the grounds that the Council had not followed the rules and procedures as set out in the Treaty. In particular, the ECJ made clear that the Council could not, by itself, take initiatives in the absence of an appropriate recommendation by the Commission and could not replace a 'procedure' with 'political conclusions'.[15]

It would be wrong, however, to paint a totally negative picture of the experience under the original SGP. Fiscal deficit ratios in the euro area did not return to their pre-Maastricht levels and earlier trends of rapidly rising public debt and expenditure ratios were mostly brought to a halt. A number of countries did moreover succeed in complying with the rules. Among these, Belgium, Spain and Austria all consolidated their fiscal positions further and managed to reach close to balance or in surplus budgetary positions. Meanwhile, Ireland, Luxembourg and Finland, while loosening fiscal policy, did so having entered EMU with large budget surpluses, and their fiscal positions have remained broadly sound. Also, the Netherlands, after breaching the deficit ceiling in 2003, has since turned this round to again reach a close-to-balance budgetary position. While overall fiscal consolidation may have largely stalled after 2000, there was no generalized or significant loosening of fiscal policies in the euro area. It can therefore be argued that, even if the original SGP did not fully attain its objectives, it did have a constraining effect on fiscal policies.

Another criticism that was made of the SGP in its original form was that it gave rise to pro-cyclical fiscal policies. This was due to the fact that its 'softer' preventive arm failed to ensure that countries reached sound fiscal positions in good times, while the much 'harder' corrective arm then forced fiscal retrenchment in bad times. In truth, however, this may be a criticism of the failure to implement the Pact correctly rather than any shortcoming in the rules themselves. To illustrate this point, Figure 2.2 plots changes of the fiscal stance as measured by the change in

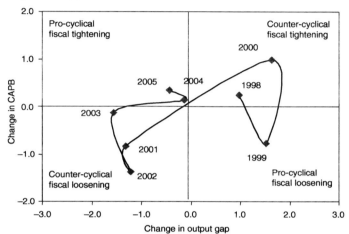

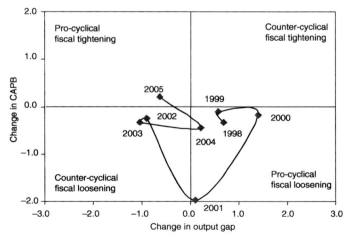

Figure 2.2 Fiscal policy stance under the SGP.

Source: European Commission and own calculations.

the cyclically adjusted primary balance (CAPB) in response to cyclical conditions, measured by the change in the output gap, distinguishing between seven 'compliant' countries (Belgium, Spain, Ireland, Luxembourg, the Netherlands, Austria and Finland) and five 'non-compliant' countries (Germany, Greece, France, Italy and Portugal) and taking the simple average for each group. Figure 2.2 shows that in the countries that have generally complied with the requirements of the SGP, this has created the necessary room for fiscal policy to play a role in smoothing output fluctuations. By contrast, in the countries that have struggled to respect the 3% deficit limit, fiscal policy has tended to respond less well to cyclical developments. More specifically, the difficulty that some countries have encountered in complying with the rules owes at least in part to a pro-cyclical loosening of fiscal policy during the upturn of 1999–2000.

2.3   The 2005 reform of the SGP

As actual fiscal developments moved budgetary positions further away from the Pact's requirements, and political commitment to the rules waned, criticisms of the SGP gained prominence and became more widely accepted.

A frequent criticism of the original SGP was that it placed too much emphasis on formal compliance with rules and took too little account of economic circumstances. It was argued that the close-to-balance or in-surplus objective, which was generally interpreted as implying the maintenance of a broadly balanced budget (in cyclically adjusted terms), failed to consider the specific circumstances of each Member State, in particular with regard to long-term fiscal soundness, public investment needs or the costs of structural reforms. According to this view, it does not make sense for countries with, for example, widely diverging debt levels to target exactly the same budget balance. The emergence of excessive deficits in a number of countries suggested that the mechanisms underlying the preventive arm (i.e. monitoring and peer pressure) were too weak to ensure progress towards sound fiscal positions. Meanwhile, when countries did incur excessive deficits, the Pact's corrective arm was criticized for requiring prompt corrective action regardless of economic growth considerations. In particular, some critics of the Pact found it inappropriate to require Member States to correct excessive deficits by tightening fiscal policy during periods of low growth, since this could dampen prospects for economic recovery. The Pact was also criticized for not paying sufficient attention to debt developments, as it did not clarify the application of the debt criterion of the Treaty.

According to advocates of reform, such shortcomings contributed to a lack of commitment and ownership on the part of Member States, the Commission and the ECOFIN Council, which could partly explain difficulties in applying the rules and procedures. To address this, numerous proposals to improve or amend the rules were put forward. Prominent among these have been those suggesting more focus on the quality of public finances (Fitoussi and Creel, 2002; Blanchard and Giavazzi, 2004), to shift the emphasis of the SGP away from deficits and onto debt and sustainability (Buiter and Grafe, 2002; Pisani-Ferry, 2002), or to replace numerical rules with stronger fiscal institutions and market discipline (Wyplosz, 2005).

While some commentators called for a complete overhaul of the rules, others defended the *status quo* or at most called for more incremental adjustment (Buti *et al.*, 2003; Bini Smaghi, 2004). Defenders of the existing rules argued that they were sufficient to preserve the sustainability of public finances in EMU while also allowing room for the full operation of automatic stabilizers (Marin, 2002). The importance of relatively simple rules and limited discretion under the original SGP was stressed in particular with a view to supporting market and public monitoring of fiscal policies (Schuknecht, 2004). According to this view, the problem was not the rules *per se*, but deficient enforcement that undermined the deterrent power of the Pact (such as the need for a qualified majority in the Council and the problem of 'sinners judging sinners'). This called for improvements in the implementation and enforcement of the rules rather than changes in the rules themselves (Gros *et al.*, 2004).

Prior to the SGP reform, there had already been a number of incremental refinements to the way the Pact was implemented. Over time, more attention came to be paid to the influence of the cycle, with cyclically adjusted budget balances acquiring greater prominence, at least under the preventive arm. In November 2002, the Commission issued a communication with a broad set of proposals, some of which were subsequently adopted by the ECOFIN Council.[16] In this context, the initial emphasis on setting target dates for the achievement of balanced budgets was replaced by a Eurogroup commitment to annual improvements of underlying fiscal balances by at least 0.5% of GDP (see below). Following the procedural impasse in the context of the EDPs against Germany and France, however, the Commission decided to launch a more wide-ranging discussion on reforming the SGP, including the option of changing the Council Regulations.[17] The Commission's proposals, along with other suggestions, were discussed at length by Member States in late 2004 and early 2005. The outcome of these discussions was an agreement to make changes to the SGP as set out in the ECOFIN Council Report of March 2005 and later implemented via amendments to Council Regulations 1466/97 and 1467/97.[18] The reform adopted by the ECOFIN Council left the structure of the SGP in place and did not alter the fundamental elements of the EU fiscal framework enshrined in the Treaty, such as the 3% and 60% reference values, which were outside its scope. Within this overall framework, however, the reform did introduce a number of significant changes.

As to the changes affecting the preventive arm, the reform has introduced various refinements to the earlier provisions concerning the setting of and progress towards sound medium-term budgetary positions and to the elements that are to be taken into account when assessing Member States' fiscal positions. These include:

The definition of the medium-term budgetary objective: Rather than being required to target 'close-to-balance or in-surplus' budgetary positions, each Member State now presents its own country-specific MTO in its stability or convergence programme, which is then assessed by the Council. These country-specific MTOs are differentiated and may differ from a position of close-to-balance or in-surplus. They should provide a safety margin with respect to the 3% of GDP reference value, ensure rapid progress towards sustainability and, taking this into account, should allow room for budgetary manoeuvre, particularly with regard to the need for public investment. For euro area and ERM II Member States, an initial range for country-specific MTOs, in cyclically adjusted terms and net of one-off and temporary measures, has been set between −1% of GDP and 'in balance or surplus'.

The adjustment path to the MTO: Member States that have not yet achieved their MTOs are expected to take steps to do so over the cycle. To this end, euro area and ERM II Member States should as a benchmark pursue an annual adjustment in cyclically adjusted terms, net of one-off and temporary measures, of 0.5% of GDP. The adjustment effort should be greater in good times, but could be more limited in bad times. Good times are defined as 'periods where output exceeds its potential level, taking into account tax elasticities', while the Code of Conduct specifies that the 'change in the output gap could also be considered, especially when the output gap is estimated to be close to zero'. Member States that do not follow the required adjustment path should explain the reasons for not doing so in their programme update, and the Commission is entitled to issue 'policy advice' to encourage Member States to stick to the adjustment path.

Taking into account structural reforms: Member States may be allowed to deviate from the MTO or the adjustment path towards it if they undertake structural reforms, and in this context special attention is paid to pension reforms which introduce multi-pillar systems that include a mandatory, fully funded pillar. However, 'only reforms which have direct long-term cost-saving effects, including by raising potential growth, and therefore a verifiable positive impact on the long-term sustainability of public finances, will be taken into account,' and a safety margin with respect to the 3% reference value must be preserved at all times.

With regard to the corrective arm, the changes introduced go in the direction of introducing more flexibility into the EDP, in particular by relaxing, adding specificity to or clarifying the availability of various escape clauses. The changes include:

- *The definition of a 'severe economic downturn'*: The benchmark for a severe economic downturn is now a negative annual real GDP growth rate or an accumulated loss of output during a protracted period of very low annual real GDP growth relative to potential growth.
- *Specification of the 'other relevant factors'*: The Treaty specifies that, in its report that constitutes the first step of an EDP, the Commission should take into account '*all other relevant factors, including the medium-term economic and budgetary position of the Member State*'. However, neither the Treaty nor the original SGP further elaborated what these other relevant factors might be. The reformed SGP now more explicitly spells out the relevant factors that should be taken into account. Regarding the medium-term economic position, these include in particular potential growth, the prevailing cyclical conditions, the implementation of the Lisbon Agenda, and policies to foster research and

development and innovation. Relevant developments in the medium-term budgetary position include fiscal consolidation efforts in 'good times', debt sustainability, public investment, and the overall quality of public finances. Attention should also be given to any other factors which, in the opinion of the Member State concerned, are relevant to a comprehensive assessment of the excess over the reference value in qualitative terms. Special consideration will be given to budgetary efforts towards increasing or maintaining a high level of financial contributions with the aim of fostering international solidarity and achieving European policy goals, notably the unification of Europe, if they have a detrimental effect on growth and the fiscal burden of the Member State. However, when assessing whether or not a deficit above 3% of GDP is to be considered excessive, the other relevant factors are only taken into account if the general government deficit remains 'close to' the reference value, and if the excess over the reference value is 'temporary'. If the Council has decided that an excessive deficit exists, the other relevant factors will be considered when issuing recommendations or notices to the Member State concerned.

- *Extension of procedural deadlines*: A number of procedural deadlines have been extended. These include the deadline for the Council to issue its recommendation to the Member State in excessive deficit (extended from three to four months after the date on which the excessive deficit was first reported), the deadline for effective action in response to a Council recommendation (extended from four to six months), the deadline for the Council to issue a notice if it has established that no effective action has been taken in response to its recommendation (extended from one month to two months), and the deadline for taking effective action in response to a notice (extended from two to four months).

- *Extension of the deadlines for the correction of excessive deficits*: The standard deadline for correcting an excessive deficit remains the 'year following its identification unless there are special circumstances'. However, the consideration of whether there are special circumstances justifying an extension by one year should take into account a balanced overall assessment of the 'other relevant factors' mentioned above. Moreover, the initial deadline for correction should be set such that the Member State with an excessive deficit will have to achieve a minimum annual improvement in its cyclically adjusted balance of 0.5% of GDP as a benchmark, net of one-off and temporary measures.

- *Unexpected adverse events and repeated recommendations or notices*: The original SGP did not explicitly provide for the reissuance of Council recommendations or for the extension of deadlines for the correction of excessive deficits, and these issues were at the heart of the procedural deadlock in the EDPs for Germany and France. The SGP reform has now clarified such matters by explicitly stating that if effective action has been taken in compliance with a recommendation under Article 104(7) of the Treaty or a notice under Article 104(9) of the Treaty, and if '*unexpected adverse economic events with major unfavourable consequences for government finances*' occur after the adoption of the recommendation or notice, the Council may decide to issue a revised recommendation or notice, which may also extend the deadline for the correction of the excessive deficit by one year.

- *Increasing the focus on debt and sustainability*: The ECOFIN Council report of March 2005 also called for a strengthening of debt surveillance, for example by applying the Treaty concept of a debt ratio that is 'sufficiently diminishing and approaching the reference value at a satisfactory pace'. However, no agreement could be reached on a quantitative definition of the satisfactory pace of debt reduction, as had been proposed by the Commission, and no changes to the Pact regulations were introduced.

Finally, concerning governance, the reform of the SGP did not, in itself, introduce major changes in the area of governance. In particular, it did not change the basic procedures and voting rules, which in any case would require changes to the Treaty. However, the ECOFIN Council report of March 2005 did make a number of proposals and suggestions for improving governance and strengthening national ownership of the rules. In this context, it called for closer co-operation between Member States, the Commission and the Council, as well as for improved peer support and peer pressure. It called for the development of complementary national budgetary rules, the continuity of budgetary targets when a new government takes office and greater involvement of national parliaments. It also stressed the importance of reliable macroeconomic forecasts and budgetary statistics.

2.4   The implementation of the reformed SGP: initial experiences and challenges

Reactions to the reform of the SGP were quite diverse. The proliferation of escape clauses under the EDP led some to conclude that the reform represented a significant watering-down of the rules while not having addressed the essential problem of weak enforcement provisions (e.g. Calmfors, 2005; Feldstein, 2005). Others, by contrast, emphasized positive elements. The Commission considers that the reform has increased the economic rationale of the SGP and should therefore lead to increased ownership on the part of Member States, although it also points out that the Council deviated from its initial reform proposals in certain respects (European Commission, 2005).

More important than the precise wording of the revised EU fiscal rules is their effective implementation. Even if the new rules may, on the whole, be more flexible and less stringent than the old ones, they can, presumably, still enhance fiscal discipline if they are implemented in a rigorous manner. But this will depend on whether the reform achieves the objective of renewing ownership and strengthening political commitment to the rules on the part of Member States. Alternatively the reform may merely serve as a green light for opportunistic behaviour, minimalist efforts, and an implementation of the rules that is determined by political pressure and horse-trading (Coeuré and Pisani-Ferry, 2005; Buti, 2006). Bearing this in mind, this section examines the first experiences with the implementation of the new framework in the first year and a half or so after the reform. It should be stressed, however, that at this stage any assessment of the implementation of the reformed Pact has to focus primarily on *ex ante* fiscal plans and decisions and in this sense has to be seen as preliminary. Ultimately, the success or failure of the reformed SGP will be judged on *ex post* fiscal outcomes, in particular on whether it actually delivers a timely correction of excessive deficits and the achievement of sound public finances in the euro area notably in the context of the next cyclical downswing.

2.4.1 The implementation of the reformed preventive arm

Between December 2005 and February 2006, all euro area Member States submitted their first updated stability programmes under the revised framework. The content of these programmes and the assessment and opinions of the Commission and the ECOFIN Council provided the first indications as to the impact of the changes to the preventive arm on Member States' medium-term fiscal plans.[19]

MTOs in the updated stability programmes

According to the revised SGP, MTOs should ensure rapid progress towards fiscal sustainability. As soon as an appropriate methodology has been agreed, MTOs should take into account implicit liabilities stemming from future age-related spending. In the meantime, however, and in accordance with the ECOFIN Council report of March 2005, MTOs are differentiated primarily in the light of countries' debt/GDP ratios and potential growth. Moreover, in this context, it has been decided to give more weight to the debt ratio in determining country-specific MTOs (see Commission, 2006). Bearing these clarifications in mind and given the predefined range for euro area MTOs of between −1% of GDP to 'in balance or surplus', the following three reasonable working assumptions concerning the MTOs can be made. First, only countries with debt/GDP ratios below the 60% reference value should be allowed to target deficits of up to 1% of GDP. Second, countries with debt ratios above the 60% of GDP reference value should aim for budgets that are at least 'close to balance' (i.e. a deficit of no more than 0.5% of GDP) in order to bring their debt ratios towards the reference value at a satisfactory pace. Third, countries with very high debt ratios should be more ambitious and target budgetary positions that are 'in balance or surplus'.

Adopting these working assumptions, the MTOs presented by euro area Member States in their stability programmes all seem to be at least consistent with the requirements of the reformed Pact. The countries targeting deficits of up to 1% of GDP (Luxembourg and the Netherlands) have debt ratios below the 60% reference value. Portugal is targeting a deficit of up to 0.5% of GDP, which is consistent with the fact that its debt ratio currently lies within a medium range of 60–80% of GDP. All the other countries are targeting either balanced or in-surplus budgetary positions.

The picture that emerges from the stability programmes in terms of actual and planned compliance with MTOs is less satisfactory, however. In 2005 only four out of 12 euro area Member States (Spain, Ireland, the Netherlands and Finland) reported outcomes that were in line with their MTOs. Three out of the remaining eight Member States (Belgium, Austria and Luxembourg) plan to achieve their MTOs by the end of the period covered in their stability programmes. Extrapolating planned consolidation progress towards the end of the programme periods into the future suggests that all countries that are currently in excessive deficit at the time (Germany, Greece, France, Italy and Portugal) do not intend to achieve their MTOs until (in some cases well into) the next decade. This horizon clearly calls into question the relevance of these targets for policymaking (which typically looks at most at the next three to four years as the medium-term horizon) and, hence, for assessing medium-term fiscal positions.

It is also important to bear in mind that the MTOs presented in the updated stability programmes do not yet take into account implicit liabilities related to future ageing-related expenditures. At present, the Council opinions on the stability programmes provide an assessment of the sustainability of public finances in the light of such liabilities, and categorize their positions as being either low, medium or high risk. As can be seen from Table 2.3, however, there is no obvious link between this assessment and the MTOs.

The adjustment path towards the MTO

The benchmark adjustment path introduced by the new Pact represents a development of previous commitments rather than an entirely new initiative. Responding to proposals by the Commission, in October 2002 the Eurogroup agreed that euro area Member States with budgetary imbalances should improve their underlying fiscal positions by at least 0.5% of GDP per annum. At the time, it was hoped that expressing consolidation requirements in terms of an annual adjustment effort, rather than setting a date for achieving a close-to-balance budget, would prevent any undue

Table 2.3 Main elements of updated stability programmes and Council opinions

	MTO	*Year in which MTO achieved*	*Sustainability risk*	*Recommendation on national institutions*
Belgium	0.5% Surplus	2007	Medium	No
Germany	Budget balance	~2011–12	Medium	Yes
Greece	Budget balance	~2013	High	Yes
Spain	Budget balance	Already	Medium	No
France	Budget balance	2010	Medium	Yes
Ireland	Budget balance	Already	Medium	No
Italy	Budget balance	~2011–2012	Medium	Yes
Luxembourg	0.8% deficit	2007	Medium	No
Netherlands	−1% to −0.5% deficit	Already	Medium	No
Austria	Budget balance	2008	Low	No
Portugal	−0.5% deficit or better	~2011	High	Yes
Finland	1.5% surplus	Already	Low	No

Source: Updated stability programmes December 2005-February 2006, and Council opinions.

back-loading of fiscal adjustment. Moreover, expressing the adjustment effort in structural terms was intended to ensure that consolidation would not compromise the stabilization function of fiscal policy, since the automatic fiscal stabilizers can be allowed to operate around a predefined structural adjustment path (provided that there is a sufficient safety margin to prevent breaches of the 3% deficit threshold).

The provisions introduced by the SGP reform differ slightly from the earlier Eurogroup agreement. It has now been made more explicit that the adjustment effort should be measured net of one-off and temporary measures. This can be seen as a strengthening of the adjustment requirement with the welcome intention of reducing, if not excluding, the recourse to measures that do not contribute to sustainable consolidation. At the same time, there is more flexibility in that the 0.5% annual adjustment path is now described as a benchmark around which efforts can vary in good times and bad times. A reasonable interpretation of the reformed SGP provisions is that the overall adjustment effort should be the same over the medium term as in the case of a constant annual adjustment of 0.5%. However, fluctuations in the nominal balance could be greater, with more scope for differentiating consolidation efforts in response to the cyclical position of the economy. Figure 2.3 illustrates two scenarios with identical starting and end points, but with very different adjustment paths for the nominal and structural balance.

Examining the adjustment path towards MTOs presented in the first set of post reform stability programmes, it appears that planned compliance with the new adjustment path benchmark is only partially satisfactory (see Table 2.4). All of the seven euro area countries with budgetary imbalances at least plan to adhere to the 0.5% annual adjustment benchmark on average over the course of the programme period. In the cases of Greece, Italy and Portugal, planned consolidation is some-what more ambitious than the benchmark adjustment path, reflecting the setting of fiscal targets to comply with Council recommendations and notices under the EDP. For the remaining four countries with budgetary imbalances (Germany, France,

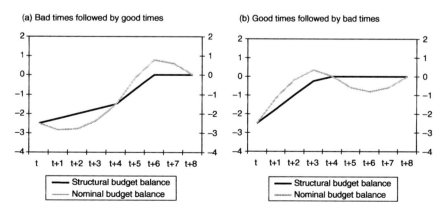

Figure 2.3 Stylised representation of the adjustment path towards the MTO (as a % of GDP).

Table 2.4 Fiscal developments under the revised SGP (as a % of GDP)

	Outcomes		Plans in 2005–6 stability programmes			
	2005	2006	2005	2006	2007	2008
General government budget balance						
Belgium	−2.3	0.2	0.0	0.0	0.3	0.5
Germany	−3.2	−1.7	−3.3	−3.3	−2.5	−2.0
Greece	−5.5	−2.6	−4.3	−2.6	−2.3	−1.7
Spain	1.1	1.8	1.0	0.9	0.7	0.6
France	−3.0	−2.5	−3.0	−2.9	−2.6	−1.9
Ireland	1.0	2.9	0.3	−0.6	−0.8	−0.8
Italy	−4.2	−4.4	−4.3	−3.5	−2.8	−2.1
Luxembourg	−0.3	0.1	−2.3	−1.8	−1.0	−0.2
Netherlands	−0.3	0.6	−1.2	−1.5	−1.2	−1.1
Austria	−1.6	−1.1	−1.9	−1.7	−0.8	0.0
Portugal	−6.1	−3.9	−6.0	−4.6	−3.7	−2.6
Finland	2.7	3.9	1.8	1.6	1.6	1.5
Euro area	**−2.5**	**−1.6**	**−2.5**	**−2.3**	**−1.8**	**−1.4**
Structural budget balance						
Belgium	0.0	−0.4	0.0	−0.3	0.4	0.7
Germany	−2.4	−1.5	−3.0	−2.9	−1.8	−1.5
Greece	−6.1	−3.9	−4.8	−3.7	−2.8	−2.4
Spain	1.6	2.3	1.2	1.2	1.2	0.9
France	−3.2	−2.3	−3.3	−2.9	−2.3	−1.5
Ireland	1.0	2.9	1.1	0.1	0.1	0.1
Italy	−3.9	−2.6	−4.1	−3.2	−2.3	−1.7
Luxembourg	1.0	0.5	−1.5	−1.2	−0.6	0.1
Netherlands	0.7	1.1	0.1	−0.7	−0.6	−0.6
Austria	−1.1	−1.0	−1.6	−1.2	−0.4	0.2
Portugal	−5.0	−2.9	−5.0	−3.4	−2.6	−1.8
Finland	3.6	3.7	2.1	1.7	1.7	1.8
General government debt						
Euro area	**70.5**	**69.0**	**71.0**	**70.8**	**69.6**	**64.7**

Sources: European Commission. Member States' updated stability programmes.

Luxembourg and Austria), planned consolidation is in line with (but does not go far beyond) the 0.5% annual adjustment on average. What is much less satisfactory, however, is an apparent back-loading of consolidation efforts, with these four countries targeting adjustments of less than 0.5% of GDP in 2006.

Interpreting fiscal plans under the new preventive arm

One way of assessing the impact of the SGP reform on fiscal plans under the preventive arm is to compare the implications for the euro area of the fiscal plans presented in the stability programmes prior to and after the reform. Figure 2.4 compares how euro area real GDP growth and the main euro area fiscal aggregates

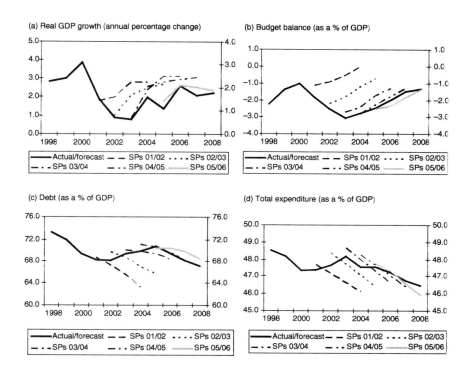

Figure 2.4 Euro area fiscal outlook: new versus old stability programmes.

Sources: Member States' updated stability programmes 2001–6 and own calculations, European Commission Autumn 2006 economic forecasts (AMECO database).

are assumed to evolve in the first post-reform round of stability programme updates compared to pre-reform programme updates, as well as vis-à-vis actual developments (up until 2005) and the European Commission's autumn 2006 forecasts (for the period 2006–8).

According to the post-reform programmes, real GDP growth is assumed to pick up to around its potential rate and then remain close to that level in the coming years (see Panel *a* of Figure 2.4). This is broadly in line with the Commission's forecast, although the stability programmes are slightly more optimistic with respect to 2007 and 2008. These growth assumptions are similar to those presented in pre-reform programmes, although they appear to have become slightly more moderate and more realistic, especially with respect to the later years of the programme horizon. Indeed, according to the Commission assessments of the post-reform programmes, most Member States did base their fiscal plans on realistic or plausible macroeconomic assumptions.

As for the euro area budget balance (Panel *b* of Figure 2.4), the envisaged adjustment in the post-reform stability programme updates is smaller than in previous programme updates, amounting to around 1% of GDP over three years (2006–8), compared to around 1.5% of GDP in previous programmes. Moreover, Figure 2.4 illustrates the above-mentioned very limited planned improvement in the budget balance in 2006 and an increase in the degree of back-loading of consolidation efforts. The slower decline in the planned deficit is also reflected in a more gradual decline in the debt/GDP ratio, which is planned to fall by only around 1% of GDP between 2005 and 2008.[20] Finally, in terms of the composition of planned fiscal consolidation, there is little change compared with previous years, with most Member States focusing on expenditure restraint, as can be seen from the projected reduction in the expenditure/GDP ratio (see Panel *d*).

One way of interpreting these numbers is that, having missed targets in previous years, Member States have decided to use the additional flexibility provided by the reformed SGP to present more realistic (i.e. achievable) deficit and debt targets. If such targets were actually achieved, this would constitute a strengthening of the preventive arm. However, the reduced ambition of the programmes also implies that unless compliance with fiscal plans genuinely improves, actual fiscal outcomes may develop less favourably (or at least not better) than before the SGP reform, which would imply that the preventive arm has been adjusted to accommodate existing policies rather than the other way around.

In fact the reform of the SGP has coincided with a much-improved economic outlook. In 2005 and even more so in 2006, most euro area governments benefited from significant revenue windfalls loading to budget outcomes that were significantly better than planned. This stands in stark contrast to the distinctly less favourable environment in 2001–3 that culminated in the breakdown of the 'original' SGP. Indeed, since the first stability programmes were submitted in 1998, there now appears to have been more or less a full economic and budgetary cycle so that the conditions facing the revised SGP are akin to those faced in the first years by its predecessor. This should perhaps serve as a warning not to draw premature conclusions regarding the success of the revised SGP on the basis of just fiscal plans and one or two years of fiscal outcomes. Rather, the revised Pact will ultimately need to be judged on how it performs in good and bad times. For now, the challenge for implementing the revised preventive arm is to avoid repeating past mistakes and to ensure that significant consolidation progress is actually made to reach safe budgetary positions before 'good times' come to an end.

Since the SGP reform five euro area countries (Germany, Greece, France, Italy and Portugal) have been the subject of ongoing EDPs. Among these, Germany and France first exceeded the 3% of GDP reference value in 2002 and, in the following year, received recommendations from the Council to correct the situation by 2004 at the latest. Following the procedural deadlock of November 2003, this deadline was *de facto* extended to 2005.[21]

France's deficit was marginally below 3% of GDP in 2005 (and the EDP for France was abrogated in January 2007). Germany's deficit remained above 3% of GDP in 2005 and towards the end of that year the German government announced a package of fiscal measures which effectively targeted the correction of its excessive deficit only in 2007. In the light of the continued breach of the reference value, the Council decided to move to the next step of the EDP by issuing a notice to

Germany under Article 104(9) of the Treaty.[22] Flexibility was shown, however, by granting an extension until 2007 to correct the excessive deficit, in line with the German government's announced fiscal plans. The reasons stated for this extension included the fact that Germany's budgetary adjustment was embedded in a comprehensive strategy, that measures were well advanced in the legislative process and that some measures already implemented would only produce results with a lag. It was also deemed sufficient that Germany would comply with the 0.5% annual adjustment path on average in 2006 and 2007 rather than in each individual year. Following the Council's decision, however, the budgetary situation in Germany evolved more favourably and the deficit was brought well below 3% of GDP already in 2006.

The EDP against Greece was launched in 2004 (following an initial breach of the reference value in 2003), and the Greek government was given until 2005 to correct the excessive deficit. By early 2005 it became clear that Greece was facing severe difficulties in complying with this deadline, in particular given that statistical revisions had pushed Greece's deficit well above the 3% threshold (and also confirmed breaches of the reference value in earlier years). The Council therefore issued a notice to Greece to take measures to correct its excessive deficit by 2006, which on the basis of fiscal data available in early 2007 appears to have been achieved.

EDPs against Italy and Portugal were launched shortly after the SGP reform. In the case of Italy, this was due to a breach of the 3% reference value being confirmed for 2004. Moreover, due to low growth and a phasing-out of temporary measures, the government announced that it planned an even higher deficit of around 4% of GDP in 2005. Portugal, meanwhile, announced that it would no longer take temporary measures to keep its deficit below 3% of GDP as it had done in the previous three years and that, as a result, its deficit in 2005 would rise to around 6% of GDP.

In July and September 2005 respectively, the Council decided that Italy and Portugal had excessive deficits and issued recommendations for their correction.[23] Since neither Italy nor Portugal could be considered to have deficits that were close to and only temporarily above 3% of GDP, the revised exceptional circumstances clause was not applicable, and the Commission's assessment of the other relevant factors was not taken into account when deciding whether or not the deficits were excessive.

When setting the deadlines for the correction of the excessive deficits, however, in both cases 'special circumstances' were found to warrant extensions. In the case of Italy, the cyclical weakness of the economy and the size of the required adjustment were deemed sufficient grounds to grant a one-year extension of the deadline to 2007. After realizing the deterioration of Italy's budgetary position in 2005, the Council recommended that Italy undertake a structural consolidation effort amounting to 1.6% of GDP by 2007, with at least half of this adjustment occurring in 2006. In the case of Portugal, the same reasons as well as the intention to no longer rely on temporary measures were considered as warranting an extension by two years to 2008.

Interpreting the implementation of the new corrective arm

The initial experience outlined above suggests that the changes introduced by the SGP reform have facilitated decision-making under the corrective arm. Procedural deadlocks such as the one that occurred in the context of the EDPs for Germany and France in November 2003 have not been repeated. All deficits above 3% of GDP have been considered excessive. In the case of Germany, a decision to issue a Council notice under Article 104(9) of the Treaty (which was the main stumbling block in November 2003) was taken without any controversy. Fiscal targets in the affected countries are mostly in line with minimum requirements under the respective EDPs. Moreover, recourse to temporary measures appears to be significantly reduced, which is encouraging given that the extended use of one-off measures and creative accounting was a factor that undermined the implementation of the original SGP.

With regard to the use of the additional flexibility and broader escape clauses, it may be premature to draw any firm conclusions, particularly since initial experiences may reflect a transition from the old to a new steady state. However, in all three countries for which important decisions have been taken, the invoking of special circumstances (in the case of Portugal and Italy) and *ad hoc* justifications (in the case of Germany) to extend deadlines could be viewed as a lenient implementation of the new rules.

Another conclusion that can be drawn from the experience so far is that the new rules introduced by the reform are themselves malleable. For example, while the reformed Pact refers to the possibility of extending deadlines 'by one year', deadlines have been extended by two years in the cases of Portugal and Germany. In the case of Germany, the 'annual' 0.5% of GDP adjustment benchmark was applied in cumulative terms over a two-year period (hence becoming a 'biennial' benchmark) in order to accommodate a longer deadline. Even if one rationale behind the SGP reform was to clarify and codify the flexibility or judgement that had previously been exercised under the EDP, room for (additional) discretion remains.

From the perspective of governance, it is notable that all recommendations issued so far under the reformed corrective arm have effectively endorsed the budget plans of the Member States concerned, although in some cases the latter may already have reflected the interests and concerns of the Commission and the other Member States. The emphasis has thus been on peer support for previously announced policies (with the Member State in question acting as leader, and the Council as a follower). Moreover, the call for 'closer co-operation between the Member States, the Commission and the Council' seems to be implemented by the Commission trying to strike a balance between issuing recommendations that boost consolidation in line with the revised Pact while also achieving qualified majority support in the Council. In this way the Commission acts as a 'consensus builder', which not only has the advantage of facilitating a smooth implementation of the EDP, but also limits the Commission's ability to act as an independent arbiter.

2.5 Conclusions

In the run-up to EMU, fiscal positions in euro area Member States improved significantly as Member States sought to comply with the 3% of GDP reference value of the Maastricht Treaty for participation in the single currency. The SGP, adopted shortly prior to the introduction of the euro, was intended to promote fiscal discipline once the incentive of EMU membership had disappeared by subjecting Member States' fiscal policies to clear rules and surveillance procedures.

Experience with the implementation of the SGP has been mixed, however. While some countries managed to achieve and maintain sound budgetary positions, in accordance with the rules, six euro area Member States (including the largest three, Germany, France and Italy) have incurred excessive deficits. Moreover, as fiscal positions deteriorated, the implementation of the SGP procedures became beset with difficulties and criticisms of the rules themselves also became louder.

The 2005 reform of the SGP did not fundamentally change the Pact's original two-armed (i.e. its preventive/corrective) structure, but it did respond to criticisms by making the rules and procedures more flexible. While the changes to the preventive arm could essentially be considered as a shift in favour of sophisticated as opposed to simple rules, in the context of the corrective arm the increased flexibility is associated with less stringent rules and procedures. Compared to the original framework, there are now more grounds for permitting deficits above 3% and extending deadlines for their correction. For this reason, the reform has been criticized as a weakening of the EU fiscal framework and there is a risk that it will result in more frequent and more persistent deficits above 3% of GDP and less favourable debt developments.

Ultimately, what matters, however, is how effectively the revised SGP will be implemented. Notwithstanding some additional flexibility of the rules, a rigorous implementation of the revised framework would be conducive to fiscal discipline and sound public finances in EMU. So far, the implementation of the new rules has been smooth, but there are also worrying signs of consolidation efforts in some countries again tending to be back-loaded. A full and proper assessment of the revised SGP will only be possible when its implementation can be assessed over a full economic cycle. The agreement on the SGP reform appears to have coincided with the re-emergence of economic good times and significant revenue windfalls, which has not only contributed to improving fiscal balances but also risks giving rise to complacency in the short-term. In order for the revised SGP to be deemed a success in the longer term, the revised preventive arm needs to deliver more in 'good times' while the increased room for judgement under the corrective arm needs to be backed by appropriate, credible and timely enforcement. In short, much depends on whether the reform gives rise to enhanced ownership of the rules on the part of the Member States, the Council and the Commission and to an intelligent but 'strict' and 'symmetric' use of the additional flexibility that they imply.

Notes

1 This chapter partly draws on and updates (until spring 2007) previous work, in particular Morris *et al.* (2006). The views expressed in this paper are those of the authors and do not necessarily reflect those of the ECB. JEL classification: E61, E62, H6. Key words: Stability and Growth Pact, Fiscal policy, Fiscal rules, EMU.

2 See ECB (2001).

3 For a more detailed overview of fiscal developments since the early 1990s, see Briotti (2004).

4 For an inside account of the negotiations leading to the agreement on the SGP, see Stark (2001). For an analysis of the economic and political factors that led to the SGP, see Heipertz and Verdun (2004).

5 The two Council Regulations are Council Regulation 1466/97 'on the strengthening of the surveillance of budgetary positions and the surveillance and coordination of economic policies' (the preventive arm), and Council Regulation 1467/97 'on speeding up and clarifying the implementation of the excessive deficit procedure' (the corrective arm). These are supplemented by a European Council Resolution on the SGP and a Code of Conduct, although these are not legally binding.

6 Resolution of the European Council on the SGP, Amsterdam, June 1997.

7 Non-euro area Member States submit convergence programmes.

8 On the role of budgetary policy in responding to cyclical developments in the context of the SGP see Stark and Manzke (2002).

9 In this sense, recent experience in the euro area appears to support the findings of a growing body of literature on fiscal consolidation which argues that revenue-based fiscal adjustments tend to be less successful (i.e. less sustainable) than consolidations based primarily on expenditure restraint (Alesina and Perotti, 1995; von Hagen *et al.*, 2001). See also Briotti (2004) for an overview.

10 Regarding one-off measures and creative accounting see Koen and van den Noord (2005).

11 ECOFIN Council conclusions of 12 February 2002.

12 In the case of Portugal, a public finances audit in spring 2002 showed that the deficit had already exceeded 3% of GDP by a considerable margin back in 2001. Hence, the Commission's recommendation for an 'early' warning actually followed the breaching of the reference value.

13 Commission recommendations of 18 November 2003 for Council decisions giving notice to Germany and France to take measures to correct their excessive deficits.

14 ECOFIN Council conclusions of 25 November 2003.

15 Ruling of the ECJ of 13 July 2004 on the affair C-27/04 by the Commission of the European Communities against the Council of the European Union.

16 See the Commission Communication to the Council and the European Parliament of November 2002 on strengthening the co-ordination of budgetary policies, and the ECOFIN Council report of March 2003 on strengthening the implementation of the SGP.

17 See the Commission Communication to the Council and the European Parliament of September 2004 on strengthening economic governance and clarifying the implementation of the SGP. See also Deroose and Langedijk (2005) for an overview of the European Commission's motivations for and approach to reforming the SGP.

18 The changes are laid down in two new Council Regulations, No 1055/2005 and No 1056/2005 amending Regulations 1466/97 and 1467/97 respectively.

19 As far as actual fiscal outcomes are concerned, 2005 budget balances turned out to be somewhat better than expected in the autumn of 2005 while falling marginally short of the target implied by the 2004/5 vintage of stability programmes (see panel b of Figure 2.4). It seems premature to attribute this development to the reform of the SGP, however, since the relevant fiscal policy decisions and plans were adopted prior to the reform,

while fiscal balances in some countries were boosted by unexplained, non-discretionary increases in tax revenues.

20 The comparison of previous stability programme targets and actual fiscal outcomes in Figure 2.4 is affected by recent changes to national accounts. The latter have resulted in upward revisions of GDP and corresponding downward revisions in government revenue, expenditure and debt when expressed as a percentage of GDP. This explains why debt/GDP ratios and expenditure/GDP ratios were initially observed to be at higher levels in the 01/02 to 04/05 programme vintages than currently recorded by actual data.

21 Following the annulment by the ECJ of the ECOFIN Council conclusions of 25 November 2003, the Commission issued a Communication in December 2004 setting out its approach in the context of the EDPs against Germany and France. In its Communications the Commission concluded that the Council's initial recommendation under Article 104(7) remained in force. However, in the light of subsequent events, it argued that the 2004 deadline should be extended to 2005. The ECOFIN Council endorsed this approach at its meeting on 18 January 2005.

22 Council Decision of 14 March 2006 giving notice to Germany to take measures to correct its excessive deficit.

23 Council Recommendation of 28 July 2005 with a view to bringing to an end the situation of an excessive deficit in Italy; Council Recommendation of 20 September 2005 with a view to bringing to an end the situation of an excessive deficit in Portugal.

References

Alesina, A. and Drazen, A. (1991), 'Why are stabilisations delayed?', *American Economic Review*, 82: 1170–88.

Alesina, A. and Perotti, R. (1995), 'Fiscal expansions and adjustments in OECD countries', *Economic Policy*, 14(2): 210–48.

Bini Smaghi, L. (2004), 'What went wrong with the Stability and Growth Pact?' Paper presented at the conference on Monetary Union in Europe: Historical Perspectives and Prospects for the Future, Copenhagen.

Blanchard, O. J. and Giavazzi, F. (2004), 'Improving the SGP through a proper accounting of public investment', CEPR Discussion Paper no. 4220.

Briotti, M. G. (2004), 'Fiscal adjustment between 1991 and 2002: stylised facts and policy implications', ECB Occasional Paper no. 9.

—— (2005), 'Economic reactions to public finance consolidations: a survey of the literature', ECB Occasional Paper no. 38.

Buiter, W. and Grafe, C. (2002), 'Patching up the Pact: some suggestions for enhancing fiscal sustainability and macroeconomic stability in an enlarged European Union', CEPR Discussion Paper no. 3496.

Buti, M. (2006), 'Will the new Stability and Growth Pact succeed? An economic and political perspective', European Commission Economic Paper no. 241.

Buti, M. and van den Noord, P. (2003), 'Discretionary fiscal policies and elections: the experience of the early years of EMU', OECD Economic Department Working Paper no. 351.

Buti, M. Eijffinger, S. and Franco, D. (2003), 'Revisiting the Stability and Growth Pact: grand design or internal adjustment?', CEPR Discussion Paper no. 3692.

—— (2005), 'The Stability Pact pains: a forward-looking assessment of the reform debate', CEPR Discussion Paper no. 5216.

Buti, M., Franco, D. and Ongena, H. (1998), 'Fiscal discipline and flexibility in EMU: the implementation of the Stability and Growth Pact', *Oxford Review of Economic Policy*, 14: 81–97.

Calmfors, L. (2005), 'What remains of the Stability Pact and what next?', Swedish Institute for European Policy Studies, 2005:8.

Coeuré, B. and Pisani-Ferry, J. (2005), 'Fiscal policy in EMU: towards a Sustainability and Growth Pact', Bruegel Working Paper no. 2005/01.

Creel, R. and Fitoussi, J.-P. (2002), 'How to reform the European Central Bank', Centre for European Reform.

Deroose, S. and van Langedijk, S. (2005), 'Improving the Stability and Growth Pact: the Commission's three pillar approach', European Economy Occasional Paper no. 15.

European Central Bank Monthly Bulletin (2001), 'The economic policy framework in EMU', Frankfurt, November.

—— (2002), 'The operation of automatic stabilisers in the euro area', Frankfurt, April.

—— (2005), 'The reform of the Stability and Growth Pact', Frankfurt, August.

—— (2006), 'Fiscal policies and financial markets', Frankfurt, February.

European Commission (2005), 'Public finances in EMU', *European Economy*, 3/2005.

—— (2006a), 'Economic forecasts – spring 2006', *European Economy*, 2/2006.

—— (2006b), 'Public Finances in EMU', *European Economy*, 3/2006.

Fatás, A., von Hagen, J., Hughes-Hallet, A., Sibert, A. and Strauch, R. (2003), 'Stability and growth in Europe: Towards a better pact', CEPR – ZEI Monitoring European Integration, 13.

Feldstein, M. (2005), 'The euro and the Stability Pact', NBER Working Paper no. 11249.

Gros, D., Mayer, T. and Ubide, A. (2004), 'The nine lives of the Stability and Growth Pact: a special report of the CEPS Macroeconomic Policy Group', Centre for European Policy Studies, Brussels.

von Hagen, J., Hughes-Hallet, A. and Strauch, R. (2001), 'Budgetary consolidation in EMU', European Commission Economic Paper no. 148.

von Hagen, J., Halleberg, M. and Strauch, R. (2004), 'Budgetary forecasts in Europe – the track record of stability and convergence programmes', ECB Working Paper no. 307.

Heipertz, M. and Verdun, A. (2004), 'The dog that would never bite? What we can learn from the origins of the Stability and Growth Pact', *Journal of European Public Policy*, 11: 765–80.

Koen, V. and van den Noord, P. (2005), 'Fiscal gimmickry in Europe: one-off measures and creative accounting', OECD Economics Department Working Paper no. 417.

Marín, J. (2002), 'Sustainability of public finances and automatic stabilisation under a rule of budgetary discipline', ECB Working Paper no. 193.

Morris, R., Ongena, H. and Schuknecht, L. (2006), 'The reform and implementation of the Stability and Growth Pact', ECB Occasional Paper no. 47.

Pisani-Ferry, J. (2002), 'Fiscal discipline and policy coordination in the Eurozone: Assessment and proposals', Paper for the European Commission President's Group for Economic Analysis.

Schuknecht, L. (2004), 'Stability and Growth Pact: issues and lessons from political economy', *International Economics and Economic Policy*, 2: 65–89.

Stark, J. (2001), 'Genesis of a Pact', in A. Brunila, M. Buti and D. Franco (eds), *The Stability and Growth Pact: The Architecture of Fiscal Policy in EMU*, New York Palgrave.

Stark, J. and Manzke, B. (2002), 'Which role should budgetary policy play in response to cyclical developments?', Paper presented at the seminar of the Netherlands' ministry of finances on 'Budgetary policy in E(M)U: design and challenges', Mimeo.

Wyplosz, C. (2005), 'Fiscal policy: institutions versus rules', *National Institute Economic Review*, 191: 64–78.

3 Macroeconomic adjustment in the euro area

The role of fiscal policy

A. Muscatelli, T. Ropele and P. Tirelli

3.1 Introduction

There is a general consensus that national fiscal policies should play an enhanced role in adjusting to macroeconomic shocks within EMU. The absence of national monetary policies and the potentially destabilizing impact of inflation differentials on national real interest rates only leave fiscal policy as a tool to offset asymmetric shocks. Some economists have gone as far as advocating a greater emphasis on fiscal policy as a key policy instrument in macroeconomic adjustment (see Ball, 1997; Wren-Lewis, 2000, 2002). In the context of EMU, this has also led to calls to radically reform the Stability and Growth Pact and render fiscal policy-making more transparent. Calmfors (2003) argues for a more transparent institutional framework for national (discretionary) fiscal policies within EMU, with clear objectives and a solution based on national fiscal committees. Other economists have challenged this perspective and see automatic stabilizers, within the constraints of a reformed SGP, as the key to macroeconomic adjustment within EMU (Buti *et al.*, 1997, 2001; European Commission, 2001). This 'Brussels consensus' is based on the view that the ECB alone should stabilize the union-wide economy (Buti *et al.*, 2001). The key question which we ask is whether fiscal policy, modelled as feedback rules on output, that is, automatic stabilizers, adds value to the stabilization role played by monetary policy in the euro area.

In this chapter we examine the validity of this proposition and assess the performance of fiscal stabilizers within EMU. We do this using a small two-country DSGE model of EMU, estimated using the synthetic euro-data collected over the period 1970–98. While the structural model used in this chapter has many elements in common with other New Keynesian DSGE models, our analysis differs in a number of respects. First, relative to similar New Keynesian models, we include a wider range of fiscal policy transmission channels, including 'non-Ricardian' effects on consumption due to rule-of-thumb (RoT, henceforth) consumers (as in Galí *et al.*, 2007; Amato and Laubach, 2003; and Muscatelli *et al.*, 2003) and supply-side distortions. Second, our model is estimated, whereas others use calibration or numerical simulations (see Andres and Domenech, 2003). Third, our two-country model features a home bias in consumption which, as we shall demonstrate, impacts on how automatic fiscal stabilizers interact with monetary policy in a monetary union.

Earlier contributions (Andres and Domenech, 2006; Gordon and Leeper, 2003; Muscatelli *et al.*, 2004) found that counter-cyclical fiscal policy can be welfare-reducing in the presence of optimizing consumers. Muscatelli *et al.* (2003) estimate the proportion of RoT consumers in the United States and show that automatic stabilizers based on taxation improve the performance of the economy. Here we find that the proportion of RoT consumers is far larger in the euro area, possibly due to financial market imperfections. This result is in line with a relatively large body of empirical evidence. Asdrubali and Kim (2004) find that, following an output shock, EU capital markets enable a very limited degree of consumption smoothing relative to the United States. Fair (2001) finds that, unlike the United States, in most EU countries there is little evidence of real interest rate effects on aggregate consumption. This is easily reconciled with our result about the large share of RoT consumers who do not directly react to interest rate shocks. Finally, our estimate is consistent with the cross-country evidence about the share of current income consumers presented in Sarantis and Stewart (2003).

We use our estimates to simulate a two-country version of the model with a single central bank and independent fiscal authorities. We find that the stabilizing effects of fiscal policy in response to EMU-wide shocks carry over to the case of asymmetric disturbances only if a significant home bias characterizes national consumption bundles. Thus, our results suggest a novel approach to the philosophy of EMU macroeconomic policy-making. At the euro area level, the action of automatic stabilizers should be regarded as a useful complement to the ECB actions. On the other hand, the usual case for fiscal stabilization of within-EMU asymmetric shocks is confirmed only if the composition of national aggregate demand functions is sufficiently biased towards domestic production. This is in sharp contrast with the 'Brussels consensus' based on the view that the ECB alone should stabilize the union-wide economy (Buti *et al.*, 2001).

In the next section we outline our model and the empirical methodology. In Section 3.3 we report our econometric results and illustrate the properties of the model by looking at its impulse responses. In Section 3.4 we consider the value-added of having national fiscal stabilizers in EMU using our two-country monetary union model. Section 3.5 concludes.

3.2   A two-country New Keynesian model with home-biased consumer preferences

3.2.1   *General approach*

Early vintages of New Keynesian DSGE models involved a limited role for fiscal policy, by assuming lump-sum taxation and representative agents with infinite planning horizon. Another strand of literature has modelled more complex supply-side effects for fiscal stabilization policies by allowing distortionary taxation (see Andres and Domenech, 2003 and the references therein).

Studies of the business cycle using VAR-type models do not provide empirical support for this simple description of demand-side effects in the New Keynesian model. Giavazzi *et al.* (2000) show that both Keynesian and neoclassical (Ricardian) effects are present. Fatas and Mihov (2001), Blanchard and Perotti (2002) and Muscatelli *et al.* (2004) show that fiscal shocks have conventional Keynesian effects, in that an increase in government spending causes a persistent rise in output[1] and consumption. Galí *et al.* (2007) demonstrate that this problem can be addressed by adding non-optimizing behaviour to the conventional New Keynesian model. They assume that a proportion of consumers are constrained to consume out of current income and show that, under plausible parameterizations, this provides an explanation for the positive response of consumption to a temporary government spending shock. The increase in government spending generates an increase in real wage (providing the substitution effect between consumption and leisure dominates the wealth effect), and causes an increase in aggregate consumption because RoT consumers spend out of current income.[2] Introducing non-optimizing consumers also potentially allows for other transmission channels for fiscal policy. Even if taxes are lump sum, they will impact on aggregate consumption behaviour through their effect on the current nominal income of RoT consumers. Furthermore, payroll taxes affect marginal costs and inflation. This, in turn, has an obvious impact on aggregate consumption if wages are sticky.

There are other ways, however, to model non-Ricardian consumers. Debt-financed fiscal deficits will have an impact on aggregate demand in versions of the New Keynesian model which depart from Ricardian equivalence because of the presence of finite horizons, as in the classic Blanchard–Yaari model (Leith and Wren-Lewis, 2000). Other effects of government debt on consumer behaviour can also be considered, such as the impact that financial wealth has on household transaction costs, which can explain the observed positive correlation between public expenditure shocks and consumption (see Schabert, 2004).

Unfortunately, there is a trade-off between estimating New Keynesian models which contain all these channels of fiscal policy transmission and maintaining the model sufficiently parsimonious in terms of structural parameters to allow the use of classical econometric techniques. A complex model will typically be under-identified with respect to the structural parameters of interest or will result in poorly defined (in a statistical sense) estimated parameters. In modelling the transmission of fiscal policies, we have therefore chosen to restrict the demand side to the inclusion of non-optimizing (RoT) consumers. On the supply side, we allow for taxation effects on firms' marginal costs (through payroll taxes). This allows for a richer range of transmission channels for fiscal policy than with early attempts to estimate structural New Keynesian models.[3]

3.2.2 The model

The global economy (monetary union) consists of two countries of equal size: Home country (H) and Foreign country (F). We ignore third-country effects. The two economies are totally symmetric. The structural model will then reduce to a small forward-looking New Keynesian DSGE model, comprising, for each country, a dynamic "IS" equation for output and a 'New Keynesian Phillips Curve' specification for inflation. In addition to the channels for fiscal policy transmission outlined above, we allow for habit formation in consumption, which is necessary to capture the observed persistence in the output-gap response to shocks (see Leith and Malley, 2005). We model a hybrid Phillips curve, allowing for partly backward-looking inflation expectations (see Galí *et al.* 2001, 2003).

Consumers

We follow Galí *et al.* (2007) in assuming two types of households: those in the first group, denoted by i, benefit from full access to national and international capital markets and as such are free to optimize. The proportion of optimizing consumers in each country is given by $(1 - \vartheta)$. The representative Home optimizing households have the following instantaneous separable utility function:

$$U_t(C^{oi}, N^{oi}) = \frac{(C_t^{oi}/H_t^i)^{1-\sigma_c}}{1 - \sigma_c} - \frac{(N_t^{oi})^{1+\sigma_n}}{1 + \sigma_n} \tag{3.1}$$

where C_t^o represents consumption of a basket of goods (to be defined below), H_t is an index of external habits and N_t^o is the level of employment. $\beta \in (0, 1)$ represents the subjective rate of time preference, σ_c the coefficient of relative risk aversion, σ_n the inverse of the elasticity of labour supply with respect to real wage. Following Smets and Wouters (2003), we assume that habits depend on past aggregate consumption, C^T:

$$H_t = \left(C_{t-1}^T\right)^\lambda, \tag{3.2}$$

with $\lambda > 0$.

Optimizing consumers maximize (3.1) subject to their intertemporal budget constraint, which in real terms reads as

$$\frac{a_{t+1}^i}{r_t} = a_t^i - C_t^{oi} + \frac{W_t}{P_t}N_t^{oi} + D_t^i - T_t^i. \tag{3.3}$$

Their financial wealth (a_t) is held in the form of one-period state-contingent securities, which yield a return of r_t. Home households can hold their wealth in bonds issued in country H, $B_{H,t}$, and bonds issued in country F, B_F, which offer the same return $(a_t = B_{H,t} + B_{F,t})$. The optimizing consumer's disposable income is defined as consisting of labour income $W_t/P_t N_t^{oi}$ plus the dividends from the profits of the imperfectly competitive firms D_t^i, minus personal taxes T_t^i, which are lump-sum by assumption.

The second group of households, a proportion ϑ of the total, follows a RoT behaviour. RoT households consume out of current disposable income, and supply a constant amount of labour,[4]N^{RoT}. This admittedly *ad hoc* assumption may be justified assuming myopia or limited participation to capital markets. Thus, the consumption function of the representative Home RoT consumer is simply

$$C_t^{RoTj} = N^{RoT} \frac{W_t}{P_t} - T_t^j. \tag{3.4}$$

The Home country household's optimization problem

Rearranging the first-order conditions associated to the optimizing consumers' problem and aggregating across consumers over $i \in (\frac{\vartheta}{2}, \frac{1}{2}]$ yields the consumption intertemporal Euler equation:

$$\frac{\left(C_t^o / C_{t-1}^\lambda\right)^{-\sigma_c}}{C_{t-1}^\lambda} = E_t \left\{ \beta \frac{\left(C_{t+1}^o / C_t^\lambda\right)^{-\sigma_c}}{C_t^\lambda} (1 + i_t) \frac{P_t}{P_{t+1}} \right\}. \tag{3.5}$$

Given the symmetry of the model, equations (3.5) and (3.4) hold true also for country F, that is

$$\frac{\left(C_t^{*o} / C_{t-1}^{*\lambda}\right)^{-\sigma_c}}{C_{t-1}^{*\lambda}} = E_t \left\{ \beta \frac{\left(C_{t+1}^{*o} / C_t^{*\lambda}\right)^{-\sigma_c}}{C_t^{*\lambda}} (1 + i_t) \frac{P_t^*}{P_{t+1}^*} \right\} \tag{3.6}$$

and

$$C_t^{*RoT} = N^{*RoT} \frac{W_t^*}{P_t^*} - T_t^*$$

where $C_t^{*o} \equiv \int_{(1+\vartheta)/2}^1 C_t^{*oi} di$ and $C_t^{*RoT} \equiv \int_{1/2}^{(1+\vartheta)/2} C_t^{*RoTi} di$.

At a given time, t, each household is called to solve an intratemporal allocation problem for the optimal choice of consumption bundles and differentiated consumption goods, indexed by $z \in [0, 1]$. We let goods indexed by $z \in [0, \frac{1}{2}]$ and by $z \in [\frac{1}{2}, 1]$ be produced in country H and F respectively.[5] Preferences over consumption bundles are modelled according to a constant elasticity of substitution (CES) specification with parameter $\chi \in (0.5, 1)$ capturing idiosyncratic taste or *home bias*:

$$C_t = \left[\chi^{\frac{1}{\eta}} C_{H,t}^{\frac{\eta-1}{\eta}} + (1 - \chi)^{\frac{1}{\eta}} C_{F,t}^{\frac{\eta-1}{\eta}} \right]^{\frac{\eta}{\eta-1}} \tag{3.7}$$

Subindexes $C_{H,t}$ and $C_{F,t}$ are themselves constructed as CES aggregators, that is

$$C_{H,t} = \left[\int_0^{1/2} C_{H,t}(z)^{(\theta-1)/\theta} dz \right]^{\theta/(\theta-1)} \quad \text{and} \quad C_{F,t} = \left[\int_{1/2}^1 C_{F,t}(z)^{(\theta-1)/\theta} dz \right]^{\theta/(\theta-1)}.$$

Parameters η and θ, both assumed greater than one, respectively measure the elasticity of substitution between consumption bundles $C_{H,t}$ and $C_{F,t}$ and the elasticity of substitution among each of the differentiated goods being produced in either country H or F.

Solving the cost minimization problem for the purchase of one unit of the composite consumption C_t gives the Home household's demand schedules for $C_{H,t}$ and $C_{F,t}$:

$$C_{H,t} = \chi \left(\frac{p_{H,t}}{P_t} \right)^{-\eta} C_t \quad \text{and} \quad C_{F,t} = (1 - \chi) \left(\frac{p_{F,t}}{P_t} \right)^{-\eta} C_t. \tag{3.8}$$

In the same vein, Home household's demand schedules for good z produced in country H and F are given by

$$c_{H,t}(z) = \left(\frac{p_{H,t}(z)}{P_{H,t}} \right)^{-\theta} C_{H,t} \quad \text{and} \quad c_{F,t}(z) = \left(\frac{p_{F,t}(z)}{P_{F,t}} \right)^{-\theta} C_{F,t}. \tag{3.9}$$

Two things are noteworthy. First, demand functions for consumption bundles $C_{H,t}$ and $C_{F,t}$ are affected by the home bias parameter χ. Even in the instance of $p_{H,t} = p_{F,t}$ the ratio of H-produced goods to F-produced goods is higher in the Home country. Second, in the case $\eta = \theta$, demand functions for $c_{H,t}(z)$ and $c_{F,t}(z)$ reduce to

$$c_{H,t}(z) = \chi \left(\frac{p_{H,t}(z)}{P_t} \right)^{-\theta} C_t \quad \text{and} \quad c_{F,t}(z) = (1 - \chi) \left(\frac{p_{F,t}(z)}{P_t} \right)^{-\theta} C_t. \tag{3.10}$$

In the rest of the analysis we continue to assume that $\eta = \theta$.

By symmetry, in country F the following relations hold true:

$$C^*_{H,t} = (1 - \chi) \left(\frac{p^*_{H,t}}{P^*_t} \right)^{-\eta} C^*_t; \quad C^*_{F,t} = \chi \left(\frac{p^*_{F,t}}{P^*_t} \right)^{-\eta} C^*_t; \tag{3.11}$$

$$c^*_{H,t}(z) = (1 - \chi) \left(\frac{p^*_{H,t}(z)}{P^*_t} \right)^{-\theta} C^*_t \quad \text{and} \quad c^*_{F,t}(z) = \chi \left(\frac{p^*_{F,t}(z)}{P^*_t} \right)^{-\theta} C^*_t. \tag{3.12}$$

Consumption-based price indices

Consumption price indices, which minimize the cost of purchasing one unit of C_t and C^*_t, are given by

$$P_t = \left[\chi P_{H,t}^{1-\eta} + (1 - \chi) P_{F,t}^{1-\eta} \right]^{1/(1-\eta)} \quad \text{and} \quad P^*_t = \left[\chi P_{F,t}^{1-\eta} + (1 - \chi) P_{H,t}^{1-\eta} \right]^{1/(1-\eta)},$$

where

$$P_{H,t} = \left[\int_0^{1/2} p_{H,t}(z)^{1-\theta} dz \right]^{1/(1-\theta)} \quad \text{and} \quad P_{F,t} = \left[\int_{1/2}^1 p_{F,t}(z)^{1-\theta} dz \right]^{1/(1-\theta)}.$$

Because there are no impediments to trade and the two countries share the same currency, the price of each differentiated good is the same in both countries, that is, $p_{H,t}(z) = p^*_{H,t}(z)$ and $p_{F,t}(z) = p^*_{F,t}(z)$ for each variety z. Thus, it also follows that $P^*_{H,t} = P_{H,t}$ and $P^*_{F,t} = P_{F,t}$. However, due to the idiosyncratic taste introduced in the preferences over consumption bundles, purchasing power parity does not hold in general. Hence: $P_t \neq P^*_t$.

Firms

In both economies there is a continuum of firms producing varieties of goods. Firms act as monopolistic competitors and use a Cobb–Douglas production technology which depends on employment, N, and a technology parameter A_t:

$$Y_t(z) = [N_t(z)]^{1-\alpha}. \tag{3.13}$$

We introduce a channel for fiscal policy by assuming that taxes on labour take the form of a uniform payroll tax.[6] Firms' demand for labour in each country for each good variety is therefore defined as

$$p_{j,t}(z) \left\{ (1-\alpha)A_t [N_t(z)]^{-\alpha} - t^{PR}_t \right\} = W_t, \text{ with } j = F, H, \tag{3.14}$$

where t^{PR}_t is the tax rate per unit of employed labour, that is, $t^{PR}_t = \frac{T^{PR}_t}{N_t}$, where T^{PR}_t are the total revenues from the payroll tax.

Turning next to firms' pricing behaviour, we consider a standard model of monopolistic competition with sticky prices, as in Galí *et al.* (2001) and Leith and Malley (2005).[7] More precisely, sticky prices are incorporated into this model by assuming a Calvo pricing mechanism. At any given time, only a fraction $1 - \xi$ of firms can adjust prices, whereas the remainder supplies output on demand at a constant price. A share γ of the adjusting firms is assumed to follow a RoT,[8] while the remainder $1 - \gamma$ set prices optimally to maximize expected discounted real profits.[9] The profit maximization problem can be formulated as

$$p^f_t(z) \max E_t \sum^{\infty}_{j=0} \alpha^j \Delta_{t,t+j} \left[\frac{p^f_t(z)}{P_{H,t+j}} Y_{t+j}(z) - TC^r_{t+j}(Y_{t+j}(z)) \right] \tag{3.15}$$

$$\text{s.t.} \quad Y_{t+j}(z) = \left[\frac{p^*_t(z)}{P_{H,t+j}} \right]^{-\theta} Y_{t+j}$$

where $p^f_t(z)$ denotes the new optimal price of producer z, $TC^r_{t+j}(Y_{t+j}(z))$ the real total cost function and $\Delta_{t,t+j}$ is the stochastic discount factor. The solution to this problem yields the familiar formula for the optimal reset price in a Calvo's setup:

$$p^f_t(z) = \frac{\theta}{\theta - 1} \frac{E_t \sum^{\infty}_{j=0} \alpha_j \Delta_{t,t+j} \left[P^\theta_{H,t+j} Y_{t+j} MC^r_{t+j}(i) \right]}{E_t \sum^{\infty}_{j=0} \alpha_j \Delta_{t,t+j} \left[P^{\theta-1}_{H,t+j} Y_{t+j} \right]} \tag{3.16}$$

where $MC_t^r(i)$ denotes the real marginal costs function. Moreover, it is possible to show that

$$
P_{H,t} = \left[\xi P_{H,t-1}^{1-\theta} + (1-\xi)(1-\gamma)\left(p_t^f\right)^{1-\theta} + (1-\xi)\gamma\left(p_t^b\right)^{1-\theta} \right]^{\frac{1}{1-\theta}}
$$

(3.17)

where $p_t^b = \bar{p}_{t-1}(P_{H,t}/P_{H,t-1})$ and $\bar{p}_{t-1}$ is the index of prices set at time $t-1$. Similar expressions apply for country F.

Fiscal authority

In modelling the fiscal authorities' behaviour in each country there are two possible alternatives. On the one hand, we can consider fiscal authorities as having the same households' preferences (with the bias parameter as well). In this case, total demand for the generic good z stems from domestic and foreign households' consumption and from domestic *and* foreign governments' consumption. In this case

$$
g_{H,t}(z) = \chi \left(\frac{p_{H,t}(z)}{p_{H,t}} \right)^{-\theta} \left(\frac{p_{H,t}}{P_t} \right)^{-\eta} G_t.
$$

On the other hand, we can model domestic fiscal authority's preferences as defined only on domestically produced goods and similarly for the foreign fiscal authority. In this case

$$
g_{H,t}(z) = \left(\frac{p_{H,t}(z)}{p_{H,t}} \right)^{-\theta} G_t.
$$

For the sake of simplicity we shall model public expenditures according to the latter specification.

The global economy

The solution method first requires to derive expressions for the world weighted averages: $X_t^W = \frac{1}{2}[X_t + X_t^*]$. Country-specific variables are thus given by the simple transformation: $X_t = X_t^W + \frac{1}{2}[X_t - X_t^*]$. Let us define two other variables that will be useful throughout the analysis: the CPI-based real exchange rate $Q_t = P_t^*/P_t$ and the terms of trade $S_t = P_{F,t}/P_{H,t}$. At the world economy level, the resource constraint implies that

$$
Y_t^W = C_t^W + G_t^W
$$
$$
Y_t + Y_t^* = C_t + C_t^* + G_t + G_t^*
$$

where, according to our notation: $Y_t^W = \frac{1}{2}[Y_t + Y_t^*]$, $G_t^W = \frac{1}{2}[G_t + G_t^*]$.

World demand schedules for Home and Foreign differentiated good

World demand schedules for the generic z Home-produced differentiated good is given by $y_t(z) = c_{H,t}(z) + c_{H,t}^*(z) + g_{H,t}(z) + g_{H,t}^*(z)$, which can be rewritten as

$$
y_t(z) = \chi \left(\frac{p_{H,t}(z)}{P_t}\right)^{-\eta} (C_t + G_t) + (1 - \chi)\left(\frac{p_{H,t}^*(z)}{P_t^*}\right)^{-\eta}(C_t^* + G_t^*).
$$

(3.18)

Integrating the above expression over $z \in [0, 1/2]$ and log-linearizing around the deterministic zero inflation steady state leads to

$$
\hat{Y}_t = \chi\eta\left[\frac{C + G}{Y}\right](\hat{P}_t - \hat{P}_{H,t}) + \chi\left(\frac{C}{Y}\right)\hat{C}_t + \frac{G}{Y}\hat{G}_t
$$
$$
+ (1 - \chi)\eta\left[\frac{C^* + G^*}{Y}\right](\hat{P}_t^* - \hat{P}_{H,t}) + (1 - \chi)\left(\frac{C^*}{Y}\right)\hat{C}_t^*.
$$

(3.19)

Hatted variables are defined as $\hat{x} = \log(x_t/x)$, where x is the steady state value. As the quantities $(\hat{P}_t - \hat{P}_{H,t})$ and $(\hat{P}_t^* - \hat{P}_{H,t})$ can compactly be written in terms of $\hat{S}_t$ as $\hat{P}_t - \hat{P}_{H,t} = (1 - \chi)\hat{S}_t$ and $\hat{P}_t^* - \hat{P}_{H,t} = \chi\hat{S}_t$, expression (3.19) becomes

$$
\hat{Y}_t = \Gamma\hat{S}_t + \chi\left(\frac{C}{Y}\right)\hat{C}_t + \frac{G}{Y}\hat{G}_t + (1 - \chi)\left(\frac{C^*}{Y}\right)\hat{C}_t^* + \frac{G^*}{Y}\hat{G}_t^*
$$

(3.20)

where $\Gamma = (C + G + C^* + G^*)\chi(1 - \chi)\eta/Y$.

The IS and the Phillips curves

Derivation of the approximated IS curves requires a number of steps. Consider country H. First, log-linearize equations (3.4) and (3.5) to obtain

$$
\hat{c}_t^{RoT} = \left[\frac{N^{RoT}\left(\frac{W}{P}\right)}{C^{RoT}}\right]\hat{w}_t - \vartheta\left(\frac{T}{C^{RoT}}\right)\hat{T}_t,
$$

(3.21)

$$
\hat{C}_t^o = E_t\hat{C}_{t+1}^o - \lambda\left(\frac{1 - \rho}{\rho}\right)\left[\hat{C}_{t-1} - \hat{C}_t\right] - \frac{1}{\rho}(\hat{i}_t - E_t\hat{\pi}_{t+1}),
$$

(3.22)

where $\hat{w}_t$ denotes the log-linearized real wage and $\hat{i}_t = \log\left([1 + i_t]/[1 + \bar{i}]\right)$. Then, approximate the definition of aggregate consumption:

$$
\hat{C}_t = \left[\frac{C^o}{C}\right]\hat{C}_t^o + \left[\frac{C^{RoT}}{C}\right]\hat{C}_t^{RoT}.
$$

(3.23)

Note that imposing no habit, that is, $\lambda = 0$, and no RoT consumers, that is, $N^{RoT}/N = \vartheta = 0$, our specification would collapse to a purely forward-looking IS curve (see Carroll, 2000). More importantly, note also that the presence of non-optimizing consumers establishes a link between the demand for goods, net personal taxes, $\widehat{T}$, and the real wage. Analogously, in country F we have

$$\hat{C}_t^* = \left[\frac{C^{o*}}{C^*}\right]\hat{C}_t^{o*} + \left[\frac{C^{RoT*}}{C^*}\right]\hat{C}_t^{RoT*} \tag{3.24}$$

$$\hat{C}_t^{RoT*} = \left[\frac{N^{RoT*}(\frac{W^*}{P^*})}{C^{RoT*}}\right]w_t^* - \vartheta\left(\frac{T^*}{C^{RoT*}}\right)\hat{T}_t^* \tag{3.25}$$

$$\hat{C}_t^{o*} = E_t\,\hat{C}_{t+1}^{o*} - \lambda\left(\frac{1-\rho}{\rho}\right)\left[\hat{C}_{t-1}^* - \hat{C}_t^*\right] - \frac{1}{\rho}(\hat{i}_t - E_t\,\hat{\pi}_{t+1}^*). \tag{3.26}$$

Consolidating equations (3.21), (3.22) and (3.23) and making use of (3.20), we obtain the IS curve for country H (in what follows, Δ denotes the first difference operator):

$$E_t\Delta\,\hat{Y}_{t+1} = \kappa_1(\hat{i}_t - E_t\,\hat{\pi}_{t+1}) + \kappa_2 E_t\Delta\,\hat{S}_{t+1} - \kappa_3 E_t\Delta\,\hat{S}_t + k_4 E_t\Delta\,\hat{C}_t^{RoT} +$$
$$+ \kappa_5 E_t\Delta\,\hat{G}_{t+1} + k_6 E_t\Delta\,\hat{Y}_{t+1}^* - k_6\frac{G}{Y}\Delta E_t\,\hat{G}_{t+1}^* + \chi\kappa_3 E_t\Delta\,\hat{Y}_t +$$
$$- (1-\chi)\kappa_3\Delta\,\hat{Y}_t^* - \chi\frac{G}{Y}\kappa_3 E_t\Delta\,\hat{G}_t + (1-\chi)\frac{G}{Y}\kappa_3 E_t\Delta\,\hat{G}_t^* \tag{3.27}$$

and similarly for country F:

$$E_t\Delta\,\hat{Y}_{t+1}^* = \kappa_1(\hat{i}_t - E_t\,\hat{\pi}_{t+1}^*) - \kappa_2 E_t\Delta\,\hat{S}_{t+1} + \kappa_3 E_t\Delta\,\hat{S}_t + k_4 E_t\Delta\,\hat{C}_t^{RoT*} +$$
$$+ \kappa_5\Delta\,\hat{G}_{t+1}^* + k_6\Delta\,\hat{Y}_{t+1} - k_6\frac{G}{Y}E_t\Delta\,\hat{G}_{t+1} + \chi\kappa_3 E_t\Delta\,\hat{Y}_t^* +$$
$$- (1-\chi)\kappa_3 E_t\Delta\,\hat{Y}_t - \chi\frac{G}{Y}\kappa_3 E_t\Delta\,\hat{G}_t^* + (1-\chi)\frac{G}{Y}\kappa_3 E_t\Delta\,\hat{G}_t \tag{3.28}$$

where $\kappa_1 = (C^O/C)\rho^{-1}(2\chi - 1)/\chi$, $\kappa_2 = (\Gamma/\chi)$, $\kappa_3 = [\lambda C^O/C(\rho - 1)/\rho]1/\chi^2$, $k_4 = (2\chi - 1)/\chi$, $k_5 = G/Y$, $k_6 = ([1 - \chi]/\chi)$. The variables $\hat{\pi}_t$ and $\hat{\pi}_t^*$ respectively define domestic and foreign consumer price inflation rates in terms of the inflation rates of domestically- and foreign-produced goods, that is,

$$\hat{\pi}_t = \chi\,\hat{\pi}_{H,t} + (1-\chi)\hat{\pi}_{F,t} \tag{3.29}$$

$$\hat{\pi^*}_t = (1-\chi)\hat{\pi}_{F,t} + \chi\,\hat{\pi}_{H,t} \tag{3.30}$$

and, moreover, $\Delta\,\hat{S}_t = \hat{\pi}_{F,t} - \hat{\pi}_{H,t}$.

Fiscal policy directly impacts on output in this model through three channels. First, through the usual resource withdrawal effect of government consumption, $\hat{g}_t$. Second, through the impact of net personal taxes, $\widehat{T}$, on the current disposable income of RoT consumers. Third, through the impact of payroll taxes, T^{PR}, on the real wage of RoT consumers.[10] Finally, RoT consumers weaken the impact of interest rate policy on aggregate demand. As shown in Galí *et al.* (2007), this may have important implications for the conduct of monetary policy. Indeed, our estimates confirm that RoT consumers weaken the output response to interest rate changes. It is important to note that whilst government spending impacts on the consumption behaviour of optimizing consumers via the resource-withdrawal effect, taxation impacts through its effect on disposable income for RoT consumers, and hence via the external habit (total consumption) variable. As we shall see below, this drives some of the results of the model.

Turning to the Phillips curve, the log-linearization of the firms' optimal pricing decision together with the dynamic equation for the price index under the Calvo mechanism with indexation, leads to a New Keynesian Phillips Curve (NKPC). See Galí *et al.*, 2001 and Muscatelli *et al.*, 2003 for details. For each country, the Phillips curves are defined for the bundle of domestically produced goods:

$$\widehat{\pi}_{H,t} = \frac{\gamma\widehat{\pi}_{H,t-1} + \beta\xi E_t\widehat{\pi}_{H,t+1}}{\xi + \gamma(1 - \xi(1 - \beta))} + \frac{(1 - \gamma)(1 - \xi)(1 - \beta\xi)}{[\xi + \gamma(1 - \xi(1 - \beta))]\left(1 + \frac{\alpha\theta}{1-\alpha}\right)}\widehat{s}_{H,t}$$
(3.31)

$$\widehat{\pi}_{F,t} = \frac{\gamma\widehat{\pi}_{F,t-1} + \beta\xi E_t\widehat{\pi}_{F,t+1}}{\xi + \gamma(1 - \xi(1 - \beta))} + \frac{(1 - \gamma)(1 - \xi)(1 - \beta\xi)}{[\xi + \gamma(1 - \xi(1 - \beta))]\left(1 + \frac{\alpha\theta}{1-\alpha}\right)}\widehat{s}_{F,t}$$
(3.32)

$$\widehat{s}_{H,t} = \frac{N\left(\frac{W}{P}\right)}{N\left(\frac{W}{P}\right) + T^*}\left(\widehat{W}_t - \widehat{p}_{H,t}\right) + \frac{T^*}{N\left(\frac{W}{P}\right) + T^*}(\widehat{t}_{H,t}^* - \widehat{n}_{H,t}) + \widehat{n}_{H,t} - \widehat{y}_{H,t}$$
(3.33)

$$\widehat{s}_{F,t} = \frac{N\left(\frac{W}{P}\right)}{N\left(\frac{W}{P}\right) + T^*}\left(\widehat{W}_t^* - \widehat{p}_{F,t}\right) + \frac{T^*}{N\left(\frac{W}{P}\right) + T^*}(\widehat{t}_{F,t}^* - \widehat{n}_{F,t}) + \widehat{n}_{F,t} - \widehat{y}_{F,t}$$
(3.34)

where $\widehat{s}_{H,t}$ and $\widehat{s}_{F,t}$ are the percentage deviations from steady state of the labour cost share in country H and F respectively.

It is important to note that in estimating the parameters of the Phillips Curves, we do not explicitly model wage-setting behaviour, and the determination of employment is given by the static production function. Other recent contributions (Leith and Malley, 2005; Smets and Wouters, 2003) estimate wage equations, and adding a wage equation would have enabled us to consider the possibility of sticky wage dynamics with some forward-lookingness in wage-setting. However, this would have also added to the complexity of the model. In simulating our model, as we shall see below, we introduce an element of adjustment in nominal wages.

This amplifies the inertia generated by RoT consumers as the flexible wage introduces an immediate change in RoT consumption.

3.3   Estimates

3.3.1 Data

In order to simulate our model, we need to estimate or calibrate the parameter values. As we intend to employ a symmetric model of the EMU area, the best approach is to estimate the values of the parameters using aggregate euro-area data, and use these parameters for our two representative countries (H and F). The data employed is the aggregated euro-area data produced by the European Central Bank (see Fagan *et al.*, 2001). The time series are quarterly over the sample period 1970(3.1)–98(3.2). While we obtain new estimates of the structural parameters present for the global IS curve, for the NKPC we use the estimates reported in Galí *et al.* (2001, 2003), as these were obtained using the same data set.[11]

To capture the spirit of the New Keynesian models as log-linearizations, the data are transformed so that the variables are expressed in deviations from the 'steady state'.[12] Both real and nominal variables are de-trended using the Hodrick–Prescott filter with smoothing parameter set to 1600. Note that, as the inflation rate and interest rate always enter the model together, all the equations are 'balanced' in terms of the levels of integration of the dependent and explanatory variables.[13]

3.3.2 Estimation methods

The New Keynesian model consists of equations that are non-linear in parameters. Following Hansen (1982), a model with rational expectations suggests some natural orthogonality restrictions that can be used in the generalized methods of moments (GMM) framework. Each equation estimated using GMM is of the form:

$$\mathbf{y}_{it} = \mathbf{f}_i(\theta_i, \mathbf{z}_{it}) + \mathbf{u}_{it} \tag{3.35}$$

where, for each equation i, $\mathbf{y}_{it}$ is the vector of dependent variables, θ_i is the $(a_i \times 1)$ vector of unknown parameters to be estimated, and $\mathbf{z}_{it}$ is the $(k_i \times 1)$ vector of explanatory variables. The GMM approach is based on the fact that $\widetilde{\theta}_i$, the true value of θ_i, has the property $E[\mathbf{h}_i(\widetilde{\theta}_i, \mathbf{w}_{it})] = 0$, where $\mathbf{w}_{it} \equiv (\mathbf{y}'_{it}, \mathbf{z}'_{it}, \mathbf{x}'_{it})$, and $\mathbf{x}_{it}$ is an $(r_i \times 1)$ vector of instruments that are correlated with $\mathbf{z}_{it}$. GMM then chooses the estimate θ_i so as to make the sample moment as close as possible to the population moment of zero. The validity of these instruments can be tested for each equation by using Hansen's J-test, which is distributed as a $\chi^2(r_i - a_i)$ statistic under the null of valid orthogonality conditions.

GMM or IV estimation has been used by a number of authors to estimate NK models.[14] One problem is that the estimated IS and NKPC equations are highly non-linear in parameters, and the rank condition for identification is not met unless a number of parameters in these two equations are fixed. To begin with, in estimating the IS equation we impose that steady-state ratios for the global economy are

Table 3.1 Steady state ratios [sample period 1990(1)–1998(2)]

$\frac{C^W}{Y^W}$	$\frac{G^W}{Y^W}$	$\frac{(T^{PR})^W}{N^W(W/P)}$	$\frac{T^W}{Y^W}$	$\frac{(T^{PR})^W/N^W}{(W/P)+(T^{PR})^W/N^W}$
0.8	0.2	0.353	0.121	0.260

Table 3.2 Structural parameters estimates

Parameter	Estimate	Description
ϑ	0.508^* (0.036)	Share of rule of thumb consumers
$(N^{Rot})^W/N^W$	0.617 (0.310)	Rule of thumb employment over total employment
$(C^O)^W/C^W$	0.658 (0.156)	Optimising consumption over total consumption
β	0.923^+ (0.071)	Subjective discount factor
ξ	0.843^+ (0.066)	Calvo parameter
γ	0.307^+ (0.128)	Share of rule of thumb firms

Notes
Standard errors are reported in brackets.
* estimated in the first step of our procedure.
+ estimates taken from Gali *et al.* (2001, 2003).

given by their average values computed over the sub-sample period 1990(3.1)–98(3.2).[15] Results are reported in Table 3.1 (superscript W refers to the global economy).

Furthermore, in order to increase the accuracy of the estimation we calibrate some structural parameters at values taken from other empirical studies. We impose the habit formation parameter on aggregate consumption to be equal to unity, that is, $\lambda = 1$, the coefficient of relative risk aversion to be equal to two, that is, $\sigma_c = 2$.

3.3.3 Model estimates

Table 3.2 reports our results obtained using GMM over the full sample period for the model expressed in world variables terms. Our vector of instruments include a constant plus de-trended output, government spending excluding government transfers, direct taxes per worker, nominal exchange rate, wage rate, inflation rate and nominal interest rate. Our results are obtained imposing six lags on the instruments.

In estimating the NK output equation we employ a two-step procedure. Initially, we estimate a reduced form of IS curve for the global economy rewritten as

$$\widehat{Y}_t^W = b_1 E_t(\Delta\widehat{w}_{t+1}) + b_2 E_t\Delta\widehat{T}_{t+1}^W + b_3\widehat{G}_t^W + b_4\left(\widehat{Y}_{t-1}^W - \frac{G}{Y}\widehat{G}_{t-1}^W\right)$$

$$+ b_5\left(\widehat{i}_t - E_t\widehat{\pi}_{t+1}^W\right) + b_6\left(E_t\widehat{Y}_{t+1}^W - \frac{G}{Y}E_t\widehat{G}_{t+1}^W\right) \tag{3.36}$$

where

$$b_1 = -\frac{k_4(N^{RoT})^W(W/P)}{(1+\chi\kappa_3)(C^{RoT})^W}; \quad b_2 = \vartheta\,\frac{k_4 T^W}{(1+\chi\kappa_3)(C^{RoT})^W};$$

$$b_3 = \frac{\kappa_5 + \chi G^W/Y^W\kappa_3}{1+\chi\kappa_3}; \quad b_4 = \frac{\chi\kappa_3}{1+\chi\kappa_3};$$

$$b_5 = -\frac{\kappa_1}{1+\chi\kappa_3}; \quad b_6 = 1/(1+\chi\kappa_3).$$

In (3.36) we thus restrict the coefficients on $\widehat{Y}_{t-1}^W$ and $E_t\widehat{Y}_{t+1}^W$ to be respectively equal to negative the coefficients on $(G^W/Y^W)\widehat{G}_{t-1}^W$ and $(G^W/Y^W)E_t\widehat{G}_{t+1}^W$. Dividing the estimated coefficient on $\Delta\widehat{T}_{t+1}^W$, that is, $\hat{b}_2$, by the coefficient on $E_t\widehat{Y}_{t+1}^W - (G^W/Y^W)E_t\widehat{G}_{t+1}^W$ multiplied by $-(T^W/Y^W)$, that is, $-\hat{b}_6(T^W/Y^W)^{-1}$, one retrieves a point estimate for the share of RoT consumers. In particular, it turns out that $\hat{\vartheta}$ is 0.508 with asymptotic standard error of 0.036.[16] In the second step we re-estimate (3.36) imposing the values of σ_c, λ and $\hat{\vartheta}$ and the steady state ratios and obtain structural estimates for the parameters $(N^{RoT})^W/N^W$ and $(C^o)^W/C^W$.

We find that 65% of total consumption in steady state is generated by optimizing consumers. RoT consumers account for about 61% of total employment. The overall fit for the estimated equation is good: the R^2 statistic for (3.36) is 0.83. The Hansen statistic for over-identifying restrictions test is 59.39, which is distributed as a $\chi^2(41)$ under the null hypothesis of valid instruments. The null hypothesis of valid instruments is not rejected at the 5% significance level. In the following table we report parameter estimates for the NKPC. Point estimates of the Calvo parameter suggest that about 84% of firms do not adjust their prices every period and of those who adjust prices, about 30% simply index prices.

In addition to the estimated parameters, we set χ, the proportion of home-produced goods in the consumption of each country, as equal to 0.7, which reflects a bias towards home-produced goods in most large Euroland countries and the parameter θ, the elasticity of demand for consumption goods, as equal to 4. In order to close the model we need to describe the behaviour of the monetary and fiscal authorities. As noted above, we do not consider strategic interactions between the ECB and the two countries' fiscal authorities. Instead, we examine the interaction between a central bank which operates a forward-looking inflation targeting framework, and fiscal authorities which rely on fiscal rules based on automatic stabilizers. In this model, monetary policy has a relatively weak effect due to the relatively large proportion of RoT consumers, who only indirectly react to the interest rate rule.[17] In addition, fiscal policy operates through a wider number of channels: taxation effects on consumption through liquidity-constrained consumers, taxation wedge effects on inflation, and interaction effects due to the presence of RoT consumers.

3.3.4 Monetary rule

In contrast to the numerous papers on the behaviour of the Federal Reserve and other central banks, the empirical literature on the behaviour of the ECB is limited, mainly due to its short history. We assume that the ECB's monetary policy rule for the nominal interest rate $\widehat{i_t}$ is similar to the standard forward-looking Taylor rule specification which has become commonplace in the literature[18] (see Clarida *et al.*, 1998, 2000; Muscatelli *et al.*, 2002; Giannoni and Woodford, 2002a,b):

$$\widehat{i_t} = \phi_1 E_t \widehat{\pi}_{t+q} + \phi_2 E_t \widehat{y}_{t+s} + \phi_3 \widehat{i}_{t-1} \tag{3.37}$$

where we also allow for inertia, due to interest-rate smoothing, if $\phi_3 \neq 0$. As shown by Sauer and Sturm (2003), this forward-looking inertial Taylor rule fits the Euroland data reasonably well for the post-EMU period. We use their estimates of the ϕ_i parameters to simulate our model. This provides a benchmark to assess the performance of different designs for automatic fiscal stabilizers in our structural model.

3.3.5 Fiscal rules

Unlike Muscatelli *et al.* (2003a), we consider a simple format for our fiscal policy rules and let automatic stabilizers depend on current real activity condition and lagged debt accumulation (relative to output). Thus

$$\widehat{g}_t = -\delta_1 \widehat{y}_t - \delta_2 (\widehat{b}_{t-1} - \widehat{y}_{t-1}) \tag{3.38}$$

$$\widehat{g}_t^* = -\delta_1 \widehat{y}_t^* - \delta_2 (\widehat{b}_{t-1}^* - \widehat{y}_{t-1}^*) \tag{3.39}$$

and

$$\widehat{\tau}_t = \varphi_1 \widehat{y}_t + \varphi_2 (\widehat{b}_{t-1} - \widehat{y}_{t-1}) \tag{3.40}$$

$$\widehat{\tau}_t^* = \varphi_1 \widehat{y}_t^* + \varphi_2 (\widehat{b}_{t-1}^* - \widehat{y}_{t-1}^*) \tag{3.41}$$

where $\widehat{\tau}_t$ is the vector of our two tax measures, personal taxes $\widehat{t}_t$ and payroll taxes $\widehat{t}_t^{TR}$. Our taxation rule therefore imposes the same adjustment pattern on both taxes, and does not look at how a mix of tax measures might improve the design of policy.[19] The importance of the fiscal policy mix is considered further below. We have a limited feedback to the debt accumulation, through a debt/GDP term which approximates to a response to the debt/GDP ratio. For our baseline case, we set $\delta_1 = \varphi_1 = 0.5$ and $\delta_2 = \varphi_2 = 0.05$. A coefficient of 0.5 on output is consistent with the empirical evidence in Van den Noord (2000) and adopted in studies on fiscal stabilization (e.g. Westaway, 2003). The coefficient on debt ensures stability but ensures that this does not swamp the impact of fiscal stabilizers given the configuration of the temporary shocks.

3.4   Dynamic simulations

Having obtained the structural parameter estimates, we can perform dynamic simulations of our two-country New Keynesian model[20] and examine the transmission mechanism of fiscal and monetary policies. We focus on the dynamic model solution under rational expectations and examine impulse response functions to a number of shocks. As we do not have an estimated wage equation, we assume a minimum amount of nominal inertia in the model by stipulating that nominal wages adjust gradually towards the initial real wage equilibrium with an autoregressive parameter of 0.5 per quarter. Employment is determined by the log-linearization of the production technology (3.13).

We examine the extent to which national fiscal policies can assist with macroeconomic adjustment in EMU. The key issues we consider are: do automatic stabilizers actually assist the ECB's function of stabilizing output and inflation in the union, that is, do the fiscal authorities assist or impede the efforts of the ECB? Which fiscal instruments are more effective in stabilizing the union and the individual economies? How do the stabilization properties of fiscal policy vary in response to symmetric and asymmetric shocks?

3.4.1   Government spending rules versus taxation rules in the global economy

We first perform some dynamic simulations for the global economy. In each simulation we consider four different policy scenarios:

1   where fiscal policy is kept exogenously fixed, that is, the automatic stabilizers (3.38), (3.39), (3.40) and (3.41) are switched off (labelled 'M');
2   where only the government spending rule is switched on (labelled 'M+G');
3   where only the taxation feedback rule is switched on (labelled 'M+T');
4   where both rules are switched on (labelled 'M+G+T').

Figure 3.1 displays the impulse response functions for output gap, inflation, nominal and real interest rate following a unit negative supply shock, modelled as a disturbance appended to the aggregate Phillips curve, with 0.5 autoregressive parameter. Consider first the case 'M'. A negative supply shock on impact increases inflation (about 6% relative to steady state) and calls for a restrictive monetary policy. The rise in both nominal and real interest rate engineers a series of negative output gaps which gradually take the economy back to long-run equilibrium. As shown in the Figure 3.1, the role of automatic stabilizers is clear. When the government spending rule operates alone (M + G), there is initially a more pronounced recession for the first three quarters, but then it tends to mildly stabilize output. Inflation dynamics is essentially unaffected. Fiscal rules based on taxation (M + T) instead achieve a sizeable stabilization of output and inflation. This is obtained both through the direct effect of lump-sum taxes on disposable income, and through the impact of the payroll tax on inflation. By contrast, government expenditure only

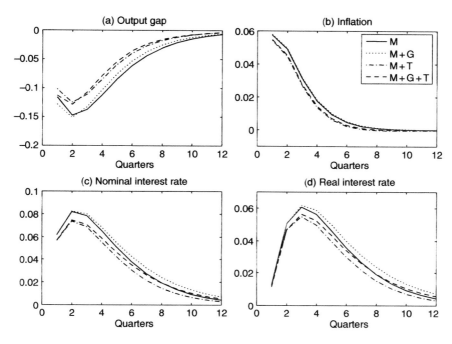

Figure 3.1 Impulse response function to a unit negative supply shock $\rho^a = 0.5$.

has an indirect effect on RoT consumption, by marginally stabilizing output. The performance is relatively good when the three rules operate contemporaneously, $(M + G + T)$, although again government spending has initially adverse effects on output and inflation.

Figure 3.2 displays the impulse response functions for output gap, inflation, nominal and real interest rate following a positive preference shock modelled as a disturbance appended to the aggregate IS curve, with 0.5 autoregressive parameter. In this case the fiscal rules have very different effects on output and inflation. In general, spending rules and taxation rules do guarantee output stabilization (and it turns out that having all the three rules active is better) but might have distorting effects on inflation. In particular, this is true for taxation rules.

Rather than assuming a particular form of welfare loss function, in what follows we consider how the introduction of a fiscal policy rule impacts on output and inflation variability (variance frontiers) when it is combined with a monetary policy rule such as (3.37). Conducting welfare analysis is complex in this model, due to the presence of heterogeneous consumers (optimizers and RoT consumers),[21] but computing variance frontiers allows a certain ranking of policy rules, where it is apparent that one rule dominates the other in terms of reducing both output and inflation variability. To construct the variance frontiers we apply a monetary policy rule where we keep fixed parameters ϕ_2 and ϕ_3 and we allow ϕ_1 to vary.[22] We

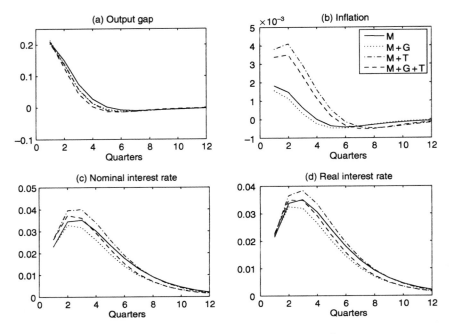

Figure 3.2 Impulse response function to a unit preference shock $\rho^c = 0.5$.

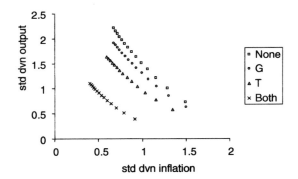

Figure 3.3 Variance frontiers and monetary-fiscal interaction.

then compute the standard deviation of output and inflation in dynamic simulations following a shock to the Phillips Curve, and report these 'variance frontiers' in the figure which follows.

Figure 3.3 shows the variance frontiers when the model is simulated following a temporary negative technology combining the forward-looking monetary policy rule with the four fiscal regimes outlined above (M, M + G, M + T, M + G + T). There are three points to note about these results. The first is that, in contrast with

Muscatelli *et al*. (2003), automatic stabilizers are no longer welfare-reducing. In particular, counter-cyclical taxation policy seems able to reduce the variance of both output and inflation. The second point to note is that also government spending does not have an unambiguous welfare-enhancing effect: introducing a feedback rule for government spending tends to shift the variance frontier, although less than in the previous case, towards the origin lowering the variability of both output inflation. The explanation for this result lies in the different ways in which government spending and taxation operate in the model: government spending varies the profile of output but its impact is ultimately reversed, as the distributed lag effect sums to zero. In contrast, taxation has an impact through the wedge (a level effect) and through the IS curve (in difference terms), and this is not reversed because of its impact on external habits. The third point is that introducing both automatic stabilizers is still preferable to having none. In this case the westwards shift in the variance frontier is even more visible, suggesting that a combination of both automatic stabilizers can have a much greater impact on the variance frontier.

To investigate the importance of personal taxes relative to payroll taxes in stabilizing output and inflation, we repeated the above experiment using only personal taxes and then using only payroll taxes. In general, we found that most of the stabilization effect comes from payroll taxes through their impact on the wedge, especially for cases where ϕ_1 is high. The intuition for this is straightforward: following an adverse shock to the Phillips curve, payroll taxes fall, stabilize both inflation (through the wedge effect) and output (through the disposable income of RoT consumers). In contrast, personal taxes act only through the IS curve and hence stabilize output at the expense of inflation stability. Only when ϕ_1 is low, so that the monetary authority reacts less forcefully to the inflation shock, personal taxes help to stabilize output and inflation. In other words, payroll taxes are generally more complementary to monetary policy in this model.

3.4.2 What is the value added from fiscal automatic stabilizers in individual countries?

We now simulate the model in response to a temporary demand (to the IS curve) and a temporary supply (to the NKPC curve) shock to one of the two countries. We consider a shock of 1% in the first period which then decays over time with an autoregressive parameter of 0.5. The reason for not considering pure asymmetric shocks (shocks of equal and opposite sign on each EMU country) is that, given the identical structure of the two countries, and that the ECB is assumed to target EMU average outcomes, monetary policy will not react to such shocks. Following the asymmetric demand and supply shocks considered here, the union's inflation and output levels will change, thus triggering a response from the ECB. This will allow us to compute the value added in terms of the impact on output and inflation variability. We report the results in Tables 3.3 and 3.4 for both asymmetric demand and supply shocks (modelled respectively as transitory shocks to the IS and the Phillips curve in country H), and symmetric demand and supply shocks (transitory shocks to IS curves in both countries and Phillips curves in both

Table 3.3 Relative variances to asymmetric shocks

	Asy. demand shock			Asy. supply shock		
	$T + G/M$	T/M	G/M	$T + G/M$	T/M	G/M
Var(Y)	0.216	0.960	0.885	0.834	0.955	0.868
Var(Y^*)	0.191	0.913	0.768	0.809	0.942	0.845
Var(Y-Y^*)	0.211	0.951	0.863	0.824	0.949	0.858
Var(π)	0.204	0.922	0.889	0.982	0.992	1.001
Var(π^*)	0.181	0.853	0.426	1.150	1.217	0.970
Var(πc)	0.214	0.949	0.659	0.995	0.992	1.001
Var(πc*)	0.141	0.728	0.187	1.009	1.014	0.998

Table 3.4 Relative variances to symmetric shocks

	Sym. demand shock			Sym. supply shock		
	$T + G/M$	T/M	G/M	$T + G/M$	T/M	G/M
Var(Y) = Var(Y^*)	0.894	0.973	0.920	0.894	0.984	0.922
Var(π) = Var(π^*)	1.005	1.059	0.964	0.999	0.999	1.000
Var(πc) = Var(πc*)	1.005	1.058	0.964	0.999	0.999	1.000

countries respectively). The results in Tables 3.3 and 3.4 are reported as the ratio of the variances of output (for each country and for the output differential) and inflation (for both product prices π and consumer prices π^c) and in the scenarios 2–4 relative to scenario 1. Thus, for instance G/M gives the relative variance of output and inflation under policy scenario 2 relative to scenario 1, and $(T + G)/M$ reports the relative variances for scenario 4 relative to scenario 1. A value of the variance ratio in excess of unity suggests that adding the fiscal instrument(s) is destabilizing relative to using ECB policy alone, and vice versa.[23] In the case of the symmetric shocks, the variability of output and inflation is obviously identical across countries because of model symmetry.

Turning first to Table 3.3, we immediately see that both fiscal instruments stabilize output and that simultaneous activation enhances their role. The latter result is particularly strong in the case of asymmetric demand shock, where the variability of domestic output is reduced by approximately 80%. To a much lesser extent, this conclusion also holds for asymmetric supply shocks. Turning to Table 3.4, 3.5, 3.6, the results for symmetric shocks also suggest a complementarity between the two fiscal policy instruments. This is in sharp contrast with the 'Brussels consensus' based on the view that the ECB alone should stabilize the union-wide economy (Buti *et al.*, 2001).[24]

3.5   Conclusions

This chapter has used a two-country New Keynesian DSGE model to examine the extent to which national fiscal policies can assist macroeconomic adjustment

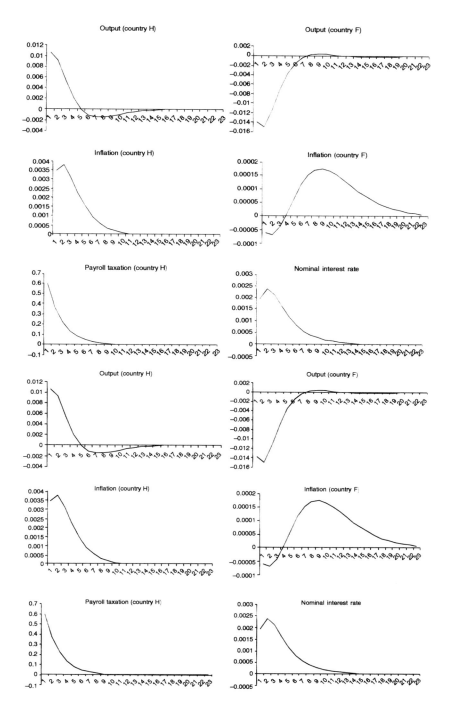

Figure 3.4 Impulse response functions to a 1% payroll taxation shock.

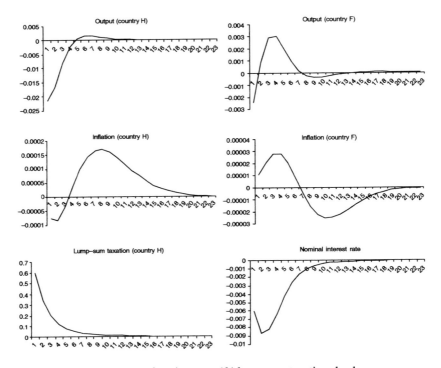

Figure 3.5 Impulse response functions to a 1% lump-sum taxation shock.

within EMU, in response to a variety of shocks. We use a model which embodies liquidity-constrained (RoT) consumers and home bias in consumption, and use some recent estimates of the structural model on euro area data to calibrate our model. The key conclusion which emerges from our analysis is that automatic stabilizers based on both government spending and taxation policy seem to combine efficiently with forward-looking (inertial) Taylor rules on the part of the ECB in the case of symmetric shocks. In contrast with the popular view that takes for granted the effectiveness of automatic stabilizers in the face of asymmetric shocks, we find that national stabilizers play a role only if private consumption and/or government spending exhibit a significant home bias. Further research should consider the possibility that progressive income tax rates could help to stabilize inflation through the well-known fiscal drag mechanism.

Notes

1 The implied fiscal multiplier is close to or greater than unity.
2 Whether consumption actually increases in such models depends crucially on the assumptions made about labour supply and price-stickiness, given the linkage between consumption and leisure (and hence the real wage) via the consumer's optimization problem.

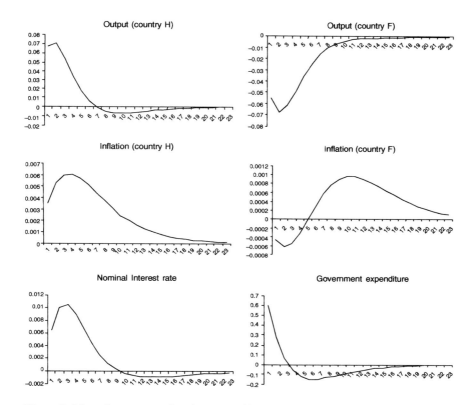

Figure 3.6 Impulse response functions to a 1% government expenditure shock.

3 See Galí *et al.* (2001); Smets and Wouters (2003); Leith and Malley (2005).
4 Galí *et al.* (2007) show that supplying a constant amount of labour is optimal when personal taxes, T_t, levied on RoT consumers are always nil. This result would never obtain in our model, where taxes and transfers are explicitly modelled. Thus, for the sake of simplicity we assume a constant labour supply. Since consumption cannot be negative, this implies that we impose a lower bound on T_t for any given level of the real wage.
5 In what follows, subscript H or F denote the country where differentiated consumption goods are produced.
6 This implies that the optimizing consumer's choice between leisure and consumption is not affected.
7 See also Erceg *et al.* (2000) and Sbordone (2002).
8 This was pioneered by Galí and Gertler (1999). Similar backward-looking elements can be introduced to the NKPC equation by introducing indexation of all non-re-optimized prices (Woodford, 2002, chapter 3; and Christiano *et al.*, 2005).
9 A similar specification for the NKPC can be obtained by making the indexation process part of the optimization process (see Smets and Wouters, 2003).
10 From equations (3.4) and (3.14) it should be clear that, in each period, the equilibrium real wage is inversely related to employment and the payroll tax.

11 The estimation was carried out using RATS, version 5.
12 Which is commonplace in this literature (see Smets and Wouters, 2003; Leith and Malley, 2005).
13 The government spending data (G) is total government spending excluding transfers and interest payments, whilst we use employers' social security contributions as payroll taxes (T^{PR}), and personal taxes as (T).
14 For instance, Galí *et al.* (2001); Kara and Nelson (2002); Muscatelli *et al.* (2003) and Leith and Malley (2005).
15 $N(W/P)/Y$ is simply equal to the labour share in equilibrium, which we set equal to $(1 - \alpha) = 0.6$.
16 The standard error has been computed using the delta method.
17 As shown in Galí *et al.* (2007), RoT consumers are affected by interest rate changes only to the extent that the real wage adjusts following the new labour conditions determined by the optimizing consumers' reaction to such interest rate changes.
18 The main difference is that we use a contemporaneous value of the output gap (see Muscatelli *et al.* (2002)) as opposed to expected future values, as in Clarida *et al.* (1998, 2000). For a detailed discussion of these issues, see Giannoni and Woodford (2002a,b). For an alternative approach to modelling interest rate responses involving non-linearities in reaction functions, see Cukierman and Muscatelli (2001).
19 Andres and Domenech (2003) provide an analysis of how different tax measures might impact on output and inflation variability.
20 The model is solved using Winsolve version 3.0 (see Pierse (2000)), which provides numerical solutions for linear and non-linear rational expectations models. We solve our model using the Stacked Newton method in Winsolve. In solving the models with structural shocks (and further below with policy shocks) these are treated as unanticipated by economic agents.
21 See for instance Benigno and Woodford (2004). We are currently considering the extension of our modelling framework to include some welfare analysis.
22 The variance frontiers are plotted for values of ϕ_1 which vary between 0.2 and 1.5. The reason for focusing on higher values of ϕ_1 compared to the estimated value is that it is often argued that estimated monetary policy rules tend to underestimate the response of the central bank to shifts in expected inflation (and conversely overestimate the degree of inertia) because central banks do not continuously change their monetary stance.
23 To facilitate the understanding of how fiscal policy tools affect individual economies. in Figures 3.4, 3.5, 3.6 at the end of the chapter we show the impulse response functions to fiscal variables in the home economy.
24 Following Van den Noord (2000); Andres and Domenech (2003) and Westaway (2003), in our simulation exercises we also experimented backward-looking specification, where fiscal instruments depend on y_{t-1}. Our results are robust to this modification. However, some important differences arise when the fiscal rules include an autoregressive term with coefficient 0.5. In this case, the stabilizing properties of automatic stabilizers are significantly weakened.

References

Amato, J. D. and Laubach, T. (2003), 'Rule-of-thumb behavior and monetary policy', *European Economic Review*, 47: 791–831.

Andres, J. and Domenech, R. (2006), 'Automatic stabilisers, fiscal rules and macroeconomic stability', *European Economic Review,* 50: 1487–1506.

Asdrubali, P. and Soyoung Kim (2004), 'Dynamic risksharing in the United States and Europe', *Journal of Monetary Economics*, 51: 809–36.

Ball, L. (1997), 'A proposal for the next macroeconomic reform', *Victoria Economic Commentaries*, March, 1–7.

Benigno, P. and Woodford, M. (2004), 'Optimal monetary and fiscal policy: a linear-quadratic approach', in NBER Macroeconomics Annual 2003, 18: 271–333 Cambridge (US).

Blanchard, O. J. (1985), 'Debt, deficit and finite horizons', *Journal of Political Economy*, 93: 223–47.

Blanchard, O. J. and Perotti, R. (2001), 'An empirical characterization of the dynamic effects of changes in government spending and taxes on output', *Quarterly Journal of Economics*, 117: 1329–68.

Buti, M., Franco, D. and Ongena, H. (1997), 'Budgetary Policies during Recessions – Retrospective Application of the "Stability and Growth Pact" to the Post-War Period', European Commission, Economic Paper no. 121.

Buti, M., Roeger, W. and in't Veld, J. (2001), 'Stabilizing output and inflation in EMU: policy conflicts and cooperation under the Stability Pact', *Journal of Common Market Studies*, 39: 801–28.

Calmfors, L. (2003), 'Fiscal policy to stabilise the domestic economy in the EMU: what can we learn from monetary policy?', *CESifo Economic Studies*, 3: 3–25.

Christiano, L. J., Eichenbaum, M. and Evans, C. (2005), 'Nominal rigidities and the dynamic effects of a shock to monetary policy', *Journal of Political Economy*, 113: 1–45.

Clarida, R., Galí, J. and Gertler. M. (1998), 'Monetary policy rules in practice: some international evidence', *European Economic Review*, 42: 1033–67.

—— (2000), 'Monetary policy rules and macroeconomic stability: evidence and some theory', *Quarterly Journal of Economics*, vol. CXV, issue 1, 147–80.

Cukierman, A. and Muscatelli, V. A. (2001), 'Do central banks have precautionary demands for expansions and for price stability? – theory and evidence', CESifo Discussion Paper no. 764.

Erceg, C. J., Henderson, D. W. and Levin, A. T. (2000), 'Optimal monetary policy with staggered wage and price contracts', *Journal of Monetary Economics*, 46: 281–313.

Fagan, G., Henry, J. and Mestre, R. (2001), 'An area-wide model (AWM) for the Euro area', ECB Working Paper no. 42.

Fair, R. (2001), 'Estimates of the effectiveness of monetary policy', Cowles Foundation and International Center of Finance, Yale University. Discussion Paper no. 1298.

Fatás, A. and Mihov, I. (2001), 'Government size and automatic stabilizers: international and intranational evidence', *Journal of International Economics*, 55: 3–28.

Favero, C. A. and Monacelli, T. (2003), 'Monetary-fiscal mix and inflation performance: evidence from the US', CEPR Discussion Paper no. 3887.

Galí, J. (2003), 'New perspectives on monetary policy, inflation, and the business cycle', in M. Dewatripont, L. Hansen and S. Turnovsky (eds), *Advances in Economic Theory*, vol. III, 151–97, Cambridge: Cambridge University Press.

Galí, J. and Gertler, M. (1999), 'Inflation dynamics: a structural econometric analysis', *Journal of Monetary Economics*, 44: 195–222.

Galí, J., Gertler, M. and López-Salido, D. (2001), 'European inflation dynamics', *European Economic Review*, 45: 1237–70.

—— (2003), 'Erratum to "European inflation dynamics"', *European Economic Review*, 47: 759–60.

Galí, J., López-Salido, D. and Valles, J. (2007), 'Understanding the effects of government spending on consumption', *Journal of the European Economic Association*, 5(1): 227–70.

Giannoni, M. P. and Woodford, M. (2002a), 'Optimal interest-rate rules: I. general theory', NBER Working Paper no. 9419.

Giannoni, M. P. and Woodford, M. (2002b), 'Optimal interest-rate rules: I. applications', NBER Working Paper no. 9420.

Giavazzi, F., Jappelli, T. and Pagano, M. (2000), 'Searching for non-linear effects of fiscal policy: evidence from industrial and developing countries', *European Economic Review*, 44: 1259–89.

Gordon, D. B. and Leeper, E. M. (2003), 'Are countercyclical fiscal policies counterproductive?', Paper presented at 5th Bundesbank Spring Conference, May.

Hansen, L. P. (1982), 'Large sample properties of generalized method of moments estimators', *Econometrica*, 50: 1029–54.

Kara, A. and Nelson, E. (2002), 'The exchange rate and inflation in the UK', Bank of England, External MPC Unit, Discussion Paper no. 11.

Leith, C. and Malley, J. (2005), 'Estimated general equilibrium models for the evaluation of monetary policy in the US and Europe', *European Economic Review*, 49: 2137–59.

Leith, C. and Wren-Lewis, S. (2000), 'Interactions between monetary and fiscal policy rules', *The Economic Journal*, 110: C93–C108.

Linnemann, L. and Schabert, A. (2003), 'Fiscal policy in the new neoclassical synthesis', *Journal of Money Credit and Banking*, 35: 911–29.

Muscatelli, V. A., Tirelli, P. and Trecroci, C. (2002), 'Does institutional change really matter? Inflation targets, central bank reform and interest rate policy in the OECD countries', *The Manchester School*, 70: 487–527.

—— (2003), 'Can fiscal policy help macroeconomic stabilization? evidence from a New Keynesian model with liquidity constraints', CESifo Working Paper no. 1171.

—— (2004a), 'The interaction of fiscal and monetary policies: some evidence using structural models', *Journal of Macroeconomics*, 2: 257–280.

—— (2004b), 'Monetary and fiscal policy interactions over the cycle: some empirical evidence', in R. Beetsma, C. Favero, A. Missale, V. A. Muscatelli, P. Natale and P. Tirelli (eds), *Fiscal Policies, Monetary Policies and Labour Markets. Key Aspects of European Macroeconomic Policies after Monetary Unification*, Cambridge: Cambridge University Press: 256–296.

Pierse, R. (2000), Winsolve, version 3.5. University of Surrey.

Sarantis, N. and Stewart, C. (2003), 'Liquidity constraints, precautionary saving and aggregate consumption: an international comparison', *Economic Modelling*, 20: 1151–73.

Sauer, S. and Sturm, J. E. (2003), 'ECB monetary policy: how well does the Taylor Rule describe it?', Mimeo, University of Munich.

Sbordone, A. G. (2002), 'Prices and unit labor costs: a new test of price stickiness', *Journal of Monetary Economics*, 49: 265–92.

Smets, F. and Wouters, R. (2003), 'An estimated dynamic stochastic general equilibrium model of the euro area', *Journal of the European Economic Association*, 1: 1123–75.

Van den Noord, P. (2000), 'The size and role of automatic fiscal stabilizers in the 1990s and beyond', OECD Working Paper no. ECO/WKP 2000.

Westaway, P. (2003), 'Modelling shocks and adjustment mechanisms in EMU', HM Treasury, EMU Studies.

Woodford, M. (2002), *Interest and Prices: Foundations of a Theory of Monetary Policy*, Princeton: Princeton University Press.

Wren-Lewis, S. (2000a), 'The limits to discretionary fiscal stabilization policy', *Oxford Review of Economic Policy*, 16: 92–105.

—— (2002b), 'Fiscal policy, inflation and stabilisation in EMU', Working Paper, University of Exeter.

Part II

Empirical analyses of national fiscal stances

4 Measuring and assessing fiscal automatic stabilizers*

J. Mélitz

4.1 Introduction

Studies of discretionary fiscal policy often centre on the 'cyclically-adjusted budget balance', or the budget balance following an adjustment for the part that depends on an automatic response to events. It is also often assumed that all of the adjustments to the cycle come from taxes and unemployment compensation. In addition, following cyclical adjustment, the analysis of discretionary fiscal policy frequently concerns the ratio of the cyclically adjusted government balance to output or potential output rather than the level. I shall put forward two criticisms of this procedure. First, many of the automatic responses to events result from other transfer payments besides unemployment compensation, including payments for pensions, sickness, subsistence, invalidity, childcare and subsidies of all sorts to firms. Second, if the issue is the ratio of the cyclically adjusted budget balance, the cyclical adjustment should be for the ratio rather than the level. Otherwise, the estimates of the cyclical adjustment are inefficient. According to both arguments, the usual estimates of the series for discretionary fiscal policy are often incorrect. The first criticism always applies when there is recourse to official sources for figures for the 'cyclically-adjusted budget balances' since those figures are constructed on the assumption that taxes and unemployment compensation are the sole elements of the budget that respond to the cycle. The second criticism follows whenever the subsequent analysis focuses on ratios.

If the analysis relates to the ratio of the budget balance to output, then the problem of estimation is not the only issue. Some important conceptual differences also arise. Interestingly, the recent report of the European Commission on Public Finances in EMU for 2004 (European Commission, 2004) recognizes these differences (Part II, chapter 3 and Annexe II). As the report observes, if the ratio of the government balance to output is the issue, then only progressive taxes can contribute much to stabilization over the cycle. Proportional taxes will do little, if anything, to stabilize. Any stabilizing response of the budget to the cycle probably will come mostly from the spending side and will arise because of inertia in government expenditures on goods and services. During a recession, the ratio of government spending on goods and services to output will automatically rise if the spending is unaffected while output falls. Not only are these observations in the recent report correct, but it is also difficult to know how well they are understood since they are rarely acknowledged.

A further conceptual issue must be raised right at the start. The part of the budget balance that responds without delay to the cycle independently of any fresh political decision-making might not be entirely beyond potential discretionary control and therefore might not be 'automatic' in the full sense of the word. This applies especially to government spending on goods and services, which we usually consider to be under potential discretionary control. For this reason, I will refer to 'non-discretionary fiscal policy' as a more general term than 'automatic fiscal policy' or 'automatic stabilization'. On the other hand, within the same calendar year the cyclical responses of transfer payments for health, retirement, subsidies to firms, or anything else, result predominantly from the application of existing laws apart from any discretionary behaviour by government officials. By and large, whatever is automatic about the immediate responses of taxes and unemployment compensation to the cycle is also automatic about the immediate responses of the rest of transfer payments. Thus, I will treat all responses of transfer payments to the cycle as automatic.

The tests in this study rest on the annual data in the OECD CD-Rom for 2003 containing the *Economic Outlook* databank. The official estimates of automatic stabilization generally distinguish five different elements of the government budget balance and then study each of them separately: household direct taxes, business direct taxes, social security contributions, indirect taxes and unemployment compensation (see Giorno *et al.*, 1995). It is also official practice to estimate the cyclical response of the five respective bases on which these five tax and spending items rest, and then to apply the national tax code or else to assume a unitary elasticity of response to the base in order to derive the five items, whichever seems more appropriate. Van den Noord (2000) offers an up-to-date, clear and detailed review of the method (in the OECD version, used by the EC as well).[1] I will deviate from this official procedure in three ways. First, I will abandon the preconception that unemployment compensation is the only type of transfer payment that responds automatically to the cycle. Second, I will examine the non-discretionary responses of government balances in levels and as ratios of output separately. Both of these deviations follow from my opening remarks. As a third deviation, I will also rely entirely on simultaneous-equation methods of estimation. This next departure deserves a separate word.

Simultaneous-equation estimation methods have several advantages. The four relevant classes of taxes depend on distinct tax schedules of varying complexity that change over time and have different collection periods and delays. From this standpoint alone, there is something to be said in favour of estimating tax responses directly rather than inferring them from some preset figures after studying the responses of the tax bases, however well founded those preset figures may be. In addition, the cyclical responses of different tax bases and unemployment (the relevant base concerning unemployment compensation) will tend to be correlated. Hence, the residuals in the separate estimates of these bases will be correlated too. On this ground, seemingly unrelated regression would appear to be fitting. Finally, taxes and government spending could have a reciprocal effect on the cycle, even within a year. Thus, simultaneous-equation estimation may be proper.

4.2 The framework

At issue then is the response of government revenues and expenditures to environmental factors independently of discretionary policy. Therefore, we want a specification that does not reflect the aims of the authorities. Nothing concerning official expected values and official objectives, as such, should enter. In addition, the focus should be on reactions to changes in a short enough period to preclude discretionary policy. Changes in tax regulations take significant time. So do fresh spending decisions. As regards spending, the European Commission (2004) underlines the delays:

> Taking into account relatively long recognition lags, the complexity and slowness of budgetary processes and the political economy of political inaction, a viable working hypothesis over the short term, for instance one year, is to assume full inertia or full adherence to spending plans, i.e. to assume that spending is not adjusted for unexpected short- [*sic*] or windfalls of growth
> (Annexe II.2)

Canzoneri *et al.* (2002) take the same view. There are three variables that are likely to affect government revenues and expenditures even within a year and to do so fairly automatically: output, inflation and the nominal rate of interest. Deviations of output (Y) from potential output (Y^*) are of particular interest, since the ultimate aim is to distinguish between discretionary and non-discretionary fiscal policy.

On these general principles, I decided to study the current yearly impact of *first differences* in $Y - Y^*$ (as present in the OECD database), or the output gap, on *first differences* in government receipts and expenditures. Especially because of the first-difference form, this focuses on short-run responses. I also admitted non-discretionary effects of inflation and the interest rate into the analysis. But while using first differences for inflation, I kept the interest rate in levels, on the ground that any automatic influence of this variable on the government budget would depend largely on initial debt and therefore could be cumulative. If the interest rate does have a cumulative effect on the interest payments on the debt, its level could affect the first difference of the budget balance just as well as the level. While I stuck to these initial choices throughout, it turns out that the use of levels or first differences for inflation and the rate of interest makes almost no difference. In addition, better estimates of current responses may result from the presence of lagged influences. Thus, I also included the lagged level and the lagged first difference of the dependent variable in the estimates. Further, I added a trend and dummies for six-year intervals (1973–8, 1979–84, 1985–90, 1991–6, 1997–2002). Since the data concerns a panel of different countries, I included country-fixed effects too.

All of the country data entering into the statistical analysis goes up through 2002. Most of it begins in the early seventies. But though some of the series in the database begin in 1960, only a scattering of observations dating prior to 1970 enters in the econometric tests (because of lack of other required series starting as early). The results concern 20 OECD countries, and include 14 of the 15 members of the EU. The missing EU member is Luxembourg, and the 6 OECD countries outside the EU are Australia, Canada, Japan, New Zealand, Norway and the United States.

4.3   The estimates in levels and ratios

In general, the lagged level and first difference of the dependent variable as well as the time trend are almost always insignificant and do not affect the results. Therefore, even though the analysis allows for some delays in responses, the dynamics are totally negligible. No lagged effects occur. On the other hand, the six-year intervals often matter and the country-fixed effects generally do. Table 4.1 contains the most aggregative results. Table 4.1 does so for the 20 OECD countries, as well as for the 14 members of the European Union. The top half shows the results in levels; the bottom half in percentages. The notes to Table 4.1 recapitulate the entire specification from start to finish. Let us examine the levels first.

4.3.1 Levels

In the case of levels, the dependent variable on the left and the output gap on the right are in identical units; namely, home currency at current prices. Thus, the coefficient of the output gap gives a meaningful figure. For example, for the members of EMU, it states by how many cents the budget will respond to a movement of the output gap of one euro. But the coefficients of the change in inflation ($\Delta \pi$) and the interest rate (r_L) do not have any clear meaning and are not reported. The measure of the inflation rate is the implicit price of GDP; that of the interest rate r_L is the long-term interest rate. I experimented with both the short-term and the long-term interest rate in the OECD database, and the long-term one is much more important. The Table omits the coefficients of all the explanatory variables besides the output gap, inflation and the rate of interest. The parenthetical figures concern statistical significance: t statistics in case of single-equation estimates, z ones in the 3SLS analysis.

In row 1, the dependent variable is the net public surplus. The results are simple least squares. As seen, according to the estimate, a one-euro rise in output above potential output increases the net surplus by 55 cents in the OECD 20 and by 35 cents in the EU 14 alone. Both coefficients are highly significant. Both estimates are also comforting, since they are in the general vicinity of the typical figures. These typical figures are remarkably close to 0.5 for either grouping, at least in previous applications of the OECD method (see Giorno *et al.*, 1995; Buti and Sapir (eds), 1998: 132; and van den Noord, 2000). However, the estimates in row 1 ignore any reciprocal influence. The next ones, in row 2, correct for this neglect by introducing instruments for $\Delta(Y - Y^*)$, $\Delta\pi$ and r_L. The chosen instruments are listed in the notes to Table 4.1. They include, among others, the lagged values of aggregate taxes and spending – the two variables whose reciprocal effect on $\Delta(Y - Y^*)$, $\Delta\pi$ and r_L is our main concern. The instruments designed to take account of the output gap require a special word, since this variable is particularly difficult to forecast by construction. With regard to the gap, I made two special choices. First, I assumed that fiscal policy does not affect unemployment within the current year. Accordingly, I included current unemployment among the instruments. Second, in line with Galí and Perotti (2003), I used the current output gap in the United States as an instrument for the other 19 countries in the study and the current output gap in the EU (as reported by the OECD) as an instrument in the case of the United States. These particular two instruments, which relate to contemporary values (unlike the rest), notably improve the fit. In their presence, the R^2s for $\Delta(Y - Y^*)$ approximately double, going up to around 50–60%. The R^2s for $\Delta\pi$ that result from the instruments are always a bit worse, closer to 40%, and those for r_L notably higher, around 90%.

As seen from rows 2, after introducing the instruments, the estimates of the influence of the output gap on the net public surplus rise from 0.55–0.64 for the OECD 20 and from 0.35–0.44 for the EU 14. This is not a satisfactory result. The failure to consider the reciprocal influence of fiscal policy on current performance in row 1 should have led to overestimates, not underestimates, of non-discretionary fiscal policy. To explain, suppose that a cyclical rise in output raises net government receipts. In principle, the rise in the government surplus should limit the increase in output. If it does, then the correction for the reciprocal influence means raising the swings in $\Delta(Y - Y^*)$ above observed levels: that is, substituting higher positive values of $\Delta(Y - Y^*)$ in expansions and higher negative values of it in contractions. On the other hand, following the cyclical corrections, the series for the net government surplus stay the same. Thus, regressing the latter series on the corrected (larger absolute) values for $\Delta(Y - Y^*)$ should yield lower coefficients. The opposite happens. Notwithstanding, I consider the estimates with the instruments preferable on general statistical grounds.

The next four equations relate to the elementary decomposition of the net government surplus between taxes and spending. In rows 3 and 4, taxes and spending are estimated separately with the same instruments as before for $\Delta(Y - Y^*)$, $\Delta\pi$ and r_L. The decomposition yields precisely the same estimate as before for the impact of the output gap on the net public surplus for the OECD 20 (0.47 in row 3 minus -0.17 in row 4 gives 0.64) and a somewhat higher estimate of this impact for the EU 14 (0.54 instead of 0.44).

The trouble with these last estimates, however, as indicated earlier, is that the equations for taxes and spending should be estimated simultaneously. Rows 5 and 6 provide the correction. The results rest on three-stage-least-squares for a five-equation system containing equations for $\Delta(Y - Y^*)$, $\Delta\pi$ and r_L in addition to taxes and spending. These three additional equations depend on the earlier instruments. Following the use of 3SLS, we can see that the separate effects of $\Delta(Y - Y^*)$ on taxes and expenditures in the OECD 20 (Table 4.1) appear exactly as before in rows 3 and 4, but the precision of the estimates shoots up. In the case of the EU 14, the precision of the estimates also goes up, though not as spectacularly. But things are more complicated in the case of EU 14. The impact of the cycle on taxes stays the same while that on expenditures rises (in absolute terms, from −0.22 to −0.3). Taking stock of both the estimates as a whole, the basic outcome of using 3SLS is to improve precision and to narrow the differences between the estimates of the impact of the output gap on the net public surplus in the EU 14 and the OECD 20. After introducing 3SLS, the impact on the public surplus approximates 0.6 in both cases. Still, in the strictly European part of the sample, taxes respond notably less and expenditures notably more than in the full sample.

It is interesting to compare these last results in rows 5 and 6, for taxes and expenditures, with received ideas. Automatic stabilization is currently supposed to come essentially through taxes. Unemployment compensation – the only relevant spending item – makes up less than 10% of tax receipts in most countries (often much less), and therefore cannot compare in importance with taxes under proportional taxation (or anything resembling it). Thus, the results conform better to standard views on automatic stabilization on the tax than the spending side. The coefficient of the output gap of 0.47 for taxes in the OECD 20 (line 5) is particularly close to what we would anticipate from earlier work on automatic stabilization (though the 0.3 estimate for the EU 14 is on the low side). However, the −0.17 estimate for expenditures in the OECD 20 looks high, to say nothing of the −0.3 estimate in the EU 14 (lines 6) (compare Giorno *et al.*, 1995; and van den Noord, 2000). We shall come back to this issue below, but for the moment let us turn our attention to the revised estimates if we simply substitute ratios of output as the dependent variables and correspondingly substitute Y/Y^* as the output gap.

4.3.2 Ratios

Ratios often serve in the analysis of fiscal policy. Quite apart, the case for using them is strong. Stabilization policy relates to smoothing economic performance or keeping output close to potential. It does not essentially concern long-run production and growth in the level of output. Accordingly, analysis of fiscal policy often focuses on keeping the ratio of output to potential output close to one. As a result, even in cases where study focuses on a single country (and there is therefore no interest in using ratios simply to promote international comparison), the critical fiscal policy variable is often the ratio of the net budget balance to output, and the critical problem is to determine this ratio in the absence of non-discretionary responses to the environment. In line with these remarks, the European Commission centres on the ratio of the budget balance to output in its surveillance of country members' adherence to the Stability and Growth Pact (European Commission, 2004, Part II, chapter 3).

Notwithstanding, in analysing discretionary fiscal policy, studies often correct the budget balance in levels for non-discretionary responses and subsequently merely divide by output in order to obtain the ratios of cyclically adjusted figures to output or potential output. The European Commission is not the only one to do so. Two leading recent academic examples are Taylor (2000) and Galí and Perotti (2003). Both explicitly proceed from cyclically adjusted figures in levels based on official numbers (from the US Congressional Budget Office in one case, the OECD in the other) to subsequent division by potential output in order to analyse discretionary fiscal policy.

If potential output were perfectly deterministic and not subject to any shocks, there would be nothing wrong with this last practice (i.e. because of the division by *potential* instead of observed output). The division would then not call for any difference in estimation procedure at all, and the choice of dividing by potential output would be a critical one indeed. However, potential output is subject to supply shocks. Thus, if ratios of output are the matter of interest, direct estimates of the correction of this ratio for the cycle will yield more efficient estimates, regardless of whether we divide by observed or potential output. A further benefit will be to clarify the stabilizing forces at work. In the absence of a separate estimate of the ratios, as such, these forces acting on the ratios remain in the background, even in the dark.[2] As for the choice of observed or potential output, I shall centre on ratios of observed output here, since in any shift of focus on ratios, estimates of automatic effects of Y/Y^* on the original data deserve priority, in my opinion.

Row 7 of Table 4.1 repeats the OLS estimates of row 1. As evident, a cyclical expansion notably raises the ratio of the net public surplus to output. A 1% rise in Y/Y^* increases this ratio by over one-third of a per cent (0.36). So far, so good: the impact of the cycle on the government balance is stabilizing, just as it was before. Moreover, the impact of the cycle is now identical for the EU 14 and the full sample. All the better. Once again, if we introduce instrumental variables for $\Delta(Y/Y^*)$, $\Delta\pi$ and r_L (row 8), the cyclical influence goes up. It rises to 0.46 (or 0.45); that is, by a greater percentage (10/36 or 9/36) than it did previously. There is no need to pause once more on the separate IV estimates of taxes and spending (rows 9 and 10). If we go directly to the preferable simultaneous-equation estimates of the two in rows 11 and 12, we find that the impact of the cycle on the net public surplus is around 0.42 for the OECD 20 and the EU 14($-0.07 - (-0.49)$ or $-0.11 - (-0.53)$) or close to the corresponding separate estimates (of 0.45–0.46) in rows 8. However, as was also true before in levels, the response of taxes is somewhat lower in the EU 14 than it is for the OECD 20, while the opposite is true for spending (though the difference is now more muted than before).

But the most striking result of all relates to the size of the respective responses of taxes and expenditures. Taxes move moderately less than output in response to the cycle. Thus, they move in a destabilizing direction. They do so to the tune of 0.07–0.11.[3] By contrast, government spending moves in the stabilizing direction. This too is largely the outcome of a smaller percentage movement in the numerator than the denominator, but in this case the difference in movement is stabilizing. The stabilizing change of the ratio of government spending to output is also marked: on the order of 0.49–0.53.[4] This is basically in conformity with expectations, as observed near the start in connection with the Commission. Once we reason in terms of ratios, we can no longer expect much non-discretionary stabilization, if any, to come from taxation, but must expect it to come largely

Table 4.1 Taxes, spending and government deficits: the aggregates

Dependent variable: 1st differences	Test method	$\Delta(Y - Y^*)$	$\Delta\pi$	r_L	R^2	N
OECD 20						
(1) Net public surplus	OLS	0.55 (4.3)	+n.r. (1.83)	−n.r. (−0.66)	0.58	553
(2) Net public surplus	IV 2SLS	0.64 (3.8)	+n.r. (1.08)	+n.r. (0.44)	0.58	513
(3) Taxes	IV 2SLS	0.47 (4.2)	+n.r. (0.85)	−n.r. (−0.61)	0.82	513
(4) Expenditures	IV 2SLS	−0.17 (1.89)	−n.r. (−0.26)	−n.r. (−1.43)	0.89	514
(5) Taxes	3SLS	0.47 (17)	+n.r. (1.06)	−n.r. (−0.69)	0.82	513
(6) Expenditures	3SLS	−0.17 (7.5)	+n.r. (0.89)	−n.r. (−0.47)	0.89	513
(7) Net public surplus $\div Y$	OLS	0.36 (9.5)	0.16 (4.6)	~ 0 (0.08)	0.35	553
(8) Net public surplus $\div Y$	IV 2SLS	0.45 (8)	0.09 (1.95)	0.03 (0.61)	0.35	513
(9) Taxes $\div Y$	IV 2SLS	−0.07 (−1.87)	0.08 (2.6)	0.06 (1.73)	0.19	513
(10) Expenditures $\div Y$	IV 2SLS	−0.5 (−10.9)	0.02 (0.58)	0.04 (1.19)	0.52	514
(11) Taxes $\div Y$	3SLS	−0.07 (−2.15)	0.07 (2.63)	0.04 (1.74)	0.19	513
(12) Expenditures $\div Y$	3SLS	−0.49 (−13.9)	−0.1 (−0.23)	0.04 (1.24)	0.54	513
EU 14						
(1) Net public surplus	OLS	0.35 (2.9)	+n.r. (1.02)	−n.r. (−0.43)	0.49	364
(2) Net public surplus	IV 2SLS	0.44 (3.2)	+n.r. (0.84)	−n.r. (−0.66)	0.49	341
(3) Taxes	IV 2SLS	0.32 (2.2)	+n.r. (2.44)	+n.r. (2.7)	0.66	341
(4) Expenditures	IV 2SLS	−0.22 (−1.94)	+n.r. (2.3)	+n.r. (2.27)	0.74	341
(5) Taxes	3SLS	0.3 (3.9)	+n.r. (2.2)	+n.r. (2.4)	0.65	341
(6) Expenditures	3SLS	−0.3 (−3.9)	+n.r. (2.1)	+n.r. (1.9)	0.72	341
(7) Net public surplus $\div Y$	OLS	0.36 (7.3)	0.14 (4)	~ 0 (0.05)	0.35	364
(8) Net public surplus $\div Y$	IV 2SLS	0.46 (6)	0.16 (2.2)	0.06 (1.13)	0.37	341
(9) Taxes $\div Y$	IV 2SLS	−0.12 (−2.45)	0.13 (2.96)	0.04 (1.93)	0.17	341
(10) Expenditures $\div Y$	IV 2SLS	−0.53 (−8.2)	0.04 (0.81)	0.05 (1.16)	0.54	341

Table 4.1 Continued

Dependent variable: 1st differences	Test method	$\Delta(Y - Y^*)$	$\Delta\pi$	r_L	R^2	N
(11) Taxes $\div Y$	3SLS	−0.11 (−2.73)	0.12 (3.2)	0.07 (2.19)	0.18	341
(12) Expenditures $\div Y$	3SLS	−0.53 (−11.5)	−0.01 (−0.31)	0.03 (0.97)	0.57	341

Source: OECD *Economic Outlook* CD-ROM.

Notes

Y = output (GDP) in current prices Y^* = potential output in current prices
π = rate of inflation of price of GDP (percentage) r_L = long term rate of interest (percentage)
N = number of observations n.r. = not reported
All the dependent variables are in current prices. t or z statistics in parentheses (z in case of 3SLS estimates). In case of 3SLS, the R^2s are also adapted.
The general estimation form for all 12 equations is:

$$\Delta A = a_0 + a_1\Delta B + a_2\Delta\pi + a_3 r_L + a_4 t + a_5\mathbf{C} + a_6\mathbf{D} + a_7(\Delta A)_{-1} + a_8\Delta_{-1}(\Delta A) + u$$

where ΔA is the first difference of the dependent variable A: either net public surplus, taxes, expenditures as such or these three divided by Y

- ΔB is either the first difference of $Y - Y$ or Y/Y^*
- $\Delta\pi$ is the first difference of π
- t is a time trend
- $\mathbf{C}$ is a matrix of country fixed effects
- $\mathbf{D}$ is matrix of dummies for the 6-year intervals: 1973–78, 1979–84, 1985–90, 1991–96, and 1997–2002
- $(\Delta A)_{-1}$ is the lagged level of ΔA (in notation with usual time subscripts, it is $A_{t-1} - A_{t-2}$)
- $\Delta_{-1}(\Delta A)$ is the lagged first-difference of ΔA (in notation with usual time subscripts, it is $(A_{t-1} - A_{t-2}) - (A_{t-2} - A_{t-3})$)
- u is a disturbance term with the usual properties

In the case of equations (2), (3), (4), (8), (9) and (10), ΔB, $\Delta\pi$ and r_L are replaced by estimates based on instruments. The instruments for ΔB are

- t, the time trend
- $\mathbf{C}$, the country fixed effects
- $\mathbf{D}$, the dummies for the six-year time intervals
- B_{-1} and $(\Delta B)_{-1}$ and $\Delta_{-1}(\Delta B)$, the lagged level, the lagged first difference and the twice-lagged first difference of B (either $Y - Y$ or Y/Y^*)
- g_{-1} and g_{-2}, the one-period and two-period lagged growth rate of Y
- π_{-1} and $(\Delta\pi)_{-1}$, the lagged level and the lagged first difference of inflation
- G_{-1} and $(\Delta G)_{-1}$, the lagged level and the lagged first difference of public expenditures
- T_{-1} and $(\Delta T)_{-1}$, the lagged level and the lagged first difference of taxes
- U, U_{-1} and $(\Delta U)_{-1}$, the level, lagged level and lagged first difference of the rate of unemployment
- either $(Y - Y^*)_{US}$, $((Y - Y^*_{US}))_{-1}$ and $(\Delta(Y - Y^*)_{US})_{-1}$ or $(Y/Y^*)_{US}$, $((Y/Y^*)_{US})_{-1}$ and $(\Delta((Y/Y^*)_{US}))_{-1}$, regarding the level, lagged level and lagged first difference of the US GAP (except for the US, where the EU GAP serves instead)

The instruments for $\Delta\pi$ and r_L are identical except that the lagged level, the lagged first difference and the twice-lagged first difference of either $\Delta\pi$ or r_L replace B_{-1}, $(\Delta B)_{-1}$ and $\Delta_{-1}(\Delta B)$.

In the case of equations (5) and (6) and equations (11) and (12), both equations belong to a 5-equation system with extra equations for ΔB, $\Delta\pi$ and r_L. In these cases, the equations for ΔB, $\Delta\pi$ and r_L include all of the same instruments as before as the explanatory variables. The only difference is that the lagged levels, lagged first differences and twice-lagged first differences of all 3 dependent variables enter in all three equations.

from spending instead. However, major questions remain outstanding. How much of the relevant stabilization results from inertia in government consumption and investment? How much is instead the work of transfer payments and is therefore automatic in the usual sense? To answer, we must distinguish between the contribution of government spending on goods and services and the rest.

4.4   Further decomposition of government receipts and expenditures

As long as any further decomposition of government spending between goods and services and transfers is essential, why not exploit all of the information available in the OECD CD-Rom? On the tax side, the OECD provides separate figures for household direct taxes, business direct taxes, social security tax receipts, transfers received, and indirect taxes. On the spending side, it offers figures for public wages, non-wage consumption, investment, social benefits paid, subsidies, other transfer payments, and net interest payments. There is also a residual category of spending, which includes capital transfers and payments, and government consumption of fixed capital. This makes 13 rubrics in all.

The division of transfer payments between social benefits paid, subsidies and other transfer payments requires further elucidation. 'Social benefits paid' includes payments to individuals for sickness, retirement benefits, subsistence, childcare and invalidity. It also contains unemployment compensation. The 'subsidies' are payments to firms. The 'other transfer payments' are then a residual category collecting all the transfers that have not been filed into the other two and better-defined rubrics.[5]

Once again, Table 4.2 shows separate results in levels and ratios. The ones in levels correspond exactly to those in rows 5 and 6 of the preceding table and those in ratios correspond exactly to those in rows 11 and 12 of that table. More precisely, the estimates in Table 4.2 are joint estimates with further equations for $\Delta(Y - Y^*)$ or $\Delta(Y/Y^*)$, $\Delta\pi$ and r_L based on the same instruments as before. The new estimates rest on 3SLS. Thus, these estimates concern a 16-equation system, including separate equations for the 13 different tax and spending items, and three more for the sources of non-discretionary effects. For the sake of legibility, I omit the results for r_L from Table 4.2 (these are almost always insignificant except for the effects on net interest payments). The results on the left side of the table concern levels (and the impact of $\Delta(Y - Y^*)$), while those on the right side concern ratios (and the impact of $\Delta(Y/Y^*)$).

With respect to levels, all of the tax items have the expected positive signs. They are also all significant for the OECD 20 but only household and business direct taxes are so for the EU 14. On the spending side, wages are highly significant with a positive sign and non-wage consumption is highly significant with a negative sign for the OECD 20. But both influences are small and cancel each other out. As regards the EU 14, the corresponding two effects are smaller and statistically insignificant. With respect to transfer payments, social benefits paid enter very significantly with a negative sign both for the OECD 20 and EU 14. The other two categories of transfer payments also bear significant signs (marginally so in

Table 4.2 Taxes, spending: the decomposition: 3SLS estimates

Dependent variable:	Dependent variables in levels: first differences			Dependent variables as a percentage of Y: first differences		
	$\Delta(Y - Y^*)$	$\Delta\pi$	R^2	$\Delta(Y/Y^*)$	$\Delta\pi$	R^2
OEC 20						
Household Direct Taxes	0.21	+n.r	0.73	−0.04	0.015	0.14
	(21)	(2.4)		(−1.8)	(2.75)	
Business Direct Taxes	0.17	+n.r.	0.52	0.04	−0.01	0.13
	(17)	(5.2)		(2.3)	(−0.59)	
Social Security Tax Receipts	0.07	−n.r.	0.75	−0.08	∼0	0.24
	(7.9)	(−1.08)		(−5.1)	(0.39)	
Transfers Received By Government	0.001	+n.r.	0.27	−0.02	−0.01	0.09
	(3.6)	(0.86)		(−1.64)	(−1.3)	
Indirect Taxes	0.07	+n.r.	0.61	0.03	−0.02	0.12
	(7.2)	(0.34)		(1.7)	(−1.86)	
Wages	0.014	+n.r.	0.93	−0.12	0.01	0.39
	(5.3)	(3.3)		(−9.4)	(0.81)	
Non-Wage Consumption	−0.013	+n.r.	0.94	−0.06	∼0	0.21
	(−3.5)	(1.66)		(−6.2)	(0.45)	
Investment	−0.09	−n.r.	0.29	−0.02	∼0	0.14
	(−7)	(−2.03)		(−1.94)	(0.35)	
Social Benefits Paid	−0.066	−n.r.	0.94	−0.21	−0.03	0.55
	(−17.5)	(−1.92)		(−13.9)	(−2.84)	
Subsidies	0.012	+n.r.	0.34	−0.05	∼0	0.21
	(5.1)	(0.92)		(−5.5)	(0.65)	
Other Transfer Payments	0.006	+n.r.	0.24	−0.04	−0.01	0.20
	(1.89)	(∼0)		(−3.8)	(−0.98)	
Net Interest Payments	0.03	−n.r.	0.13	−0.01	−0.01	0.26
	(1.66)	(−0.42)		(−0.81)	(0.01)	
Residual Spending	−0.09	−n.r.	0.21	0.04	−0.01	0.33
	(−5.6)	(−1.2)		(1.26)	(0.25)	
EU 14						
Household Direct Taxes	0.19	+n.r	0.50	−0.04	0.04	0.15
	(5.9)	(2)		(−1.87)	(1.97)	
Business Direct Taxes	0.08	+n.r.	0.12	0.05	0.01	0.10
	(3.2)	(0.75)		(3.38)	(1.28)	
Social Security Tax Receipts	0.05	+n.r.	0.43	−0.09	0.01	0.27
	(1.3)	(−1.9)		(−4.7)	(0.49)	
Transfers Received By Government	−0.007	+n.r.	0.16	−0.01	∼0	0.15
	(−1.2)	(0.79)		(−1.2)	(−.5)	
Indirect Taxes	0.05	+n.r.	0.33	0.02	−0.03	0.10
	(1.3)	(0.47)		(.95)	(−1.78)	
Wages	0.009	+n.r.	0.68	−0.13	0.2	0.43
	(0.44)	(3.8)		(−9.33)	(1.74)	
Non-Wage Consumption	−0.005	+n.r.	0.54	−0.05	∼0	0.23
	(−0.25)	(1.92)		(−4.9)	(0.32)	
Investment	−0.003	+n.r.	0.29	−0.01	.01	0.16
	(0.35)	(−2.85)		(−1.27)	(1.37)	
Social Benefits Paid	−0.2	+n.r.	0.64	−0.23	−0.05	0.56
	(−7.2)	(−1.44)		(−13.5)	(−3.9)	
Subsidies	−0.054	−n.r.	0.24	−0.05	−0.01	0.23
	(−5.4)	(−0.96)		(−4.8)	(0.66)	
Other Transfer Payments	0.05	−n.r.	0.07	−0.05	−0.03	0.23
	(−3.12)	(−3.06)		(−3.8)	(−2.7)	
Net Interest Payments	0.03	+n.r.	0.31	−0.01	∼0	0.29
	(0.79)	(1.42)		(−0.63)	(−0.29)	
Residual Spending	−0.19	−n.r.	0.35	0.05	−0.03	0.34
	(−5.35)	(−0.17)		(1.26)	(−1.06)	

Notes

Both sets of 3SLS estimates include additional equations for $\Delta(Y - Y^*)$ or $\Delta(Y/Y^*)$ and $\Delta\pi$ and r_L. There are other regressors for the 13 dependent variables shown, and for $\Delta(Y - Y^*)$ or $\Delta(Y/Y^*)$, $\Delta\pi$ and r_L. These are the same as in Table 4.1. z statistics in parentheses. The R^2s are adapted. Number of observations: OEC 20, 415; EU 14, 335.

the case of 'other transfer payments' for the OECD 20 at conventional confidence levels). But the signs are opposed between the OECD 20 and EU 14, only those for the OECD 20 (positive) going in the destabilizing direction. These last signs are also much smaller than the corresponding ones for the EU 14, which go the 'right' way.

As an important consideration, the residual category ('residual spending') is significant both for the OECD 20 and the EU 14. Importantly, this category covers government injections of capital into enterprises and can hide many things. To make matters worse, the variable enters with opposite signs in Table 4.2, and with large coefficients to boot. In the case of the EU 14, the coefficient is enormous: 0.19. These opposite signs could well explain the conflicting signs for subsidies and other transfer payments in the two samples (those signs being much lower – that is, more negative – in the case of the EU 14, where the coefficient for residual spending is positive). Some doubt consequently surrounds the estimates of the individual spending items. Notwithstanding, it should be noted that the stabilizing movement of 'social benefits paid' on the left-hand side would be difficult to contest, since the signs of influence of $\Delta(Y - Y^*)$ on this variable are negative in the table, despite the opposite signs of the residual spending in the two. In addition, both coefficients are large, and both of them have exceedingly high statistical significance – especially the one closer to zero (-0.066) concerning the OECD 20 (and which, judging from the associated estimate of residual spending, is probably an underestimate and should be even more negative). Whatever the doubts about exact magnitudes, a stabilizing movement of 'social benefits paid' of at least 0.066 in levels can be accepted. The estimates for wage and non-wage consumption in the OECD 20 and the EU 14 are also consistent with one another and merit confidence. On the other hand, the estimates for investment are wide apart and they do not.

The results on the right-hand sides, concerning the ratios, are far more satisfactory. There the residual spending items are totally insignificant. Thus, though those items move with the cycle, they evidently do so approximately in step with output, so that when calculated as percentages of output, their importance vanishes. Very significantly too, there is a remarkable conformity all down the line between the estimates of the impact of $\Delta(Y/Y^*)$ in Table 4.2. If we add up the coefficients for taxes on the right-hand side in Table 4.2, we get the identical figure, -0.07, in both cases. The discrepancy with Table 4.1 is negligible too. Looking back at line 11 of that table, the estimates of the impact of Y/Y^* on total taxes there were respectively -0.007 and -0.11. If we repeat the same operation for the seven itemized elements of spending besides the residual element, the respective totals of the coefficients in Table 4.2 are -0.51 or -0.53. This then compares with estimates of -0.49 and -0.53 in line 12 of Table 4.1. In sum, the decomposition on the right-hand side in Table 4.2 merits confidence.

What story do those estimates tell us? First, household direct taxes move in a destabilizing way. They do not keep up with the cycle. Social security taxes do so even less. However, indirect taxes keep up, while business direct taxes do better than just keep up. These results may carry conviction. We would expect profits to move more than wages with the cycle, and therefore business direct taxes to be more stabilizing (less destabilizing) than household direct taxes. Turning to the spending side, the results for transfer payments are the most striking. Social benefit payments fall markedly as a percentage of income during cyclical upswings. Further, subsidies and other transfer payments also both move significantly in the stabilizing direction. But though they matter, the contributions of these last two rubrics to stabilization taken together are less than half as large as the contribution of social benefits paid alone. The results regarding wages and non-wage consumption also merit notice. Neither class of government expenditures keeps up with the cycle, but wages do so less than non-wage consumption – by far.[6]

With these results in hand, we may return to the question of the extent to which the aggregate stabilizing response of the budget in ratios depends on the contribution of government spending on goods and services. The overall stabilizing response of the budget as a ratio of output does indeed owe a great deal to government spending on goods and services. If we sum over all the five tax and the seven spending items other than residual spending, the stabilizing response of the budget balance is of the order of 0.42–0.45. But even when we ignore this inertia, the figure for automatic stabilization is still around 0.25. Thus, though government consumption and investment is important in explaining the stabilizing movement, transfer payments are even more so. A 1% rise in the ratio of output to potential output leads to a fall in transfer payments of 30–33% of the rise, enough by itself (apart from the inertia in government current expenditures) to overcome the associated fall in the ratio of taxes to output (7% of the rise) by around 25%.

How shall we interpret the greater stabilizing role of transfers than government consumption and investment? To answer, let us go back first to Table 4.1 concerning levels. There we see that spending adds about 17% to stabilization in levels. Next, Table 4.2 tells us that this stabilization comes essentially from transfers rather than government consumption and investment (despite some ambiguities stemming from the unreliability of the results associated with residual spending). The left-hand sides of both tables clearly indicate that government consumption adds little to the 17% while a single class of transfers alone, 'social benefits paid', adds a lot. Suppose we interpret all of the 17% as coming from transfers, as it is easy to do, then everything falls into place. Government spending on goods and services plays a stabilizing role in terms of ratios strictly because of initial size. But government transfers do so both on account of initial size and a stabilizing movement in level. While transfer payments are effectively smaller than government consumption and investment in most countries, they still amount to nearly 0.8 of this spending on average. Hence, the stabilizing response of transfer payments stemming from the combination of movement and initial size trumps the stabilizing response of government spending on goods and services coming from initial size alone.[7]

4.5 Some individual country analysis

The study would also suggest the importance of national distinctions. Such distinctions obviously matter greatly in case of the usual conception of automatic stabilization (which excludes most transfer payments), since tax structures and systems of unemployment compensation differ by country. But national distinctions are still more important if a central element in non-discretionary fiscal policy is aggregate transfer payments. Programmes of government financing of retirement, health, unemployment, poverty, childcare, regional assistance and subsidies to firms not only differ by countries but there are also cases of big programmes that do not even exist in other countries.

Unfortunately, however, it is impossible to replicate the analysis for individual countries. The national data series are too short. The previous 3SLS analysis proves impracticable. The most comparable tests by country I was able to perform depend on seemingly unrelated regressions (SUR) with instruments for the environmental factors $\Delta(Y - Y^*)$ or $\Delta(Y/Y^*)$, $\Delta\pi$ and r_L. Even then, five of the countries in the previous work needed to be dropped because of insufficiently long time series (Denmark, Greece, Ireland, New Zealand and Spain). Table 4.3 displays a few of the results for the other 15 countries in turn. These results pertain to four separate estimates per country: two in levels, two in ratios. One of the estimates in levels and one of them in ratios relate to the net government surplus. These two correspond exactly to lines 2 and 7 of Table 4.1. The other pair relates to the 13 dependent variables in Table 4.2, and rest on SUR with IV instead of 3SLS. With respect to those SUR estimates, I only display the results for 5 of the 13 variables, and I only report them for the impact of $\Delta(Y - Y)$ or $\Delta(Y/Y^*)$. This selectiveness in reporting avoids reams of pages that would be difficult to digest and to comment on seriously. The five chosen variables for display focus on the spending rubrics that may be of special interest are: wages, non-wage consumption, social benefits, subsidies and other transfer payments. Even limited in this way, the table still contains a large number of figures. Therefore, I highlight the significant z values at the 10% confidence level with the use of bold letters and the significant z values above the 5% confidence level with bold letters for the coefficients as well as the z values.

All these estimates obviously deserve much less confidence than those in Table 4.2. There are too few degrees of freedom. Each equation contains estimates of 10 or 11 separate coefficients (for ($\Delta(Y - Y^*)$ or $\Delta(Y/Y^*)$, $\Delta\pi$, r_L, the lagged level and first difference of the dependent variable, the trend, and four or five six-year dummies). But there are only around 28 observations altogether (the Table reports the exact number of observations per country (N)). As a result, the typical number of degrees of freedom is around 16. Notwithstanding, a few points can be made. The stabilizing response of the net public surplus to the cycle emerges – in levels or ratios, one or the other – for 12 of the 15 countries (all but Australia, Norway and Sweden). In eight of the countries, it emerges in both forms. Wages and non-wage consumption often appear as moving in the stabilizing direction. In addition, the stabilizing influence of at least one of the three classes of transfer payments always emerges – that is, if we go down to the 10% level of significance. In ten of the countries, the significance of one or more classes of transfer payments is clearly above the 95% confidence level.

I propose to take a closer look at the estimates for the United States. As in many other instances of closed-economy macroeconomics, the United States has been the

Table 4.3 Selected individual-country responses to $y - y^*$ or y/y^*. Levels in columns 1; percentages of y in columns 2

Dependent variable: first differences	AUS (1)	AUS (2)	AUT (1)	AUT (2)	BEL (1)	BEL (2)	CAN (1)	CAN (2)	FIN (1)	FIN (2)	FRA (1)	FRA (2)	GER (1)	GER (2)	ITA (1)	ITA (2)
Net Public Surplus	**0.036**	**0.01**	**0.105**	**0.30**	**0.29**	**0.45**	**0.40**	**0.45**	**0.94**	**0.43**	**0.39**	0.26	**0.26**	**0.46**	**0.49**	**0.50**
	(0.23)	(0.18)	(0.58)	(1.69)	**(2.52)**	**(2.15)**	**(2.94)**	**(1.97)**	**(2.59)**	**(1.97)**	**(2.84)**	(1.53)	**(2.53)**	**(1.98)**	**(2.1)**	**(3.85)**
Wages	0.024	**−0.046**	0.027	**−0.053**	−0.015	**−0.042**	0.029	**−0.09**	**−0.045**	**−0.054**	−0.016	**−0.058**	0.007	**−0.032**	−0.077	−0.021
	(1.4)	**(−4)**	(0.60)	**(−1.85)**	(−0.84)	**(−2.64)**	(1.42)	**(−4.41)**	**(−2.43)**	**(−2.18)**	(−1.03)	**(−3.77)**	(0.57)	**(−2.7)**	(−1.44)	(−0.77)
Non-Wage Consumption	**−0.13**	−0.014	−0.03	0.006	**−0.056**	**−0.058**	**−0.034**	−0.034	**−0.036**	−0.20	−0.042	−0.005	−0.018	−0.024	**−0.78**	−0.021
	(−3.1)	(−0.03)	(−1.07)	(0.32)	**(2.68)**	**(−2.8)**	**(−2.11)**	(−1.58)	**(−3.2)**	(−1.38)	(−1.17)	(−0.17)	(−0.84)	(−1.17)	**(−2.14)**	(−0.90)
Social Benefits Paid	**−0.08**	**−0.64**	**−0.11**	**−0.14**	**−0.04**	**−0.145**	—	−0.48	−0.048	**−0.065**	**−0.101**	**−0.053**	**−0.091**	−0.065	0.064	
	(−3)	**(−2.54)**	**(−3.48)**	**(−4.19)**	**(−2.51)**	**(−6.78)**		**(−1.69)**	(−1.23)	**(−3.36)**	**(−3.25)**	**(−1.85)**	**(−2.01)**	(−1.55)	(1.79)	
Subsidies	0.005	**−0.02**	**−0.05**	**−0.05**	−0.01	0.006	**−0.051**	−0.016	−0.004	0.017	**−0.024**	−0.224	**0.036**	**0.025**	**−0.045**	−0.066
	(0.63)	**(−2.9)**	**(−2.42)**	**(−3.28)**	(−1.22)	(0.81)	**(−3.06)**	(−0.99)	(−0.46)	(1.49)	**(−1.97)**	(−1.71)	**(3.8)**	**(2.66)**	**(−2.59)**	(−0.28)
Other Transfer Payments	**−0.026**	−0.01	−0.04	**−0.03**	0.001	0.001	−0.028	**−0.128**	0.025	0.001	−0.001	**0.01**	0.007	0.002	**−0.049**	−0.005
	(−2.17)	(−1.12)	(−1.66)	**(−2.15)**	(1.20)	(0.18)	(−1.54)	**(−3.63)**	(1.44)	(0.03)	(−0.16)	**(1.63)**	(0.22)	(0.93)	**(−3.48)**	(−0.49)

Continued

Table 4.3 Continued

	JAP (1)	JAP (2)	NETH (1)	NETH (2)	NOR (1)	NOR (2)	POR (1)	POR (2)	SWE (1)	SWE (2)	UK (1)	UK (2)	US (1)	US (2)	N
Net Public Surplus	**0.47**	0.175	**0.51**	**0.41**	−0.075	0.56	0.17	0.09	0.11	0.22	**0.50**	0.28	**0.42**	**0.48**	AUS 24
	(4.5)	(1.73)	**(2.65)**	**(1.94)**	(−0.12)	(1.4)	(1.59)	(0.55)	(0.35)	(0.74)	**(2.54)**	(0.99)	**(2.80)**	**(3.07)**	AUT 27
Wages	−0.003	−0.029	−0.058	−0.085	−0.042	−0.051	**0.091**	−0.048	−0.052	−0.149	−0.112	−0.069	−0.015	−0.093	BEL 28
	(−0.44)	**(−4.35)**	(−2.2)	**(−2.93)**	(−1.04)	(−0.95)	**(2.16)**	**(−3.33)**	(−1.42)	**(−3.47)**	**(−3.04)**	(−1.89)	**(−2.26)**	**(−10)**	CAN 28
Non-Wage Consumption	−0.008	−0.035	−0.107	−0.054	0.019	0.005	**0.156**	0.013	0.042	−0.002	−0.019	−0.047	−0.021	−0.061	FIN 24
	(−0.70)	**(−2.77)**	**(−2.63)**	(−1.52)	(0.57)	(0.17)	**(3.87)**	(0.58)	(1.1)	(−0.07)	(−0.36)	**(−1.83)**	(−1.54)	**(−5.48)**	FRA 28
Social Benefits Paid	**−0.031**	−0.047	**−0.127**	**−0.10**	−0.048	−0.013	0.007	−0.01	0.018	0.05	**−0.083**	−0.044	0.019	−0.041	GER 33
	(−2.71)	**(−2.78)**	**(−2.36)**	**(−2.02)**	**(−1.74)**	(−0.18)	(0.21)	(−0.60)	(0.42)	(0.71)	**(−2.08)**	(−1.1)	(0.49)	**(−1.71)**	ITA 36
Subsidies	0.002	**−0.018**	**−0.044**	−0.004	0.022	−0.01	~0	0.02	0.033	−0.007	0.008	**−0.05**	−0.01	0.002	JAP 29
	(0.28)	**(−2.22)**	**(−1.94)**	(−0.18)	(1.14)	(−0.39)	(~0)	(0.80)	**(1.60)**	(−0.41)	(0.65)	**(−3.25)**	(−1.04)	(0.38)	NETH 27
Other Transfer Payments	0.001	0.001	−0.009	−0.001	−0.058	**−0.058**	**−0.254**	−0.056	0.041	0.06	**0.048**	0.01	—	—	NOR 26
	(0.09)	(0.14)	(−0.52)	(−0.07)	(−1.72)	**(−1.98)**	**(−6.71)**	(−1.67)	(1.24)	(1.58)	**(3.48)**	(0.87)			POR 28
															SWE 31
															UK 29
															US 30

Notes

The coefficients in columns 1 are responses to $\Delta(Y - Y^*)$; those in columns 2 are responses to $\Delta(Y/Y^*)$. All dependent variables are in first-difference form. z statistics in parentheses. Denmark, Greece, Ireland, New Zealand and Spain figure in the previous estimates but not here because the time series for them are too short. In the case of net public surplus, the specifications correspond exactly to those in rows 2 and 8 of Table 4.1. They are 2SLS with the same instruments as before for $\Delta(Y - Y^*)$, $\Delta(Y/Y^*)$, Δr and r_L. The estimates of the other 5 dependent variables are obtained simultaneously, together with estimates of the other 8 dependent variables in Table 4.2. But these estimates are based on SUR (seemingly unrelated regressions) with instruments for $\Delta(Y - Y^*)$ or $\Delta(Y/Y^*)$, Δr and r_L. The regressors and the instruments are the same as those in Table 4.2 (to which the details are given in the notes to Table 4.1) except for the omission of all the twice-lagged variables as instruments in order to preserve degrees of freedom.

outstanding individual-country laboratory for studies of automatic stabilization. Some especially careful estimates are available for this country, even at the microeconomic level (see, especially, Auerbach and Feenberg, 2000). It is reassuring, therefore, that the stabilizing response of the net public surplus to the output gap comes out plainly both in levels and in ratios for the United States. The country is thus a good laboratory in this regard. However, the United States happens to be highly untypical in another respect. It is one of the few countries in the sample where the impact of transfer payments emerges faintly if at all. Measured in levels, transfer payments are totally insignificant for the United States, and in ratios the significance of these payments appears for only one of the three relevant rubrics, 'social benefits paid', and then only near the 10% confidence level.[8] Thus, the tendency to focus on the United States could have something to do with the usual failure to give proper attention to transfer payments. On the other hand, principal focus on this country will obviously not explain the typical disregard of the issue of levels or ratios. Quite apart from the matter of principle, the difference in the sources of stabilization in levels and ratios emerges clearly in the United States. When judged in terms of ratios, the government spending on goods and services in the country contributes greatly to the stabilizing movement of the budget balance. Indeed, nowhere does the significance of public wages and non-wage consumption in stabilization come out more plainly.

4.6 Conclusions

I have rejected the mere guess that 'among primary expenditures [or apart from interest payments], only unemployment benefits probably have a non-negligible built-in response to output fluctuations' (Galí and Perotti, 2003: 542–3). I have also stressed that if, for whatever reason, the interest lies in the cyclically adjusted ratio of government budget balance to observed or potential output, then the right way to proceed is to correct for the automatic impact of the cycle on the ratio itself. Basing the cyclically adjusted figures on estimates of the numerator alone is inefficient. When the proper estimates in the case of ratios take place, transfer payments appear as especially prominent in automatic stabilization. But the main point, as regards ratios as such, is the issue of estimation.

Two sorts of questions remain wide open. One relates to the specific transfer programmes that contribute to stabilization. Some programmes may not contribute at all, some may do so more than others, and some may even work in a pro-cyclical direction. The OECD classification of social benefits paid, subsidies, and other transfer payments is far from adequate. Social benefits paid embrace too many things: payments for pensions, sickness benefits, invalidity, unemployment, subsistence and childcare. We would clearly expect pensions, for example, to respond to the cycle in a stabilizing manner. Cyclical upswings are likely to induce people to work longer and to delay pension receipts. Pensions are also very expensive. In addition, unemployment compensation probably also responds counter-cyclically, though only with a lag (unless there is a rise in the number of people who qualify for benefits within a year during a contraction among those who are already unemployed, which is possible). However, it is not clear that payments for childcare should move counter-cyclically. The stabilizing influence of subsidies to firms poses similar interrogations. Subsidies can cover many diverse programmes, going from agricultural price supports to help for firms in difficulty. What are the subsidy programmes at work? Finally, it would be nice to know too where the stabilizing impact of 'other transfer payments' comes from.

The second sort of questions that demand investigation relate to discretionary fiscal policy. If the series for the cyclically adjusted budget balances should be constructed differently, measures of fiscal policy stances need to be re-estimated. In addition, so do many estimates of the impact of discretionary fiscal policy on the economy. This is true regardless of estimation in levels or ratios. But in the case of ratios, the problems go further since they relate to the estimation procedure as well as the failure to consider any transfer payments besides unemployment compensation.

A big final question is that of the policy implications. As regards the size of automatic stabilization, the answer is easy: the estimates are larger. They go up in levels from usual figures of 0.5 to around 0.6. This is only reasonable since the sources of automatic stabilization are wider and cover all transfer payments. In the case of ratios, there is still the issue whether to use the 0.42 figure inclusive of government spending on goods and services or the 0.25 one exclusive of this spending. I believe the larger estimate to be better. It is the only one consistent with the 0.6 figure in levels, which clearly depends on the response of all government spending as well as taxes to the cycle. We might be tempted to exclude the contribution of government consumption and investment in levels in order to resolve the problem. But this would be unwise. The point of no contribution of government spending on goods and services in levels is precisely the one where inertia in government spending, as such, exerts a maximum effect in the corresponding calculation in ratios. Thus, the only way to maintain coherence in the analysis in levels and ratios is to admit inertia in government spending on goods and services when reasoning in ratios. Unless we do so and thus admit all non-discretionary responses to the cycle in the case of ratios, we generate a discrepancy mainly based on terminology alone.

The 0.42 figure in ratios and the 0.6 one in levels are also easy to fit together. Taxes and government spending, individually, are mostly of the order of 0.3–0.5 of output in the OECD. Let us take 0.4 as our basis for reasoning and, only to facilitate the calculation, let us translate the entire response of the budget balance to the cycle into a change in taxes (thereby putting aside the opposite signs of taxes and expenditures in the budget balance). Consider then the case of a cyclical doubling of output. The earlier 0.42 estimate for the influence on the ratio of the budget balance to output means that the government's income share would go up from 0.4 by 0.42 or to about 0.57, close to 0.60. This then fits well with the estimate of the change in the budget balance of around 0.60 of the rise in output.

But there are other policy implications. Consider the popular advice 'let the automatic stabilizers work.' In the case of taxes and government spending on goods and services, the injunction has essentially the same interpretation as before.

When reasoning in levels, it advises not to interfere with the stabilizing effect of taxes through discretionary government spending. When reasoning in ratios, it gives similar advice, though this may not be transparent. We see it most easily by referring to the case of lump-sum taxation. In that case, the ratio of taxes to output would automatically fall in a cyclical expansion, which would then be destabilizing. But since, in fact, taxes rise with income, this does not happen (or less so). Income-related taxes thus avert a destabilizing outcome. It follows that, when reasoning in ratios, the earlier injunction to let the automatic stabilizers work can be interpreted to advise, nearly identically, not to interfere with the reduction in destabilization coming from income-related taxes through discretionary government spending. The real *policy* difference in the injunction to let everything alone regards transfer payments. Now the injunction also says 'do not interfere with the automatic stabilizing effects of transfer payments and subsidies.'

As observed many times in the past, the automatic stabilization coming from taxes is not the product of any deliberate design. Ratios of taxes to output rose greatly following World War II in the richer section of the world for reasons mostly having nothing to do with desired macroeconomic stabilization. Smoothing of business cycles resulted. However, by and large, this fortuitous outcome meets approval.[9] In contradistinction, in the case of unemployment compensation, automatic stabilization was indeed part of the design. The same cannot be said for transfer payments as a group. Some of them, like agricultural price supports, are even the subjects of political opposition. Transfer payments typically concern programmes that are intended for their redistributive effects and that carry some controversial features – if only in their detailed configuration. There is little doubt that the motto 'let the automatic stabilizers work' assumes a different political colour if it says, as the data suggests, 'let more people go into retirement or on the poverty rolls and let public aid to currently subsidized firms increase during recessions.' Already the principle of letting the automatic stabilizers work encounters some opposition because of the international differences in the sizes of stabilizers and the lack of any bearing of these different sizes on optimal stabilization (see, for example, Farina and Tamborini, 2004). Any call for unqualified reliance on transfer programmes could only stir more controversy. Yet, according to the data, that is precisely what the motto calls for.

Notes

* I would like to thank Marco Buti; the editors, Peter Wierts, Servaas Deroose, Elena Flores and Alessandro Turrini; and Julia Darby, Paul van den Noord and Charles Wyplosz for valuable comments. Paul van den Noord was of special help.
1 To quote from van den Noord's summary:

> First, the elasticities of the relevant tax bases and unemployment with respect to (cyclical) economic activity, *i.e.* the output gap, are estimated through regression analysis. Next, the elasticities of tax proceeds or expenditure [unemployment compensation] with respect to the relevant bases are extracted from the tax code

or simply set to unity in cases where proportionality may be assumed. These two sets of elasticities are subsequently combined into reduced-form elasticities that link the cyclical components of taxes and expenditure to the output gap.

2 The most recent report on public finances in EMU of the European Commission (2004) edges toward this position. First, the report recognizes major conceptual differences when study concerns the ratio of cyclically adjusted budget balances to output, as mentioned at the start. Next, the report also recognizes an issue of estimation if ratios to output serve because the predicted ratio to output then depends not only on the predicted value of cyclically adjusted budget balances, but also the predicted ratio of output to potential output Y/Y^* (section 3.3 of Part II and Annex II). In other words, based on the report, forecast errors in Y/Y^* affect both the numerator and the denominator in the ratio. But according to my reasoning, the difficulty lies deeper: it is inefficient to estimate the numerator separately.

3 Note, though, that this destabilizing movement in the ratio of taxes to output is true at a constant rate of inflation. Suppose instead a percentage-point rise (fall) in Y/Y^* that is associated with an equal percentage-point acceleration (deceleration) of inflation. Then, according to the estimates, taxes move in perfect step with output (since the −0.07 and −0.11 estimates for $\Delta(Y/Y^*)$ in line 11 of Table 4.1 are perfectly matched by (more significant) 0.07 and 0.12 respective estimates for $\Delta\pi$ on these lines).

4 Arreaza *et al.* (1999) probably deserve credit as the first to bring attention to the issue. Reasoning in ratios, they obtain similar results to those in the text and conclude that taxes are destabilizing and government spending is stabilizing in the OECD and the EU. Mélitz (2000) notes the seeming unorthodoxy of their stand (without siding with them, as might have been right).

5 More specifically, 'Other current transfers' include payments by the central government for damages resulting from natural causes, such as fires and floods (which may be associated with insurance (net of income receipts for the insurance) or with emergency relief). Another element is 'annual or other regular contributions paid by member governments to international organizations (excluding taxes payable to supra-national organizations)'. Still another element is 'fines and penalties'. Somewhat mysteriously (since the figures concern general government), the numbers include some 'transfers between different levels of government, such as frequently occur between central and state or local government units'. I quote from a text from the Statistics Division of the UN, to which the services of the OECD refer me.

6 These last results, regarding spending, compare well with Lane (2002), who concentrates on the cyclical sensitivity of government activity on the spending side.

7 The math helps to see. Let spending be x, output y, normal output y^* and suppose $x = f(y)$. Then $d(x/y)/d(y/y^*) = (1/y^*)[(dx/dy) − (1/y)(x/y)]$. The negative value of the second term varies with x/y while dx/dy is just the same regardless of x/y. Thus, if dx/dy is −0.17 and $x/y = 0.22$ (0.22 being about the right figure for government consumption plus investment relative to output in the period on average), the first term may easily dominate the second. This is the decisive consideration (even though the reasoning abstracts from differences between the estimates of $dx/d(y − y^*)$ – or dx/dy, supposedly the same – and $d(x/y)/d(y/y^*)$ stemming from the separate estimation of the two in a stochastic environment).

8 Why there is no data for the United States for 'other transfers paid' is not clear.

9 Not always. Some people worry that automatic stabilization owes much to big government. True, the size of government can be reduced without cutting down automatic stabilization by lowering taxes and spending concurrently while increasing the progressiveness of taxation. However, progressive taxes can have serious disincentive effects on supply. For an emphasis on this conundrum and related discussion, see Buti *et al.* (2003).

References

Arreaza, A., Sørensen, B. and Oved, Y. (1999), 'Consumption smoothing through fiscal policy in OECD and EU countries', in James Poterba and Jürgen von Hagen (eds), *Fiscal Institutions and Fiscal Performance*, Chicago: University of Chicago Press.

Auerbach, A. and Feenberg, D. (2000), 'The significance of federal taxes as automatic stabilizers', *Journal of Economic Perspectives*, 22: 37–56.

Buti, M. and Sapir, A. (eds) (1998), *Economic Policy in EMU: A Study by the European Commission Services*, Oxford: Oxford University Press.

Buti, M., Martinez-Mongay, C., Sekkat, K. and van den Noord, P. (2003), 'Macroeconomic policy and structural reform: a conflict between stabilisation and flexibility?', in M. Buti (ed.), *Monetary and Fiscal Policies in EMU – Interactions and Coordination*, Cambridge: Cambridge University Press.

Canzoneri, M., Cumby, R. and Diba, B. (2002), 'Should the European central bank and the Federal Reserve be concerned about fiscal policy?', Rethinking Stabilization Policy, A symposium sponsored by the Federal Reserve Bank of Kansas City, August.

European Commission (2004), 'Public Finance in EMU 2004', *European Economy*, Reports and Studies, 3.

Farina, F. and Tamborini, R. (2004), ' "Set a Sufficiently Ambitious Budget Target and Let Automatic Stabilizers Work". Will it really work in the European Monetary Union?', *Open Economies Review*, 15: 143–68.

Galí, J. and Perotti, R. (2003), 'Fiscal policy and monetary integration in Europe', *Economic Policy*, 37: 533–72.

Giorno, C., Richardson, P., Roseveare, D. and Van den Noord, P. (1995), 'Potential output, budget gaps, and structural budget balances', *OECD Economic Studies*, 24: 167–209.

Lane, P. (2003), 'The cyclical behaviour of fiscal policy: evidence from the OECD', *Journal of Public Economics*, 87: 2661–75.

Mélitz, J. (2000), 'Some cross-country evidence about fiscal policy behaviour and consequences for EMU', *European Economy Reports and Studies*, 2.

Taylor, J. (2000), 'Reassessing discretionary fiscal policy', *Journal of Economic Perspectives*, 25: 21–36.

Van den Noord, P. (2000), 'The size and role of automatic stabilizers in the 1990s and beyond', *OECD Economics Department Working Paper no. 230*, revised and abridged in L. Buti, J. von Hagen and C. Martinez-Mongay, *The Behaviour of Fiscal Authorities*, Houndmills, Basingstoke, Hampshire, UK: Palgrave, 2002, chapter 8.

5 Getting measures of fiscal stance right for the new SGP*

E. Gaffeo, G. Passamani and R. Tamborini

[...] since the second half of 2004, growth in the Euro area has been modest, below the area's potential growth rate

Jean-Claude Trichet (30 May 2005)

[...] the delivery of the new, refocused Lisbon agenda could boost Europe's natural rate of growth to around 3 percent per year and bring our goal of full employment within reach by the end of the decade

José-Manuel Barroso (2 April 2005)

5.1 Introduction

In November 2004, France and Germany obtained from the Council of the Finance Ministers (Ecofin) suspension of the 'excessive deficits procedure' recommended by the European Commission in application of the norms established by the Maastricht Treaty and the Stability and Growth Pact (SGP). The decision was unanimously viewed as the political end of the SGP in its then current form. In March 2005, the Ecofin approved a revision of the rules on the excessive deficit procedure. Was the breakdown of the SGP in 2004 due to brute political pressure applied by the major stakeholders? Was it merely by chance that it occurred after three years of stagnation, if not recession, in the euro area, and that the drive for reform was led by the two early guardians of the SGP orthodoxy? Will the new SGP be more successful in combining 'rigour and flexibility'?

The revision of the SGP in March 2005 confirmed the 3% deficit/GDP ratio as the pillar of the excessive deficits procedure. On the other hand, some of the many criticisms levelled against the original version of the SGP were recognized insofar as

- some more 'flexibility' has been injected into the procedure by allowing the deduction of a list of long-run growth-promoting expenses;
- a longer time span for the correction of excess deficits has been granted;
- a less stringent definition of 'recession' has been introduced for a country to qualify for exemption from the excess deficit procedure.[1]

The previous exemption clauses were based on the increasing 'gravity of recessions'. All of them included *negative* GDP growth rates (from less than −0.75%

('mild') to more than −2% ('exceptional')). To the negative growth rate criterion the new exemption clauses add that of *'growth gap'*, this being a growth rate that, albeit positive, *falls short of the potential rate*:

> a breach of the threshold [of 3% deficit] will now be considered exceptional if it results from a negative growth rate or *an accumulated loss of output during a protracted period of very low growth relative to potential growth*
> (Buti and Franco, 2005: 15, italics added).

However, since the deficit/GDP ceiling of 3% is still in place, research on its implications for fiscal discipline and macroeconomic stabilization in the frame of the new SGP should be taken further. We argue that the agenda largely involves empirical matters. In particular, the issues involved require careful examination and control of complex dynamic interactions between the fiscal variables and the other macro-variables. This task can be accomplished better by quantitative simulations. Hence, this chapter presents a simulation of the evolution of fiscal aggregates after a negative growth gap in two representative euro-countries: Italy and Germany. Our study addresses the following issues:

First, analyses and prescriptions concerning fiscal and monetary policy in a monetary union should be framed in a fully specified macroeconomic scenario in which the interactions between the two policies are clearly understood and identified. Favero (2002) reviews the theoretical reasons behind this claim and shows the empirical mistakes that may be generated by piece-wise analyses of monetary and fiscal policies. Developments in this direction, however, are only recent (e.g. Melitz, 2002; Muscatelli *et al.*, 2004; and this volume). By contrast, most of the empirical work on the SGP produced to date does not meet this requirement. This remark applies to studies intended to show the tendency of pre-Maastricht European governments towards 'fiscal indiscipline' (e.g. Buti and Sapir, 1998, chapter VII), to those concerned with the adequacy of domestic stabilizers within the SGP limits (e.g. Buti *et al.*, 1998; Artis and Buti, 2000; Brunila *et al.*, 2002),[2] as well as to assessments of the sufficient flexibility for stabilization purposes granted by the 3% deficit/GDP constraint based on past cyclical performances of the euro-economies (e.g. Buti and Sapir, 1998, chapter VII; Eichengreen and Wyplosz, 1998; Artis and Buti, 2000).

Second, it is well known that the deficit/GDP ratio is a variable highly sensitive to the business cycle, if anything because the numerator and the denominator are mutually correlated. Nonetheless, most applied research still uses the deficit/GDP ratio as a single variable. Moreover, the official methods employed to identify the cyclical component of the total budget are far from satisfactory. As shown by Melitz (this volume), the current practice that starts from the total deficit and proceeds by correcting for selected cyclical stabilizers is likely to miss the target. Selection of candidate items based on *ex ante* institutional information (see, for example, Perotti, 2002) soon enters a tangle of norms and practices that differ hugely from country to country.[3] The textbook distinction between 'cyclical budget/automatic stabilizers' on the one hand, and 'structural budget/discretionary interventions' on the other, is misleading in practice. Stabilization policy may be implemented by means of discretionary measures, and these measures may also have structural effects: by way of example, consider a cut of distortionary taxes during a recession (Galí and Perotti, 2003). We argue that renewed effort should be made to trace the cyclical behaviour of the deficit/GDP ratio back to its two components, especially because 'excessive deficits' measures and procedures should be based on a clear identification (and delimitation) of governments' responsibilities.

In this perspective, a third issue is budget analysis by components. Decomposition between primary and total budget is a minimal requirement, given that over the typical time horizon of the business cycle interest payments are largely predetermined by the stock of outstanding debt and by the effect of monetary policy on interest rates. Hence, a reasonable approximation to the actual fiscal stance of the government would at least require a good measure of the cyclically adjusted primary budget. In this regard it should be borne in mind that the existing evidence suggests that primary expenditure on the one hand, and total tax revenue on the other, may have different cyclical properties (see, for example, Favero, 2002; Galí and Perotti, 2003; Melitz, this volume; Muscatelli *et al.*, this volume).

Finally, the correct measurement of a country's cyclical position and the response of its fiscal variables should be carefully reconsidered. Indeed, the words of the Presidents of the European Central Bank and of the European Commission quoted above[4] provide anecdotal evidence for what seems to be an uncontroversial fact. When policy-makers consider macroeconomic performance and how it can be influenced by policy actions, they reason in terms of differences between actual and potential GDP growth rates. The stability and growth programmes they are required to submit to the Commission are based on projections of future growth rates. Thus, in the policy-makers' view, a downturn starts whenever the observed growth rate is *negative relative to the trend (potential) rate*, even though it may be *positive in absolute terms*. This requirement has to some extent been recognized, and has at the same time been made compelling, by the reformulation of exemption clauses in the new SGP in terms of growth gaps. Given that the focus of the new normative macroeconomics (Taylor, 1999) is on how policy-makers do and should behave in practice, why is it that the bias of central bankers and prime ministers towards percentage points is seldom considered by theoretical and empirical models which continue to deal with billions of euros?

Our treatment is organized as follows: Sections 5.2 and 5.3 introduce a New Keynesian macroeconomic model with monetary and fiscal policy rules suitable for econometric estimation. The model includes aggregate demand and supply for GDP and the inflation rate, a Taylor rule for the nominal interest rate, and two fiscal rules for primary expenditure and total tax revenue. The main features of the model are intended to remedy the deficiencies in the empirics of SGP pointed out above.

1   The model is specified so as to capture cycles in terms of gaps in growth rates rather than in levels of GDP. We consequently have a system of linear dynamic equations whereby we can study the evolution of the endogenous

variables over the cycle in terms of rates of deviation from their steady-state *growth paths* or target values.

2   The monetary and fiscal rules are interdependent in that each rule includes a variable determined by the other.

3   The government budget is split into its main components (primary expenditure, total tax revenue, interest payments) and each is treated separately. Primary expenditure and tax revenue are treated as the dependent variables of specific fiscal rules; interest payments are treated as an exogenous variable conditioned by monetary policy.

4   All fiscal policy variables are treated in real terms and absolute values (not as GDP ratios).

Section 5.4 reports on the econometric results for Italy and Germany with yearly data from 1962 to 2004.[5] It should be understood that the model has not been estimated in order to test hypotheses or to make forecasts, but in order to provide an empirical quantitative basis for the core part of our study, which consists of simulations. We have therefore chosen these two countries not only because they are major euro-economies but also, and especially, because they differ markedly as to their monetary and fiscal histories and may represent two different ideal types whose comparison may convey rich information on the various issues at stake. The estimation has confirmed that, while the two countries show similar structures in the determinants of their non-policy variables (GDP and inflation), they differ as far as their policy variables (interest rate, primary expenditure and tax revenue) and monetary–fiscal interactions are concerned. On the other hand, we are aware of the number of economic and institutional events that, in the period of time covered by our dataset, may qualify as sources of structural breaks for policy rules. Last but not least, the advent of the EMU, with its indisputable consequence that the national monetary authorities have been replaced by the European Central Bank (ECB). As a first step, we have not performed formal controls for structural breaks (also for the lack of sufficient observations), but we have instead resorted to dummy variables for the pre-EMU major events. Also, we have stretched the specification of independent national Taylor rules into the EMU period; first, because the available data do not allow reliable inferences about the ECB policy conduct,[6] and second, because major central banks in Europe had long pursued converging frames and practices of policy conduct in view of the creation of the single central bank, so that the institutional changeover has probably been less dramatic than it may appear (see, for example, Dornbush *et al.*, 1998; Begg *et al.*, 1999; and, for the Bank of Italy, Angeloni, 1994).

Section 5.5 presents simulations for Italy and Germany, based on the respective estimated models, of a temporary negative shock to the GDP growth rate with respect to potential growth. The simulations concern the five endogenous variables, as well as two additional variables derived from the previous ones; namely, the primary and the total budget. As explained above, the system yields the sequence of *deviations* of the variables from their baseline growth rates or target values until a new steady-state is reached. This provides information on the different dynamics of the various budget components over the cycle. These simulated data can also be used to examine the evolution of the deficit/GDP ratio, shedding light on the much-debated question of the actual control of governments over its cyclical behaviour.

The evidence can be read in two ways. Counterfactually, the simulations indicate how each economy and its public finances would perform, given its inherited macroeconomic structural relationships and policy rules. Our main findings are that (1) relatively small, and hence frequent, negative growth gaps may suffice to deteriorate the government budget up to 3% of GDP even in the absence of discretionary fiscal profligacy; (2) governments have little control over the cyclical evolution of the deficit/GDP ratio, and current methods of correction of the budget for the cycle are misconceived and deceitful; (3) the extent of the two previous results crucially depends on fiscal–monetary policy interactions, and they are more pronounced in a country like Italy, where fast-growing public debt appears among the determinants of the central bank's interest-rate policy. These findings suggest that the aforementioned studies that tested the feasibility of the old SGP against the past cyclical performances of the euro-economies were overly simplistic in their foundations and reached overly optimistic verdicts that were in fact overturned at the first serious growth slowdown in Europe. From a normative perspective, our findings also suggest that the new SGP moves in the right direction in that it re-focuses on growth gaps as a basis for exemption clauses and introduces a longer-term horizon for stability programmes centred on debt stabilization and control. Thus, maintenance of the 3% deficit/GDP ceiling as a sort of *taboo* imposed on governments appears even less justifiable and more questionable than in the old SGP. An important caveat to be borne in mind is that attention should be paid to the role of monetary–fiscal interactions, and how they will develop in the new institutional setup of the EMU with respect to the picture emerged from the past on which we have based our simulations.

The chapter closes with Section 5.6, which presents a summary of the results and makes some concluding remarks.

5.2   The core model of practical macroeconomic policy[7]

Our analysis is based on a theoretical framework rooted in the so-called New Keynesian approach. It typically consists of three main components:

- an IS curve relating current real spending with the real interest rate;
- an AS curve which relates prices and output, so that the relationship is vertical in the long-run and positively sloped in the short-run;
- one (or more) policy reaction function(s) or 'rules' showing how policy-makers react to shocks.

In this section we shall illustrate how this general framework has been extended to highlight monetary–fiscal policy interactions, and then how it has been specified with a view to empirical analysis.

5.2.1 The fundamental equations

The basic relationships in the approach under consideration can be represented in log–linear terms as follows (e.g. Allsopp and Vines, 2000),[8] where we omit time indexes that will be introduced later in the context of the testable versions of the model:

$$\text{(IS)} \quad y = y^* + \alpha r + \beta f + u_y \tag{5.1}$$

$$\text{(AS)} \quad \pi = \pi^* + \gamma(y - y^*) + u_\pi \tag{5.2}$$

$$\text{(TR)} \quad i = i^* + \delta(\pi - \pi^*) + \phi(y - y^*) + u_i \tag{5.3}$$

$$\text{(FR)} \quad f = f^* + \eta(y - y^*) + u_f \tag{5.4}$$

Equation (5.1) represents the goods-market equilibrium (IS) and it states that the actual GDP y is determined by its potential value y^*,[9] the real interest rate r (where $\alpha < 0$), a variable measuring the fiscal stance f, and possible real shocks u_y. Note that the real interest rate is a derived variable, since it is given by $r = i + \pi^e$. Under the rational expectations hypothesis, the expected inflation rate π^e is a function of other variables present in the model, and consequently r results to be entirely determined. The variable f may be a measure of expenditure, of taxation or of the overall government budget, depending on different specifications and microfoundations of the model, whereas the parameter β may be positive or negative. Equation (5.2) represents the determination of the inflation rate by the supply side of the economy (AS), according to which the actual inflation rate coincides with the official target π^* up to deviations of the level of output from its potential, and to inflationary shocks u_π. The parameter $\gamma > 0$ is usually interpreted as a measure of the flexibility of prices: the higher γ is, the more rapidly prices adjust to their market-clearing level. Temporary deviations of output from its potential imply a positively sloped relation between inflation and output, while non-zero realizations of the inflation shock when output is at its potential cause the inflation rate to shift along a vertical (long-run) relation. Note that this specification is consistent with an expectations-augmented AS, where the expected inflation rate is assumed equal to the central-bank target π^*.[10]

The next two equations constitute the policy block of the model. Equation (5.3) is a basic parameterization of a monetary rule in the form of the well known Taylor rule (TR), with the term u_i representing a monetary shock. The main idea here is that the central bank sets the nominal interest rate i in relation to a given target value i^*, while positive (negative) *deviations* of actual inflation from its target level, and of actual output from its potential, are associated with positive (negative) deviations of the interest rate from its target (i.e. $\delta, \phi > 0$). As discussed in Allsopp and Vines (2000), and more extensively in Woodford (2003, chapter 4), a monetary authority endowed with a rule like (5.3) can successfully deal with the two main functions usually assigned to monetary policy: that is, provide a nominal anchor for the economy, and stabilize output fluctuations. Finally, equation (5.4) is the fiscal authority's policy rule, and represents a more recent extension of this framework into fiscal policy analysis (e.g. Taylor, 2000a). Typically, normative as well as descriptive fiscal rules, like the monetary ones, are considered from the macro-stabilization viewpoint, and consist of a 'systematic' and an 'unsystematic' (or 'discretionary') part. In the systematic part, the government sets a target (or a 'structural') value f^* of the variable, which is then allowed to be sensitive to *deviations* of output from its potential level in a predictable way (e.g. by means of 'automatic stabilizers'); the sign of the parameter η can then be positive or negative depending on the fiscal variable chosen. The unsystematic part u_f captures discretionary and non-anticipated fiscal decisions by the government. These, in turn, may be aimed at stabilization as well as at other fiscal ends.[11] Note that the systematic relationship of the policy variables with the deviations of output and inflation from the respective targets, rather than with their levels, is regarded as a major innovation of the New Keynesian approach not only with respect to the Old one of the Sixties and Seventies, but also with respect to the New Classical Revolution of the Eighties which confined effective policy interventions only to their unsystematic part.[12]

The key to the New Keynesian interpretation of model (5.1)–(5.4) is that there exists a steady state of the economy where

$$y = y^*, \quad \pi_t = \pi^*, \quad i = i^*, \quad f = f^*.$$

In this framework, the business cycle is viewed as the transitory deviation of output and inflation from their steady-state values (i.e. a sequence of 'output gaps' and 'inflation gaps', respectively) which may be triggered by non-policy (u_y, u_π) as well as policy shocks (u_i, u_f). Under suitable conditions (which will be discussed later), the system is considered globally stable; that is, all variables tend to converge to the steady state after a shock. Among these suitable conditions are well-behaved policy rules such as (5.3) and (5.4), where it is crucial that the policy authorities set the relevant target values consistently with the steady state of the economy. In this respect, note that by imposing the steady-state condition $y = y^*$, we obtain from (5.1) the so-called neutral real interest rate:[13]

$$r* = -\frac{\beta}{\alpha} f^*. \tag{5.5}$$

Hence, the neutral real interest rate, associated with potential GDP and a constant inflation rate, is a function of the steady-state fiscal variable. As a result, given f^*, r^* and π^*, there is only one possible steady-state value of the nominal interest rate too, that is, $i^* = r^* + \pi^*$.

The system (5.1)–(5.4) can be expressed in a more compact manner that highlights this interpretation of the business cycle and of the role of policy rules. Let $\hat{x} \equiv x - x^*$ denote a 'gap' variable; that is, the deviation of the level of a variable from its target or steady-state value. Then, making use of (5.5), and considering that $r = r^* + \hat{r}, f = f^* + \hat{f}$, system (5.1)–(5.4) may be rewritten as

$$\hat{y} = \alpha\hat{r} + \beta\hat{f} + u_y \tag{5.6}$$

$$\hat{\pi} = \gamma\hat{y} + u_\pi \tag{5.7}$$

$$\hat{i} = \delta\hat{\pi} + \phi\hat{y} + u_i \tag{5.8}$$

$$\hat{f} = \eta\hat{y} + u_f. \tag{5.9}$$

The foregoing theoretical framework can be employed for empirical policy analysis by means of a general specification like the following:

$$\mathbf{A}(L)\mathbf{x}_t = \mathbf{B}(L)\mathbf{z}_t + \mathbf{v}_t \tag{5.10}$$

where $\mathbf{x}_t$ is the vector of the endogenous variables, $\mathbf{z}_t$ is the vector of the exogenous variables, $\mathbf{v}_t$ is a vector of structural errors on the equations, with $E(\mathbf{v}_t) = \mathbf{0}$ and $Var(\mathbf{v}_t) = \Omega$, L is the lag operator, and $\mathbf{A}(L)$ and $\mathbf{B}(L)$ are polynomials in L of order p, q. The elements in $\mathbf{A}(L)$ capture the interactions between the endogenous variables as well as their time structure; the elements in $\mathbf{B}(L)$ represent the impact of exogenous variables with their time structure. The conditions for dynamic stability of the model are that all the roots of the determinant polynomial lie within the unit circle. Theoretical as well as empirical elaborations may then impose *a priori* restrictions on the elements in $\mathbf{A}(L)$ and $\mathbf{B}(L)$ and add other exogenous variables.

5.2.2 Refining the Taylor rule

The policy rules embedded in the basic framework put forward above are highly stylized representations of the policy processes. When they are applied to specific countries, attention should be paid to historical periods and institutional settings. We are aware of the considerable structural and institutional differences between the two countries of interest, Italy and Germany, as well as of the number of institutional events that occurred in the time period covered by our dataset. The most important of these were the end of the Bretton Woods exchange-rates system (1971), participation in the European Monetary System (1979–1998 for Germany; 1980–1992, 1996–1998 for Italy), national reunification of Germany (1989), endorsement of the Maastricht Treaty's criteria for admission to EMU (1992) and subsequently of the SGP (1996), and inception of EMU (1999). All these events qualify as causes of structural changes in the data-generating process, especially as regards policy variables.

Owing mainly to a lack of sufficient observations, we have not performed formal tests for structural breaks. As a first step, we have introduced *a priori* information on institutional events by means of dummy variables. Those that proved to be significant or which significantly altered the quality of the estimates are reported in the next section. Of course, we do not conclude that events not associated with these selected dummies are irrelevant; simply, we leave the matter for further and more rigorous investigation. As to the advent of EMU, we have imposed no *a priori* change in the specification of national TR equations for two main reasons: First, the very small number of yearly observations available prevents reliable statistical analysis of a structural break in the TR equations of the two countries as well as estimation of an independent equation. Faced with the trade-off between curtailing the sample period at 1998 and losing observations and degrees of freedom on the one hand, and including the EMU sub-period with a structural break on the other, we have taken the second option. Hopefully, the small number of observations may also restrict the statistical importance of this break. Second, several studies point out that the convergence and harmonization process across the main central banks largely took place well before the creation of the ECB, so that the impact of the institutional changeover may have been milder than expected. This is most likely the case, as is well known, for one of our sample countries, that is, Germany (see, for example, Dornbush *et al.*, 1998; Begg *et al.*, 1999; and, for the Bank of Italy, Angeloni, 1994).

As said above, not only historical events, but also institutional specificities, should be taken into account. To begin with, the TR has been conceived with reference to a 'large', independent, almost 'closed' economy where the central bank can freely set and pursue its own targets. As regards Italy, none of these preconditions has ever existed. First, over a considerable part of the sample period (1962–1971, 1980–1992, 1996–1998), Italy was part of exchange-rate agreements (Bretton Woods and the European Monetary System, respectively) which limited her central bank's ability to manage an independent monetary policy. Second, the Bank of Italy did not adopt explicit inflation targeting policy until the second half of the 1980s, although it can be argued that an exchange-rate target implies a target on domestic inflation vis-à-vis major trading partners (Visco, 1995). Thus, we have sought a specification of equation (5.3) in consideration of the interest-rate parity constraint to which an open economy like Italy was probably subject.[14] Admittedly, this constraint was not always equally tight. In the Bretton Woods era, low and controlled capital mobility left substantial room for domestic monetary policy. By contrast, according to well-established interpretations, the monetary policies of non-German member countries in the EMS were severely constrained by interest-rate parity vis-à-vis Germany, while the anti-inflationary goal was pursued, not by choosing the domestic inflation target, but by anchoring the domestic nominal interest rate to the German one (Visco, 1995; Giavazzi and Pagano, 1988). Accordingly, the TR should in principle be replaced by the interest-rate parity (IRP) constraint with Germany. In the simplest possible form we have

$$i^{ITA} = i^{GER} + \mathrm{E}(\Delta e) + [\text{risk premium}]$$

where E is the expectation operator, e is the log of the nominal lira–DM exchange rate and $\Delta e > 0$ is the lira depreciation rate. The IRP equation may also include a risk premium on domestic bonds, to which we shall return below. Assuming that the depreciation rate is determined by the inflation differential, and leaving the risk premium aside for a moment, the IRP appears as a special TR with $i^* = i^{GER}$, $\pi^* = \pi^{GER}$, and $\delta = 1$, $\phi = 0$. On the other hand, the IRP constraint may come closer to the traditional TR to the extent that the presence of relaxing factors (e.g. capital controls, fluctuation bands of the exchange rate, realignments, etc.) allows (at least in the short run) for a limited reaction to inflation differentials, that is, $\delta < 1$, as well as for domestic GDP targeting, that is, $\phi > 0$. Therefore, the monetary rule (5.3) might be rewritten as

$$i^{ITA} = i^{GER} + \delta\hat{\pi}^{ITA} + \phi\hat{y}^{ITA} + u_i^{ITA} \tag{5.3a}$$

with $\hat{\pi}^{ITA} = \pi^{ITA} - \pi^{GER}$.

As regards Germany, her role as monetary-policy leader for the pre-EMU period admits of the use of the unconstrained TR. However, there are at least two possible regimes for the inflation target. The first includes a time-varying target; this hypothesis has required a historical reconstruction of the official inflation target of the Bundesbank (as provided, for example, by Geberding *et al.*, 2004). The second follows the widely held belief that the ECB has substantially reproduced the monetary policy framework of the Bundesbank, which amounts to assuming that the inflation target for Germany has been constantly equal to 2%. It should be noted, however, that according to the available reconstruction, although the official inflation target of the Bundesbank was not always equal to 2% until 1987, it was rarely changed. Therefore, the two specifications produce two almost coincident time series, and for the sake of simplicity we have assumed a constant $\pi^{*GER} = 2\%$, obtaining a monetary rule like the following:

$$i^{GER} = i^{*GER} + \delta\hat{\pi}^{GER} + \phi\hat{y}^{GER} + u_i^{GER} \tag{5.3b}$$

with $\hat{\pi}^{GER} = \pi^{GER} - 2\%$.

5.2.3 Refining the fiscal rules

As recalled above, investigation into fiscal rules has started more recently, and is less developed, with respect to monetary rules (e.g. Taylor, 2000a,b). On the other hand, the SGP has represented a major historical and institutional innovation that has prompted lively research on fiscal rules (e.g. Buti *et al.*, 1998; Beetsma and Uhlig, 1999; Artis and Winkler, 1999; Artis and Onorante, 2006). As a result of the (almost exclusive) focus on governments' budget deficits in the practical implementation of the SGP, empirical research initially concentrated on this variable. However, more recent developments present disaggregations of the budget into at least the two main determinants, namely total expenditure and total taxation (e.g. Favero, 2002; Perotti, 2002; Galí and Perotti, 2003; Melitz, this volume). That is to say, the FR equation (5.4) can be split into $f = g, \tau$. The main rationale for this disaggregation is that the systematic and unsystematic parts of the components of the budget may respond unequally to the cyclical position of the economy as well as to other fiscal aims. Likewise, each component may have a different impact on aggregate demand and GDP in the IS equation.

From another point of view, the government's actual fiscal stance and choices may be more precisely identified by observing expenditure and taxation separately.

A related issue is that if the aim is to establish the extent to which a government is complying with a given target or rule (as is typically the case with the SGP), it is crucial to identify the fiscal variables that can actually be traced back to direct government control. In this regard, we have also found it useful to narrow the measure of g to the sole primary expenditure, with the exclusion of interest payments (e.g. Favero, 2002). As we shall see, this is also propaedeutic to analysis of the feedback from monetary to fiscal policy.

Moreover, contrary to the common practice in both theoretical and empirical models, we have measured fiscal policy variables in absolute real terms instead of ratios to GDP. As stressed by Melitz (this volume), the two specifications yield different empirical results and lead to different policy implications. In particular, fiscal policy equations in real absolute values allow estimation of the exact elasticity of each real fiscal variable with respect to GDP gaps, whereas the cyclical elasticity of total budget can be correctly derived by compounding the partial elasticities of each component. Thanks to this estimation of the elasticities of primitive fiscal variables, also the notorious pitfall of fiscal ratios to GDP, which stir the cyclical components of the numerator and of the denominator, can easily be avoided. This yields important information, as will be shown by means of our simulations.

A final critical issue regards the targets associated with the fiscal policy variables, in our case real expenditure and taxation. The SGP targets, which naturally come to mind, are of little help for our study. First, because they were not in place for a large part of the time-span of our database, even allowing for anticipation of the new rules as early as 1992; second, because they are aggregate targets, whereas we wish to study the disaggregate components of the government budget. Further, available empirical results on fiscal target variables are less developed and more controversial than those on monetary ones. The official statistics closest to our theoretical variables are the so-called structural or cyclically adjusted fiscal items and balances released by national and international institutions. These, however, are far from satisfactory because they are fraught with arbitrariness in their *a priori* distinction between 'structural' and 'cyclical' components, as well as in the econometric methodologies employed.[15] The foregoing considerations have led us to proxy the fiscal targets by means of the least prejudged strategy that will be explained in the context of our 'growth-gap' version of the model.

5.2.4 Fiscal–monetary policy interactions

In a model like (5.6)–(5.9) there are two-way relationships between the macro and the policy variables, but no direct relationship between the latter. The direct spillovers between monetary and fiscal policy have been a matter of increasing theoretical interest, especially in relation to the inception of the euro system with its peculiar institutional setup consisting of a single supernational monetary authority vis-à-vis a number of national fiscal authorities (e.g. Beetsma and Bovenberg, 1998; Beetsma and Uhlig, 1999; Buti *et al.*, 2001; Dixit, 2001; Dixit and Lambertini, 2001; Tamborini, 2004a,b). However, empirical investigations are still relatively less developed. Among recent studies on monetary–policy interactions in the euro area, Favero (2002) and Melitz (2002) make use of macro-structural models, Muscatelli *et al.* (2004, and this volume) rely on microfounded models, all of which consist of specifications and refinements of the basic New Keynesian framework. Taking stock of these contributions, we have sought to enrich the specifications of policy rules by paying particular attention to the channels through which fiscal–monetary interactions operate.

Considering first the monetary policy rule, it should be noted that, as far as we know, no empirical model includes a fiscal term in it. Yet the basic TR includes the neutral real interest rate $r*$ as the 'real anchor' of the nominal interest rate. The direct measurement of this variable is highly problematic, and its estimates, whether as a constant or on a time-varying basis, are regarded as unsatisfactory and unreliable (see Caresma *et al.*, 2005, for a recent survey). However, theory does relate r^* to fiscal variables (see Woodford, 2003, chapter 4, and above, equation (5.5)). Hence, we have considered the hypothesis that when the national central banks were in existence, they tracked the dynamics of r^* with reference to a measure of the fiscal stance impinging upon the private sector's asset holdings which are supposed to underpin the determination of r^*. According to Woodford's model, there exists an equilibrium *stock* of public debt which, together with all other asset stocks, is associated with r^*. Following this theoretical indication, we have opted for a stock measure such as the (log) of real public debt d.[16] An additional merit of this variable is that it fits both the TR equation for a monetary independent country like Germany and that of a constrained open economy like Italy. In fact, in the case of Germany, d can be used to proxy a time-varying r^*, so that

$$i^{*GER} = \mu d^{GER} + \pi^{*GER}.$$

In the case of Italy, d can be introduced as a proxy for the risk premium that can be added to the IRP, so that

$$i^{*ITA} = i^{GER} + \mu d^{ITA}.$$

Turning to the fiscal policy rules, the main interaction channel with monetary policy is generally considered to be interest payments (Favero, 2002). In fact, given outstanding debt, changes in interest rates determined by monetary policy may affect the government budget substantially. This channel should be particularly important in countries where the government operates under a *total* budget target or constraint, since the fiscal authority should respond to changes in interest payments by adjusting their primary balance. That is to say, a monetary restriction is likely to induce a fiscal restriction as well. In the fiscal case, we found no compelling reasons to distinguish between Italy and Germany in the specification of the relevant rules. Therefore, we have limited ourselves to introducing the variable *IP*, measuring real interest payments, into the equations of expenditure and taxation for both countries.[17] Non-null estimates of the relevant coefficients would provide evidence both of a direct feedback from monetary to fiscal policy and of the government compliance with a given (implicit) budget target or constraint.

5.2.5 Other exogenous variables

The refinements of the basic model put forward above amount to including d_t and IP_t into the vector of exogenous variables $\mathbf{z}_t$. In view of empirical analysis, other exogenous variables can be added. Following Favero (2002), we have corrected the IS equation of both countries for the world business cycle represented by the US output gap, $\hat{y}_t^{US}$.

5.3 The 'growth-gaps' model

The change of perspective required to account for the attitude of policy-makers as well as of the new SGP to reason in terms of gaps in growth rates rather than of gaps in levels, may be accomplished straightforwardly within the foregoing framework.

By construction, the model (5.6)–(5.9) is fully consistent with a balanced-growth solution such that at every point in time the output level Y_t equals its potential, Y_t^*, which in turn is assumed to grow over time by the constant potential growth rate q^*, that is, $Y_t^*/Y_{t-1}^* = 1 + q^*$, all t. Hence, along this growth path:

- the inflation rate is constant and equal to the target value set by the central bank, π^*;
- the nominal and real interest rates are constant and fulfil the Fisher equation, $i^* = r^* + \pi^*$;
- for a constant real interest rate to be possible, all real asset stocks should be on a balanced growth path with GDP, which for public debt, in real terms, implies $D_t^*/D_{t-1}^* = 1 + q^*$, all t (i.e. a constant real debt/GDP ratio, $D_t^*/Y_t^* = \delta^*$, all t);
- consequently, real interest payments, $IP_t = r^* D_{t-1}$, also grow at the GDP rate, $IP_t^*/IP_{t-1}^* = 1 + q^*$ (i.e. they are constant as a ratio to GDP, $IP_t^*/Y_t^* = r^* \delta^*$);
- the government budget, in real terms, must satisfy the condition $B_t^* = -q^* D_{t-1}^*$, which implies a target value for the primary balance such that $PB_t^* = -q^* D_{t-1}^* + IP_t^*$; as a consequence, $PB_t^*/PB_{t-1}^* = 1 + q^*$ (i.e. both the total and the primary balance/GDP ratios are constant, $B_t^*/Y_t^* = -\delta^*[q^*/(1+q^*)]$, $PB_t^*/Y_t^* = \delta^*[(r^* - q^*)/(1+q^*)]$);
- a sufficient condition for targets on primary expenditure G_t^* and total tax revenue T_t^* to satisfy the primary balance constraint is that $G_t^*/G_{t-1}^* = T_t^*/T_{t-1}^* = 1 + q^*$ (i.e. constant ratios to GDP).

It is well known that the SGP arithmetic is consistent with this reference state as long as $q^* = 3\%$, $\pi^* = 2\%$, and $\delta^* = 60\%$, which yield a target deficit/GDP ratio of 3% in nominal terms. The target primary budget/GDP ratio can be close to balance on the 'classical' assumption that $r^* = q^*$. The recommendation that the target *total* budget be 'close to balance or in surplus' implies a *positive* target primary balance, and a *reduction* of any non-zero debt/GDP ratio, along the GDP potential path.

Now let q_t be the actual growth rate of a variable x_t in logs, that is, $q_t = x_t - x_{t-1}$, and $q_t^* = x_t^* - x_{t-1}^*$ its target growth rate. Clearly, the growth gap of x_t is given by $q_t - q_t^* = \Delta x_t - \Delta x_t^* = \hat{x}_t - \hat{x}_{t-1} = \Delta \hat{x}_t$. Thus, our growth-gap model can simply be obtained as the time first-difference of the basic gap model (5.6)–(5.9). With reference to the general formulation for estimation (5.10), the growth-gap model can be viewed as the result of particular constraints on the first-order elements in the coefficient matrices $\mathbf{A}(L)$ and $\mathbf{B}(L)$ or, more directly, as a respecification of the endogenous (and possibly exogenous) variables; namely, for $j = $ ITA, GER

$$\mathbf{C}(L)\Delta \mathbf{x}_t^j = \mathbf{D}(L)\Delta \mathbf{z}_t^j + \varepsilon_t^j$$
$$\Delta \mathbf{x}_t^j = [\Delta \hat{y}_t^j, \Delta \hat{\pi}_t^j, \Delta \hat{i}_t^j, \Delta \hat{g}_t^j, \Delta \hat{\tau}_t^j]' \tag{5.11}$$
$$\Delta \mathbf{z}_t^j = [\Delta \hat{y}_t US, \Delta \hat{d}_t^j \Delta \hat{I} P_t^j]'$$

Accordingly, the IS equation now gives the GDP growth gap $\Delta \hat{y}_t$ that measures the difference between the actual and the potential growth rate, while the AS equation yields the associated inflation growth gap $\Delta \hat{\pi}_t$: that is, the extent to which inflation accelerates or decelerates relative to the target. Hence, the TR equation is just the 'accelerationist' version of the basic TR: that is, $\Delta \hat{i}_t$ measures by how much the nominal interest rate increases or decreases in relation to its target. Likewise, the FR equations measure by how much the relevant fiscal variable deviates from its balanced path in response to output growth gaps and interest-payments gaps.

Before proceeding, let us draw attention to the correct interpretation of this model. It represents an economy in which all real variables and prices grow over time. In steady state, each variable grows along its balanced growth path, while the nominal interest rate is constant at its target value, as explained above. The reader can easily check that this state occurs as the vectors of shocks and of exogenous variables are null. The problem of interest is the system's dynamic response when one or more variables are shocked and display positive or negative growth gaps. A crucial part of the problem is how the policy variables react in the presence of undesired growth gaps in the relevant variables, and how changes in policy variables react back onto growth gaps.

As said above, the 'starred' variables in the model are difficult to observe and measure. Though not free from faults, the only generally accepted and officially certified variable in this category is the year potential GDP, which we have used to compute the GDP potential growth rate Δy_t^*. Our treatment of the remaining variables was already discussed in the previous section. It is worth recalling that, as a result, Italy and Germany had different specifications of some target-variables in the TR equation. In the growth-gap context these are

$$\Delta i_t^{*GER} = \mu \Delta \hat{d}_t^{GER}{}_t, \quad \Delta i_t^{*ITA} = \Delta i_t^{GER} + \mu \Delta \hat{d}_t^{ITA}{}_t,$$

$$\Delta \pi_t^{*GER} = 0, \quad \Delta \pi_t^{*ITA} = \Delta \pi_t^{GER}$$

where $\Delta \hat{d}_t^{j} = \Delta d_t^{j} - \Delta d_t^{*j}$. Germany, being a monetary independent country, follows an independent 'accelerationist' TR. The *changes* in the interest-rate target for Germany are given by changes in the neutral real interest rate and in the domestic inflation rate. The latter are zero under the assumption of a constant target at 2%. The former are proxied by the growth gap of real public debt: in fact, as explained above, as long as the public debt grows at a rate consistent with the balanced growth path of the country, Δd_t^{*GER}, the neutral interest rate does not change, while it increases or decreases as the public debt accelerates or decelerates. In the case of Italy, an IRP-constrained country, the changes in the interest-rate target are driven by changes in the German interest rate and in the risk premium on the domestic debt, according to its acceleration/deceleration relative to the balanced growth rate Δd_t^{*ITA}, whereas the changes in the inflation target are dictated by accelerations/decelerations of the actual inflation rate in Germany.

As to the target values of fiscal variables, the growth-gap model provides a consistent indication. In fact, assuming that the year before our sample started (i.e. in 1961) primary expenditure, fiscal revenue, public debt and interest payments were exactly at their target, the implication of the model is that from the following year onwards all these fiscal variables, if undisturbed, would grow along their balanced growth path, that is, at a rate equal to the potential GDP growth rate:

$$\Delta g_t^* = \Delta \tau_t^* = \Delta d_t^* = \Delta IP_t^* = \Delta y_t^*.$$

Furthermore, to account for major institutional events in the sample period, the following dummy variables were also added:

- Italy, TR equation, 1992 (breakdown of the EMS parity); FR equations, 1996 (readmission procedure to the EMS and EMU process);
- Germany, all equations, 1991 (post-reunification shock).

Finally comes specification of the dynamic structure of the estimation model (5.11). The basic theoretical relationships presented in the previous paragraph are too simple to give guidance. Yet, economic theory in general does not deliver univocal results concerning the time structure of dynamic models. Dynamic stochastic general equilibrium models stress the role of rational *forward-looking* behaviour such that expected future variables determine current ones. However, they deny the relevance of, or ignore, the role of lagged variables, which by contrast are widely used in econometric practice. Agnostically, one might conceive of a general dynamic structure like (5.11) whereby all endogenous and exogenous variables enter with current and lagged values, and 'let the data say' what the best time structure is. However, unconstrained estimation of system (5.11), and a full-blown 'general-to-specific' procedure, would have been too demanding in our case, given the insufficient amount of observations relative to the number of coefficients to be estimated. We have therefore proceeded by imposing structure regarding the endogenous variables, the exogenous variables as well as the model's time profile embedded in the matrices $\mathbf{C}$ and $\mathbf{D}$, based on *a priori* theoretical or empirical information gathered from existing studies.[18]

The two main issues in the relevant literature concern the imposition of 'leads and lags' for (1) identification of systematic policy interventions with respect to unsystematic policy innovations (the errors in the relevant equations) and (2) identification of the effects of policy on non-policy variables with respect to the reverse feed-back effects. This latter issue is particularly relevant in our case because of the simultaneous presence of fiscal and monetary variables. Among the works dealing with this problem, we have followed Favero (2002), who posits that non-policy variables and policy shocks have contemporaneous effects on policy variables, while the latter have delayed effects on non-policy variables. In other words, policy variables react quickly to their own determinants, but they take time to develop their effects on non-policy variables. A consistent endorsement of this hypothesis should exclude that policy variables have a significant autoregressive structure, which typically indicates that policy-makers adjust slowly to incoming information. By contrast, we have included a first-order autoregressive structure of the non-policy variables, since if policy variables have delayed effects, these are likely to induce dependence of non-policy variables on their own lagged values.

The resulting estimation model is reproduced below. The superscript $j = $ ITA, GER indicates specifications that are common to both countries, whereas specifications valid for a single country are indicated by the relevant country superscript.

$$\Delta \hat{y}^j_t = c_{10} + c_{11}\Delta \hat{y}^j_{t-1} + c_{12}\Delta \hat{r}^j_{t-1} + c_{13}\Delta \hat{g}^j_{t-1} + c_{14}\Delta \hat{\tau}^j_{t-1}$$
$$+ c_{15}\Delta \hat{y}_t^{USA} + c_{16}dummy91^{GER} + v^j_{1t}$$

$$\Delta \hat{\pi}^j_t = c_{20} + c_{21}\Delta \hat{\pi}^j_{t-1} + c_{22}\Delta \hat{y}^j_t + c_{23}dummy91^{GER} + v^j_{2t}$$

$$\Delta \hat{i}^j_t \begin{cases} ITA = c_{30} + c_{31}\Delta i_t^{GER} + c_{32}\Delta \hat{\pi}_t^{ITA} + c_{33}\Delta \hat{y}_t^{ITA} + c_{34}\Delta \hat{d}_t^{ITA} \\ \qquad + c_{35}dummy92^{ITA} + v^{ITA}_{3t} \\ GER = c_{30} + c_{31}\Delta \pi_t^{GER} + c_{32}\Delta \hat{y}_t^{GER} + c_{33}\Delta \hat{d}_t^{GER} \\ \qquad + c_{34}dummy91^{GER} + v^{GER}_{3t} \end{cases}$$

$$\Delta \hat{g}^j_t = c_{40} + c_{41}\Delta \hat{y}^j_t + c_{42}\Delta \hat{I}P^j_t + \begin{cases} ITA = c_{43}dummy96^{ITA} \\ GER = c_{43}dummy91^{GER} \end{cases} + v^j_{5t}$$

$$\Delta \hat{\tau}^j_t = c_{50} + c_{51}\Delta \hat{y}^j_t + c_{52}\Delta \hat{I}P^j_t + \begin{cases} ITA = c_{53}dummy96^{ITA} \\ GER = c_{53}dummy91^{GER} \end{cases} + v^j_{5t}$$

where $\Delta \hat{r}_{t-1} = \Delta i_{t-1} - E_{t-1}(\Delta \hat{\pi}_t)$.

5.4   Econometric estimations

The source for the data are yearly observations for each primitive variable in the OECD CD-Rom Database over the period 1962–2004.[19] Elaborations on primitive variables to obtain estimation variables are those described in the previous sections. The time series of selected estimation variables are reproduced in Figure 5.1.

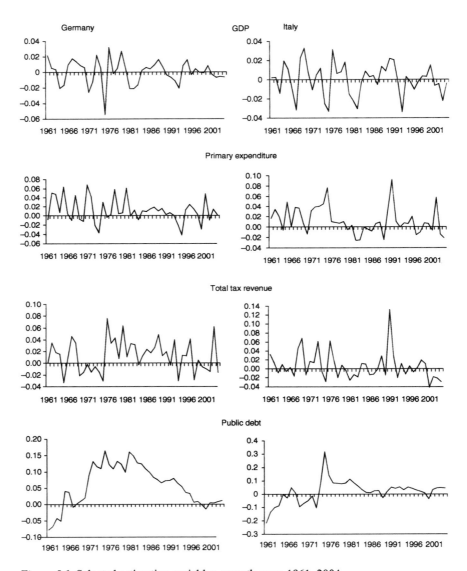

Figure 5.1 Selected estimation variables, growth gaps, 1961–2004.

We have used the 3SLS method with instrumental variables to correct for simultaneity. In the system's unrestricted reduced form (URF) for both countries, no test revealed any major problem: no evidence of significant first-order residual autocorrelation, and normality seemed a good approximation to the residuals' distributional shape. We therefore considered the system specification and its lag structure to be a congruent representation of the data. The results, with the instrumental variables employed, are presented in Table 5.1.

Equation for $\Delta \hat{y}_t$. One variable is strongly significant (p-value $< 5\%$) with the expected (negative) sign for both countries: the change in the real interest rate anticipated one year earlier (which should trigger a deviation of private expenditure from its growth path one year earlier). The US GDP growth gaps, which we interpret as world business cycles, turn out to be strongly significant for Germany, but very weakly significant or rejectable for Italy (p-value $> 10\%$). For both countries, the 1-year lagged values of the GDP growth gap itself, and of the fiscal variables, present the expected sign, but are definitely non-significant.

Though there is extensive world-wide evidence that GDP displays autocorrelation, it does not come as a surprise that GDP *growth gaps* fail to obey this empirical regularity. In fact, it is also well known that first-order differenced variables generally display low order or no autoregressive structures. As to the relationship between GDP growth gaps and fiscal variables, this is notoriously open to debate. Not only is the evidence inconclusive, but different views are deeply rooted in unresolved theoretical issues. To say the least, the international evidence allows no firmer conclusion than that the effects of fiscal variables on GDP may differ substantially across countries, being in some countries apparently weak and/or shrinking over time (see, for example, Favero, 2002; and works by Perotti, 2002; Galí and Perotti, 2003). However, as explained above, our estimation differs from most of the reference literature because it yields the exact elasticity of GDP *growth gaps* to real fiscal variables *growth gaps*. Hence, our results may have a statistical origin in that GDP growth gaps show low variability vis-à-vis remarkably high variability of rates of change in real fiscal variables. Also to be considered is that GDP growth gaps may be due to a combined deviation of observed GDP growth from the potential path and a shock to the path itself. A paradox is possible here. Suppose that both observed and potential GDP depend on real fiscal variables (see, for example, Barro, 1990); then if, say, during a downturn the government spends more and/or taxes less, the result may be that the observed GDP rises while the potential GDP is also revised upwards, with the effect that the gap is not closed.

Equation for $\Delta \pi_t$. The estimated equation supports the 'accelerationist' version of the AS curve for both countries, though Germany displays negligible persistence of changes in the inflation rate, whereas Italy shows a remarkably large effect of GDP growth gaps.

Equation for Δit. No component of our 'accelerationist' monetary policy equations is to be rejected statistically, with the theoretical sign and with high confidence (p-values $< 5\%$). As to Italy, our interpretation is that the central bank substantially tracked interest-rate parity with Germany, corrected for the risk

Table 5.1 Estimation results by 3SLS

Italy			Germany		
$\Delta\hat{y}_t$	Constant	0.002 (0.002)	$\Delta\hat{y}_t$	Constant	−0.004 (0.002)
	$\Delta\hat{r}_{t-1}$	−0.357** (0.048)		$\Delta\hat{r}_{t-1}$	−0.205** (0.089)
	$\Delta\hat{g}_{t-1}$	0.006 (0.048)		$\Delta\hat{g}_{t-1}$	0.108 (0.126)
	$\Delta\hat{\tau}_{t-1}$	−0.153 (0.136)		$\Delta\hat{\tau}_{t-1}$	−0.024 (0.062)
	$\Delta\hat{y}_t^{USA}$	0.115 (0.078)		$\Delta\hat{y}_t^{USA}$	0.261** (0.091)
				Dummy91	0.081** (0.013)
$\Delta\hat{\pi}_t$	Constant	−0.000 (0.003)	$\Delta\hat{\pi}_t$	Constant	0.000 (0.002)
	$\Delta\hat{\pi}_{t-1}$	0.807** (0.224)		$\Delta\hat{\pi}_{t-1}$	0.245 (0.161)
	$\Delta\hat{y}_t$	1.405** (0.259)		$\Delta\hat{y}_t$	0.377* (0.166)
				Dummy91	−0.020 (0.017)
Δi_t	Constant	−0.000 (0.002)	Δi_t	Constant	0.001 (0.003)
	Δi_t^{GER}	0.599** (0.209)		$\Delta\pi_t$	0.619** (0.245)
	$\Delta\hat{\pi}_t$	0.461** (0.122)		$\Delta\hat{y}_t$	0.149** (0.418)
	$\Delta\hat{y}_t$	0.682** (0.284)		$\Delta\hat{d}_t$	−0.040 (0.069)
	$\Delta\hat{d}_t$	0.223** (0.123)		Dummy91	−0.007 (0.036)
	Dummy92	0.040** (0.017)			
$\Delta\hat{g}_t$	Constant	0.010 (0.004)	$\Delta\hat{g}_t$	Constant	0.006 (0.004)
	$\Delta\hat{y}_t$	−1.018** (0.261)		$\Delta\hat{y}_t$	−1.185** (0.348)
	$\Delta\hat{I}P_t$	0.008 (0.032)		$\Delta\hat{I}P_t$	−0.009 (0.059)
	Dummy96	−0.033 (0.022)		Dummy91	0.170 (0.040)
$\Delta\hat{\tau}_t$	Constant	0.012 (0.004)	$\Delta\hat{\tau}_t$	Constant	0.003 (0.004)
	$\Delta\hat{y}_t$	0.520* (0.292)		$\Delta\hat{y}_t$	1.854** (0.297)
	$\Delta\hat{I}P_t$	0.016 (0.038)		$\Delta\hat{I}P_t$	0.091 (0.051)
	Dummy96	−0.007 (0.026)		Dummy91	−0.025 (0.034)

Instrumental variables: $\Delta\hat{r}_{t-1}$, $\Delta\hat{y}_t^{USA}$, $\Delta\hat{d}_t$, $\Delta\hat{I}P_t$, Dummy96

Instrumental variables: $\Delta\hat{r}_{t-1}$, $\Delta\hat{y}_t^{USA}$, $\Delta\hat{d}_t$, $\Delta\hat{I}P_t$, Dummy91

Notes
Standard errors in brackets. (**), (*) indicate significance at 5% and 10% level, respectively.

premium proxied by the excess growth rate of public debt, while trading-off GDP growth gaps. As to be expected, our estimated TR equations show that in Italy more weight was given to growth-targeting than to inflation-targeting, whereas the opposite was the case in Germany. On the other hand, the so-called Taylor principle did not operate in either country: that is to say, the estimated coefficient of the inflation gap is less than one. Notably, the fiscal variable turns out to be significant only for Italy. We believe that this is an informative result: in two countries with sharp differences in the speed of public-debt growth, the monetary policy rules differ. The central bank facing slow-growing debt (Germany) has given no weight to the fiscal variable, whereas the one facing fast-growing debt (Italy) has given substantial weight to it.

Equations for Δg_t *and* $\Delta \tau_t$. First of all, both countries display sizeable anti-cyclical contemporaneous components of the rate of change of real fiscal variables. In fact, the parameters of GDP growth gaps are strongly significant and with the theoretical sign (p-values < 5%). The conventional wisdom on the 'long and variable lags' of fiscal policy does not seem confirmed, or else the importance and extent of in-built stabilizers is vindicated (see also Melitz, this volume). As regards the elasticities of fiscal variables to contemporaneous growth gaps.

- expenditure elasticity is about −1.0 in both countries;
- taxation elasticity is about 0.5 in Italy and 1.8 in Germany.

At first sight, both elasticities in the two countries are much larger than in other empirical studies, where they are around 0.3 in absolute value, and where 0.5 is regarded as the typical elasticity of the *total budget* (see, for example, Giorno *et al.*, 1995; Artis and Buti, 2000; Van den Noord, 2000; Brunila *et al.*, 2002). Italy is also at variance with the received wisdom that taxation is the more elastic stabilizer. Yet, as already discussed, our results are not directly comparable with standard practice, which typically a) estimates fiscal rules *in isolation*, and b) measures the elasticity of fiscal–GDP *ratios* to output gaps, both in *levels*. A measurement (partially) comparable to ours has been proposed by Melitz (this volume, Table 4.1) who, in a panel of euro-countries, finds slightly larger values of the elasticities of first differences of both public expenditure and taxation to first differences in output gaps. It should also be considered that the difference between our estimated values and the others may simply be due to the algebra of respecification (empirically, estimates may be roughly equivalent).[20] Whatever the case may be, our aim here is not so much to dispute the magnitude of the cycle elasticities of fiscal variables as to focus on the implications of our proposed change of approach with regard to assessment of the government budget over the cycle, one implication being that knowing these elasticities, if it is ever possible, *per se* conveys little information. These implications will be clarified with the help of the simulations.

Neither Italy nor Germany pass the 'budget-target' hypothesis that implies the adjustment of the primary fiscal variables to compensate for interest payments. The respective parameters are negligible in size and non-significant. If taken at face value, only Italy displays the correct sign.[21] However, another interpretation is possible, which is consistent with the difference between the two countries' monetary rules detected above: namely, that a virtuous fiscal–monetary circle was in place in the slow-growing-debt country (Germany) and a vicious one in the fast-growing-debt country (Italy). In the former country, the mutual sensitivity between fiscal and monetary policy is negligible as slow-growing debt, low and stable interest rate and sustainable interest payments are mutually consistent. The opposite occurs in the latter country, where the fast-growing debt compels mutual sensitivity between fiscal and monetary policy.

5.5   Simulations

By means of the estimated system, it has been possible to simulate the responses of the endogenous variables to exogenous shocks.[22] Here we only report as an example the results of a -1% temporary shock to the GDP growth below potential at time 0 (1963), with no other shock thereon. The simulation has yielded, for each endogenous variable, the per cent rate of deviation from the correspondent baseline value (which, for analogy with the theoretical model, we still denote with $\Delta(\hat{\ })$).[23] Recall that in our model the baseline value is a growth rate for all real variables and the price level, and a constant for the nominal interest rate.

In order to gather information on the government budget, we also used the simulated dynamics of the endogenous variables to compute relevant compound budget variables such as

real primary balance: $\Delta \hat{P}B_t = \Delta \hat{\tau} - \Delta \hat{g}$
real interest payments: $\Delta \hat{I}P_t = \Delta i_t - \Delta \hat{\pi}_t$
total budget: $\Delta \hat{B}_t = \Delta \hat{P}B_t - \Delta \hat{I}P_t.$

Thus, in the simulation, the primary balance deviates from its baseline value by the difference between the deviations of the tax revenue and of the primary expenditure. The deviation rate of real interest payments is approximated by the change of the real interest rate on outstanding debt. As to total budget, this deviates from its baseline value by the difference between the deviations of interest payments and of the primary balance.

The graphs (Figures 5.2 and 5.3) show the post-shock dynamics of the five primitive endogenous variables ($\Delta \hat{y}_t$, $\Delta \hat{\pi}_t$, $\Delta \hat{i}_t$, $\Delta \hat{g}_t$, $\Delta \hat{\tau}_t$) and of the two generated variables ($\Delta \hat{P}B_t$, $\Delta \hat{B}_t$) for the two countries. The following comments are in order.

5.5.1 *Stability and transitory dynamics*

All variables are dynamically stable with low persistence in both countries. In fact, deviations in all variables shrink to zero in a relatively small number of rounds. In other words, each variable returns to its baseline value. Transitory dynamics is almost monotonic for all variables in both countries, except inflation in Italy. As regards Italy, on impact we see a typical pattern of demand shock: the negative growth gap triggers a deceleration in the inflation rate and anti-cyclical policy adjustments. The nominal interest rate is reduced, though less than the

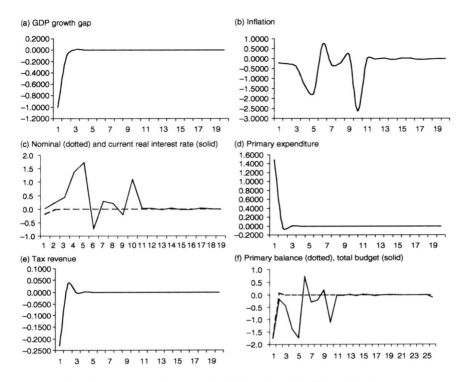

Figure 5.2 Italy. Responses (per cent deviations from baseline values) to a temporary negative 1% multiplicative shock to the GDP growth gap.

deceleration of inflation: the real interest rate deviates above the neutral rate most of the time. Fiscal stabilization consists of a sequence of impulses accelerating primary expenditure and decelerating tax revenue with respect to baseline growth rates. Consequently, the economy is set on a path of negative growth gaps of decreasing magnitude up to zero. Germany instead shows a typical pattern of supply shock: on impact of the negative growth gap, the simulation yields an acceleration of inflation. The policy variables now react in opposite directions. The nominal interest rate immediately rises, though not as much as the acceleration of inflation; yet subsequent adjustments bring the real interest rate above the neutral rate. Fiscal variables react to the negative GDP growth gap as expected, until the gap is progressively reduced to zero.

5.5.2 Elasticities and stabilization capacity: measurement puzzles

How should we measure stabilization capacity and the ensuing budget requirements correctly? Are estimated elasticities of fiscal variables to a cyclical measure of GDP really informative? If fiscal variables do respond 'automatically' to growth

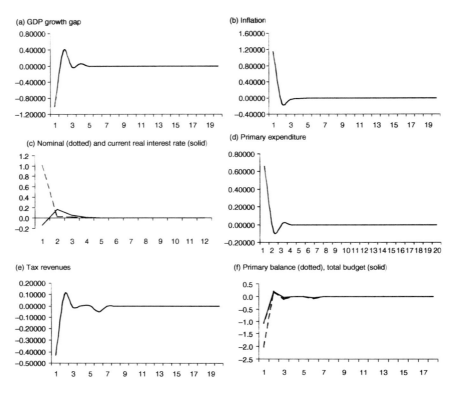

Figure 5.3 Germany. Responses (per cent deviations from baseline values) to a temporary negative 1% multiplicative shock to the GDP growth gap.

shocks, these shocks – as they are usually understood in models – are unobservable, while estimates are based on observed data which probably already embody at least some of the stabilization effects of fiscal variables on GDP and vice versa. Our simulation exercise has enabled us to disentangle this matter. First, we had a well-defined shock, and secondly we could track the response of fiscal variables precisely up to the new steady state. We could thus distinguish (at least) two measures of elasticities with respect to the shock, (1) on impact of the shock, and (2) in the new steady state, that is, the *cumulated* rates of deviation of fiscal variables from target necessary to nullify the initial GDP growth gap (the 'integrals' of the graphs in Figures 5.2 and 5.3). The respective values are reported in Table 5.2.

As can be seen, steady-state elasticities are smaller than impact ones, with one important exception. Consider the primary versus total budget. In Italy as well as in Germany, on impact both variables deteriorate relative to their baseline value by roughly the same amount (about 1.7% in Italy and 1.0% in Germany). However, the paths of the primary and total budgets differ markedly in Italy with respect to Germany (see Figures 5.2 and 5.3, panel (f)). In the latter country the

Table 5.2 Measures of elasticities to −1%
GDP growth gap

	Simulated elasticities	
	Impact	Steady-state
Italy		
Primary expenditure	−1.48	−1.45
Total tax revenue	0.23	0.20
Primary balance	1.71	1.65
Total balance	1.74	6.22
Germany		
Primary expenditure	−0.66	−0.59
Total tax revenue	0.43	0.39
Primary balance	1.09	0.98
Total balance	0.95	1.06

two measures of fiscal stance roughly follow the same monotonic path. In Italy, by contrast, the total budget worsens at higher (absolute) rates and for a longer time than does the primary budget. Hence, the steady-state elasticity of the total budget is strikingly higher in Italy than in Germany, although the underlying fiscal rules are quite similar in the two countries. The difference is due to real interest payments. As we know, although in Italy the nominal interest rate is reduced, the inflation rate decelerates even more, imposing a sequence of inflation-tax cuts. Thus, real interest payments rise most of the time, whereas the opposite occurs in Germany.

This exercise substantiates the idea that the total budget is not under the government's full control over the cycle, even when the government does 'let the automatic stabilizers work' and does not engage in discretionary activism. Even if an almighty econometrician could tell us the exact elasticities of primary fiscal variables to growth shocks, we would still be unable to infer the evolution of the government budget unless we also knew all the details of the underlying macroeconomic process. A major 'detail' is that the actual cyclical evolution of total budget is closely dependent on the concomitant monetary–fiscal interactions.

5.5.3 Monetary–fiscal interactions

Since more weight is given in Italy to growth-targeting than to inflation-targeting, whereas the opposite occurs in Germany, this may explain the handbook reactions of monetary policy both in the deflationary case of Italy and in the stagflationary case of Germany. On the other hand, the nominal interest rate does *not* over-react to deviations of inflation from target, causing, at first sight, unintended movements in the real interest rate: it *rises* in Italy and *falls* in Germany (at least initially). One reason may be that in both countries the estimated coefficient of the inflation gap is, in fact, less than one. Another reason may be that our TR equations also respond to public debt dynamics as a determinant of the neutral real interest rate.

As remarked above, the coefficient of this variable is significant and positive for Italy, whereas it is not for Germany. Since this variable in the sample period of the simulation is rapidly increasing in Italy, the ensuing 'fiscal spillover' may reduce the responsiveness of monetary policy and sustain the rise in the real interest rate. We now consider the other side of the monetary–fiscal interactions; namely, interest payments. The estimation results reject this hypothesis for both countries. Nonetheless, interest payments also exert direct influence on the evolution of the total budget, as seen above.

One is tempted to conclude from our exercise that in a slow-growing-debt country not only are fiscal and monetary policy *complements*[24] but they may also be (virtually) *independent*. By contrast, in a fast-growing-debt country the two policies may still be complements but not independent. As a consequence, in the first type of country both policies can be more aggressive with less overall impact on the total budget, whereas in the second type of country one policy checks the other, but they nonetheless have an overall negative effect on the total budget.

5.5.4 Growth gaps, levels and the SGP rules

Let us finally examine the much-debated question of the cyclical evolution of the deficit/GDP ratio. For this purpose, we have to go back from rates of deviation to levels, which also facilitates comparison between our results and existing ones. The interpretation of the foregoing results within our theoretical model is that the *growth rates* of output, tax revenue, primary expenditure and prices return to their respective initial values. This, however, does not imply that the *levels* of those variables will thereafter be equal to those that would have obtained along the growth path of the economy in the absence of the shock. To verify this property, the simulation data in rates of deviations from baseline values can easily be converted into data in levels (index numbers).[25] This exercise shows that, for instance, a *temporary* negative gap in the *growth rate* of output determines a *permanent* output gap *in levels*. Likewise, a temporary positive growth gap in public expenditure will end up with a permanent positive gap in level and so on. In this respect, important information is given by the cumulative deviations of the variables discussed above, which determine the respective gaps in levels in the new steady state. The latter are reported in Table 5.3 both for absolute fiscal variables and for their GDP ratios.

Let us first consider final output gaps, which are −1.04% for Italy and −0.57% for Germany. This means that in Italy the initial growth shock leaves behind a permanent output gap of the same magnitude, whereas in Germany it is almost halved. In both countries the bulk of stabilization is borne by primary expenditure (particularly in Italy) rather than by taxation as presumed by most studies on automatic stabilizers (on this point see also Melitz (this volume)). Remarkably, however, Germany's stronger stabilization capacity is obtained with less fiscal effort as measured by the cumulative deterioration of the primary balance, which reaches −1.57% of baseline value in Italy but stops at −0.94% in Germany. Notice that the figures are somewhat different if measured in ratios to GDP: in particular, the expenditure/GDP and taxation/GDP ratios *are larger* than the gaps in

Table 5.3 Steady-state gaps in levels after
the shock (per cent)

	Italy	Germany
Output	−1.04	−0.57
Primary expenditure	+1.38	+0.57
Ratio to GDP	+2.45	+1.14
Total tax revenue	−0.19	−0.37
Ratio to GDP	+0.86	+0.20
Primary balance	−1.57	−0.94
Ratio to GDP	−1.59	−0.94

absolute terms (overestimating the increase in expenditure and underestimating the reduction in taxation – which even appears to have been increased). The well known reason for this is that GDP ratios embody the lower level of the denominator.[26]

In any case, these figures deliver an important message concerning the new exemption clauses introduced by the SGP reform. As reported in the Introduction, these clauses correctly recognize that not only negative growth rates, but also 'prolonged' negative growth gaps (while the absolute growth rate may remain positive) may account for 'exceptional' fiscal deficits. They also give the right emphasis to the related concept of 'cumulated loss of output'. These are welcome amendments, which, however, will require careful re-examination of the criteria used to assess the fiscal stances of member countries.

First of all, unlike the sparse occurrences of the former definitions of 'exceptional conditions' found by Buti and Sapir (1998) from 1961 to 1997,[27] one should expect statistics – if not interested governments – to report negative growth gaps roughly half of the time, owing to the sheer statistical artifact that these are stationary variables around the trend (see Figure 5.1). And we have seen that econometric analysis supports the hypothesis that fiscal variables are highly sensitive to *this* measure of the business cycle. Further, cycles are typically characterized by strings of negative and positive growth gaps. Consequently, strings of negative years impinging upon fiscal balances are frequent events rather than exceptional ones. Our simulated steady-state elasticities suggest that in a country like Italy, even starting from balance, the 3% deficit/GDP ratio may be reached after two years of negative growth gaps in the order of 1%, not an infrequent occurrence in the sample. These findings raise doubts concerning the early assessments on the substantial safety margin guaranteed by the 3% deficit ceiling.

Second, we have seen that 'cumulated losses of output' have far-reaching consequences. Temporary growth gaps leave long-lasting traces in public finances, even in well-managed (simulated) ones. On looking at the statistics of our simulated economies, the SGP guardians might be tempted to conclude that, as the GDP is driven back to its potential growth rate, there is no longer justification for a deficit. However, the extant primary deficit – not to mention the total deficit – though created by 'legitimate' cyclical factors, becomes, in a sense, structural.

It is bound to last until a new positive impulse to growth overcomes the previous cumulative output loss. Admittedly, as we argued above, at each point in time there is about a 50% chance that this will happen. But what is, then, an 'excessive deficit'? And how is the return to normality ascertained? At the moment it is unclear whether the SGP institutions are ready to address these crucial questions, and how.

5.6 Conclusions

In this chapter we have sought to reframe the questions of assessment and measurement of fiscal variables in view of the Maastricht Treaty's prescriptions within a consistent macroeconomic model whereby the cyclical dynamics of GDP, inflation, monetary and fiscal variables are jointly determined. The model has been specified in terms of growth gaps, rather than level gaps, consistently with the common perception and measurement of business cycles as well as with the new exemption clauses introduced by the reformed SGP. The results from estimation of the model for Italy and Germany have been used for simulations of the effects of a negative growth gap shock on policy and non-policy variables, tracking the sequence of deviations of the variables from their baseline growth rates or target values until a new steady-state is reached. In particular, the simulated data have been used to examine the evolution of the deficit/GDP ratio as a result of the two components of the ratio, shedding light on the much-debated question of the actual control exerted by governments over its cyclical behaviour.

To begin with, the results can be read counterfactually: that is to say, how each economy and its public finances would perform after a growth gap shock, given its inherited macroeconomic structural relationships and policy rules. Our main findings can be summarized as follows:

1   Our estimations provide evidence of 'well-behaved' fiscal rules for both Germany and Italy, at least in the sense that a good number of the observed deviations of primary expenditure and total tax revenue from the respective balanced growth paths are explained by the growth cycle. Contrary to the widespread belief of unfettered fiscal indiscipline, this conforms with the Commission's popular view that the EMU governments should simply 'let the automatic stabilizers work'. As also indicated by Melitz, and by Muscatelli *et al.* (this volume), we have seen that *broad* measures of public expenditure and taxation do respond to the business cycle contributing to stabilization; hence we cannot but agree with these authors that the larger these items the better. The other side of the coin shown by our simulations is that small negative growth gaps may easily deteriorate the government budget up to the 3% of GDP even in the absence of discretionary fiscal profligacy. Moreover, growth gaps of this kind are statistically much more frequent than the *negative* growth rates that would qualify a country for exemption from the excessive deficit procedure in the old SGP.

2   Governments have little control over the cyclical evolution of the deficit/GDP ratio, while the current methods of correction of the budget for the cycle are misconceived and deceitful. On the one hand, the implication of the previous point is that not many of the observed changes in fiscal variables can indisputably be subtracted from anti-cyclical stabilization. In other words, the body of evidence required to open excessive deficits procedures may be very limited if excessive means beyond legitimate anti-cyclical deficits. We have also shown that attempts to measure the cyclical components of fiscal variables by means of estimated elasticities encounter several pitfalls. With the help of our simulations, we have obtained what we think is the theoretically correct measure of these elasticities: the steady-state rates of deviations in absolute fiscal measures in response to the initial GDP growth gap (last column, Table 5.2). True, this measure can hardly be obtained in practice; yet researchers should be aware that measures obtained on observable data, which probably contain at least part of the stabilization effect of fiscal variables on GDP, tend to overestimate the magnitude of elasticities (especially if measured as GDP ratios), and all the more so the more effective the fiscal variables are.

3   The extent of the two previous results crucially depends on fiscal–monetary policy interactions. We have seen that they are more pronounced in a country like Italy, where public debt appears among the determinants of the interest-rate policy of the central bank, and the interest rate has considerable impact on payments by the government. If it may be wise for an independent central bank to operate in this way, it is disputable that the ensuing loss of budget control of the government vis-à-vis the 3% ceiling is the best way to achieve fiscal discipline.

These findings suggest that the crisis of the old SGP was, at least in part, boosted by some internal flaws on the 'flexibility' side that had been underestimated and that became manifest at the first serious growth slowdown in Europe.

Our study can also be read, with some 'out-of-sample' caution, in the normative perspective of the new SGP. Caution is necessary because the above-mentioned role of monetary–fiscal interactions in our exercise are based on the past institutional setup of the two sample economies. If there are good reasons and some evidence to believe that the ECB will not operate in a way dramatically different from the one parametrized by our national TR equations, at present the attitude of the ECB towards specific national positions, the impact of national fiscal variables on ECB policy and the common bonds market, and the future evolution of monetary–fiscal interactions in the EMU are largely hidden from view. Bearing this caveat in mind, the new SGP is moving in the right direction in that it re-focuses on growth gaps as a basis for exemption clauses, and introduces a longer-term horizon for stability programmes centred on debt stabilization or reduction. On the other hand, the long-standing criticisms about the total deficit/GDP ratio as the pillar of the SGP rules are still valid. The relative frequency of negative strings of growth gaps, combined with the responsiveness of large fiscal aggregates to these gaps, shed doubts on the view that the 3% deficit ceiling allows a sufficient safety margin for cyclical manoeuvres. More importantly, we have shown that these episodes, even though triggered by temporary shocks, determine *permanent* output losses to which there correspond *permanent* primary deficits. These will not be reabsorbed by a mere return to 'normal' growth. Hence, it is not clear how the Commission will assess these situations. Overall, the maintenance of the 3% deficit/GDP ceiling as a sort of *taboo* imposed on governments seems at variance with the prescription set out in the recent developments of the theory of policy rules, according to which rules should make reference to, and policy-makers should be examined on, *instruments* that they can control, not on *outcomes* they do not control (Woodford, 2003, chapter 1).

Notes

* We wish to thank the participants in the conferences organized by the Jean Monnet Chair in 'European Macroeconomics' at the University of Siena, and Chris Gilbert for their comments. We remain fully responsible for this paper.
1 See Buti *et al.* (2003); Galí and Perotti (2003); Buti and Franco (2005) for brief accounts of these progressive adjustments.
2 Preliminary works that address this issue are Farina and Tamborini (2002, 2004); Tamborini (2004b).
3 And the estimates of 'fiscal shocks' obtained by Perotti are, on his own admission, not very plausible in several instances.
4 Respectively available at http:/www.bis.org/review/r050602d.pdf and at http://www.eua.be/eua/jsp/en/upload/Barroso_speech.1112693429657.pdf.
5 The year frequency of the observations has been dictated by the well known unreliability of higher-frequency data on fiscal variables.
6 Hopefully, the small number of observations may also restrict the statistical importance of this institutional change.
7 The terminology is from AEA (1997).
8 Similar equations can be derived from a microfounded dynamic general equilibrium model (e.g. Clarida *et al.*, 1999; McCallum and Nelson, 1999; Woodford, 2003; among many others), where the relations corresponding to our equations (5.1) and (5.2) are derived from households choosing optimal intertemporal paths for their consumption and firms setting prices optimally according to a Calvo-type mechanism. The main difference from the specification which we employ is that explicit microfoundations allow expectations on future output and inflation to explicitly appear in the IS and the Phillips curves, respectively.
9 There are various possible specifications of potential output (e.g. Woodford, 2003, chapters 4 and 5). Generally, it is interpreted as the level of output that would prevail with full use of resources up to the natural rate of unemployment, and it is computed as the non-cyclical component of actual GDP.
10 On the other hand, if the central bank consistently pursues its inflation target, then π^* is also the rational expectation of the inflation rate.
11 There is a tendency in the literature to identify the systematic fiscal policy with stabilization and the discretionary one with other ends. But this identification is clearly unwarranted since governments may well opt for anti-cyclical discretionary interventions (e.g. a temporary cut in taxation).
12 See Woodford (2003, chapters 1, 2) for a thorough discussion of this point.
13 Although r^* very closely resembles the Wicksellian notion of the natural real rate of interest (Woodford, 2003), it is directly influenced by fiscal policy, so that the term

'neutral' is more suitable (Allsopp and Vines, 2000). In fact, standard economic theory implies that the neutral rate of interest is a function of consumers' preferences and of the trend growth rate of output. If an endogenous growth mechanism is added to the model, fiscal policy may affect the neutral rate of interest, even in a Wicksellian world via its impact on the steady-state growth rate. Note, however, that the channel involved here is quite different.

14 An example of a New Keynesian model of a small open economy is provided by Galí and Monacelli (2005); an open-economy model applied to Italy has been employed by Chiades and Gambacorta (2004).

15 See Perotti (2002); Galí and Perotti (2003); Melitz (this volume) for recent discussions of these problems.

16 Unfortunately, the existing empirical studies do not give clear guidance in this respect; in particular, it is not yet clear whether a stock or a flow measure of government borrowing is appropriate (e.g. Schiavo, this volume).

17 Unlike Favero (2002), however, for simplicity we have taken the whole value of interest payments as a single variable without disaggregating the interest component from the debt component.

18 See, for example, Chiarella *et al.* (2005) for extended treatment of, and variations on, the New Keynesian basic framework.

19 Primitive variables are: Gross domestic product at current market prices (ITA, GER, US), Potential output at current market prices (ITA, GER, US), GDP deflator (1995 = 100) (ITA, GER, US), Government non-interest expenditure at current market prices (ITA, GER), Government interest payments (ITA, GER), Total tax revenue at current market prices (ITA, GER), Government net borrowing and lending (ITA, GER), Public debt (ITA, GER), Short-term interest rate (ITA, GER).

20 Consider any fiscal variable in isolation f_t, in relation to a cyclical measure of GDP only. Our 'growth-gaps' specification is

$$\Delta \hat{f}_t = \alpha + \beta \Delta \hat{y}_t + u_t.$$

On expanding this expression according to our definition of growth gap, and rearranging, it is possible to obtain a respecification in the following form:

$$(f_t - y_t) = \alpha + (f_{t-1} - y_{t-1}) + (1 - \beta)(y_t - y_t^*) + (1 - \beta)(y_{t-1} - y_{t-1}^*) + u_t.$$

This is the standard specification of an estimation equation for the fiscal variable/GDP ratio $(f_t - y_t)$ in level, regressed on its own lagged value and on the current and lagged value of the output gap in level (see, for example, Melitz, 2002; and Favero, 2002). Clearly, the cyclical coefficents estimated in the standard specification are complements to those estimated by means of the 'growth-gaps' specification; if the former are smaller than 0.5, the latter will be larger than 0.5.

21 On the other hand, Favero (2002) has found that both Germany and Italy display sensitivity to interest payments to some extent.

22 The simulation software was Winsolve.

23 It should be borne in mind that the simulator creates the baseline value of each endogenous variable for each point in time by means of an initial simulation of the estimated system whereby the system is fed with the 'true' times series of the exogenous variables used in the econometric estimation. These same time series are also used in the simulation. Hence, the simulation results should be understood as deviations of the endogenous variables from their 'historical' estimated values in the absence of shocks. This procedure also implies that simulation results are 'history sensitive' in that they depend on the shock date chosen and on the true historical values of the exogenous variables.

24 It should be stressed that complementarity emerged in our simulation of a GDP shock. Preliminary inspections of different shocks, such as inflationary or fiscal shocks, indicated that the two policies are used as substitutes. A similar result can be found in Muscatelli *et al.* (2004).

25 Let $X_0 = 100$ be the initial absolute value of any variable. Then for any $t = 1, \ldots$, the new level along the steady-state growth path of the economy is given by $X_t^* = X_{t-1}^*(1+q_t^*)$, whereas the new level after the shock is given by $X_t = X_{t-1}(1+q_t^*+\Delta \hat{x}_t)$. We have taken q_t^* to be the potential growth rate of GDP in the data set for each country, and, according to the theoretical model, we have used it also for fiscal variables.

26 The figures in Table 5.3 further exemplify the above-mentioned pitfalls of estimating ex-post elasticities. These figures in fact closely resemble the typical statistical information available; that is, realized output gaps on the one hand, and changes in absolute fiscal variables or in their GDP ratios on the other. Yet Table 5.3 highlights that, whereas the data have been generated by the same growth shock in the two countries, ex-post elasticities in Germany would be grossly overestimated merely because stabilization has been more effective.

27 They detected just 84 observations for all EU countries (5 for Italy, 8 for Germany).

References

AEA (1997), 'Is there a core of practical macroeconomics that we should all believe?', Panel at the American Economic Association, New Orleans, LA, 4–6 January 1997, Papers and Proceedings of the American Economic Association, *American Economic Review*, 87: 230–46.

Allsopp, C. and Vines, D. (2000), 'The assessment: macroeconomic policy', *Oxford Review of Economic Policy*, 16: 1–32.

Angeloni, I. (1994), 'Strumenti e obiettivi operativi della Banca d'Italia: verso un modello europeo', *Note Economiche*, 14: 128–61.

Artis, M. J. and Buti, F. (2000), 'Close to balance or in surplus. a policy maker's guide to the implementation of the Stability and Growth Pact', *Journal of Common Market Studies*, 38: 563–92.

Artis, M. J. and Onorante, L. (2006), 'The economic importance of fiscal rules', CEPR Discussion Paper no. 5684.

Artis, M. J. and Winkler, B. (1999), 'The Stability and Growth Pact: trading off flexibility for credibility', in A. J. Hughes Hallett, M. M. Hutchinson, S. E. Hougaard Jensen (eds), *Fiscal Aspects of European Monetary Integration*, Cambridge: Cambridge University Press.

Barro, R. J. (1990), 'Government spending in a simple model of endogenous growth', *Journal of Political Economy*, 98: 103–25.

Beetsma, R. M. and Bovenberg, A. L. (1998), 'Monetary union without fiscal coordination may discipline policymakers', *Journal of International Economics*, 45: 239–58.

Beetsma, R. M. and Uhlig, H. (1999), 'An analysis of the Stability and Growth Pact', *Economic Journal*, 109: 546–71.

Begg, D., De Grauwe, P., Giavazzi, F., Uhlig, H. and Wyplosz, C. (1999), *The ECB: Safe at Any Speed?, Monitoring the European Central Bank*, 1, London: CEPR.

Brunila, A., Buti, M. and in't Veld, J. (2002), 'Fiscal policy in Europe: how effective are automatic stabilizers?', *European Economy*, Economic Paper no. 177.

Buti, M. and Franco, D. (2005), 'The Stability Pact's pains: a forward-looking assesment of the reform debate', CEPR Discussion Paper no. 5216.

Buti, M. and Sapir, A. (1998), *Economic Policy in EMU*, Oxford: Clarendon Press.

Buti, M., Eijffinger, S. and Franco, D. (2003), 'Revisiting the Stability and Growth Pact: grand design or internal adjustment?', *European Economy*, Economic Paper no. 180.

Buti, M., Franco, D. and Ongena, H. (1998), 'Fiscal discipline and flexibility in EMU: the implementation of the Stability and Growth Pact', *Oxford Review of Economic Policy*, 14: 81–97.

Buti, M., Roeger, W. and in't Veld, J. (2001), 'Stabilizing output and inflation in the EMU: policy conflicts and co-operation under the Stability Pact', *Journal of Common Market Studies*, 39: 801–28.

Caresma, J. C., Gnan, E. and Ritzberger-Gruenwald, D. (2005), 'The natural rate of interest. concepts and appraisal for the Euro area', *Monetary Policy and the Economy*, Austrian National Bank, Q4.

Chiades, P. and Gambacorta, L. (2004), 'The Bernanke and Blinder Model in an open economy: the case of Italy', *The German Economic Review*, 5: 1–34.

Chiarella, C., Flaschel, P. and Franke, R. (2005), *Foundations for a Disequilibrium Theory of the Business Cycle*, Cambridge: Cambridge University Press.

Clarida, R., Galí, J. and Gertler, M. (1999), 'The science of monetary policy: a new Keynesian perspective', *Journal of Economic Literature*, 37: 1661–707.

Dixit, A. (2001), 'Games of monetary and fiscal interactions in the EMU', Papers and Proceedings of the European Economic Association, *European Economic Review*, 45: 589–613.

Dixit, A. and Lambertini, L. (2001), 'Monetary–fiscal interaction and commitment versus discretion in a monetary union', Papers and Proceedings of the European Economic Association, *European Economic Review*, 45: 977–87.

Dornbush, R., Favero, C. A. and Giavazzi, F. (1998), 'Immediate challenges for the European Central Bank', *Economic Policy*, 26: 15–64.

Eichengreen, B. and Wyplosz, C. (1998), 'Stability Pact: more than a minor nuisance?', *Economic Policy*, 26: 67–112.

Farina, F. and Tamborini, R. (2002), 'Le politiche macroeconomiche di stabilizzazione in Europa nel nuovo regime di unione monetaria', in F. Farina and R. Tamborini (eds), *Da Nazioni a Regioni. Mutamenti strutturali e istituzionali dopo l'ingresso nella Unione Monetaria Europea*, Bologna: Il Mulino.

—— (2004), ' "Set a sufficiently ambitious budget target and let the automatic stabilizers work". Can it really work in the European Monetary Union?', *Open Economies Review*, 15: 143–68.

Favero, C. (2002), 'How do European monetary and fiscal authorities behave?', CEPR Discussion Paper no. 214.

Galí, J. and Monacelli, T. (2005), 'Monetary policy and exchange rate volatility in an open economy', *Review of Economic Studies*, 72: 707–34.

Galí, J. and Perotti, R. (2003), 'Fiscal policy and monetary integration in Europe', *Economic Policy*, 31: 533–72.

Geberding, C., Worms, A. and Sietz, F. (2004), 'How the Bundesbank really conducted monetary policy: an analysis based on real-time data', Deutsche Bundesbank, Discussion Paper no. 25.

Giavazzi, F. and Pagano, M. (1988), 'The advantage of tying one's hands: EMS discipline and central bank credibility', *European Economic Review*, 32: 371–90.

McCallum, B. T. and Nelson, E. (1999), 'An optimizing IS-LM specification for monetary policy and business cycle analysis', *Journal of Money, Credit and Banking*, 31: 296–316.

Melitz, J. (2002), 'Some cross-country evidence about fiscal policy behaviour and consequences for EMU', in M. Buti, J. Von Hagen and C. Martinez-Mongay, *The Behaviour of Fiscal Authorities*, London: Palgrave.

—— (2007 – this volume), 'Non-discretionary and automatic fiscal policy in the EU and the OECD', in F. Farina and R. Tamborini, *Macroeconomic Policy in the European Monetary Union*, London and New York: Routledge.

Muscatelli, V. A., Ropele, T. and Tirelli, P. (2007 – this volume), 'Macroeconomic adjustment in the euro area: the role of fiscal policy', in F. Farina and R. Tamborini, *Macroeconomic Policy in the European Monetary Union*, London and New York: Routledge.

Muscatelli, V. A., Tirelli, P. and Trecroci, C. (2004), 'Monetary and fiscal policy interactions over the cycle: some empirical evidence', in R. Beetsma, C. Favero, A. Missale, V. A. Muscatelli, P. Natale and P. Tirelli (eds), *Fiscal Policies, Monetary Policies and Labour Markets. Key Aspects of European Macroeconomic Policies after Monetary Unification*, Cambridge: Cambridge University Press.

Perotti, R. (2002), 'Estimating the effects of fiscal policy in OECD countries', ECB Working Paper no. 168.

Schiavo, S. (2007 – this volume), 'Euro bonds: in search of financial spillovers', in F. Farina and R. Tamborini, *Macroeconomic Policy in the European Monetary Union*, London and New York: Routledge.

Tamborini, R. (2004a), 'One monetary giant with many fiscal dwarfs: the efficiency of macroeconomic stabilization policies in the European Monetary Union', in A. V. Deardorff (ed.), *The Past, Present and Future of the European Union*, London: Palgrave Macmillan.

—— (2004b), 'The "Brussels consensus" on macroeconomic stabilization policies in the EMU. A critical assessment', in F. Torres, A. Verdun, C. Zilioli and H. Zimmermann (eds), *Governing EMU: Political, Economic, Historical and Legal Aspects*, Florence: European University Press.

Taylor, J. B. (1993), 'Discretion versus policy rules in practice', *Carnegie-Rochester Conference Series on Public Policy*, 39: 195–214.

—— (ed.) (1999), *Monetary Policy Rules*, Chicago: Chicago University Press.

—— (2000a), 'Reassessing discretionary fiscal policy', *Journal of Economic Perspectives*, 14: 21–36.

—— (2000b), 'The policy rule mix: a macroeconomic policy evaluation', in G. Calvo, M. Obstfeld and R. Dornbusch (eds), *Robert Mundell Festschrif*, Cambridge, MA: MIT Press.

Visco, I. (1995), 'Inflation, inflation targeting and monetary policy: notes for discussion on the Italian experience', in L. Leiderman, and L. E. O. Svensson (eds), *Inflation Targets*, London: CEPR.

Woodford, M. (2003), *Interest and Prices*, Princeton: Princeton University Press.

6 Testing the fiscal theory of the price level for European countries

A cointegrated VAR approach*

F. Farina and R. Ricciuti

6.1 Introduction

In their celebrated article, Sargent and Wallace (1981) argued that Monetary Dominance takes place when the central bank rigorously pursues monetary stability. In the Chicken Game between the monetary and the fiscal authorities, the Nash equilibrium prevails in which monetary policy is 'active' and the fiscal policy is 'passive' as the government abides by the restrictive monetary stance (Leeper, 1991). In contrast, under Fiscal Dominance, fiscal authorities do not impede the dynamics of nominal variables to be affected by changes in the public budget, so that fiscal policy is 'active'. However, the price level remains a monetary phenomenon. Since fiscal laxity requires to make recourse to seignorage, the central bank keeps influencing the nominal variables.

The so-called Fiscal Theory of the Price Level (FTPL) contends this view. Although following different research lines, many contributions argue that the relationships between money, debt and prices is more complex than assessed by the quantitative theory of money (Woodford, 1995, 1996, 2001, 2003; Cochrane, 1998, 2001; Christiano and Fitzgerald, 2000; Chadha and Nolan, 2003). In fact, the FTPL claims that the intertemporal public budget constraint (IPBC) can alternatively be generated by a Ricardian (R) Regime or a Non-Ricardian (NR) Regime.

In an R Regime, the central bank acts as the Stackelberg leader. Once monetary policy is set by the monetary authorities, the price level is determined through a money demand equation, based on the quantitative theory of money. The fiscal authorities' compliance with the monetary stance implies that they cannot violate their budget constraint, on the same ground as private agents. To fulfil the IPBC, the pattern of future expected surpluses must match the present value of the budget constraint for any possible values of the price level and the interest rate. This amounts to saying that in each period of time the government determines a fiscal stance consistent with the price level resulting from the money demand equation (Leith and Wren-Lewis, 2000: C97–C98). After any exogenous shock, such as a rise in the real interest rate impinging on the total (primary plus secondary) public deficit, or a slowdown in the GDP growth rate causing a lower potential output, fiscal authorities should adjust tax revenues and/or expenditures. If this does not happen, the financial market will react to the violation of the fiscal sustainability condition, and a risk premium will increase the interest rate on the public debt (Buiter, 2001 and 2005).

In a Non-Ricardian Regime, the government acts as the Stackelberg leader. By drawing upon the volatility of the money demand function, and the consequent switch of central banks to manoeuvre the monetary stance by setting the interest rate (e.g. in the Taylor rule the real interest rate is increased, according to a coefficient bigger than one, as a response to a rise in the inflation rate), the FTPL claims that the price level is left indeterminate.

Can fiscal policy get in and provide the nominal anchor for the economy? The traditional approach stemming from the Sargent–Wallace analysis opposes the FTPL view that the IPBC is an equilibrium condition. Since 'prices clear markets, not budget constraints' (Buiter, 2005: C19), there is no alternative to the Ricardian Regime and the IPBC is always satisfied as an identity. The FTPL rejoinder emphasizes that the renege from the commitment to meet the IPBC puts fiscal authorities in the position to take hold of the determination of the price level. Whenever the government does not fulfil its intertemporal budget constraint, a Non-Ricardian Regime is established. A jump in the price level will do the business of reducing the real value of government debt, making it possible to rebalance the present value of taxes with future spending obligations.

In this chapter we evaluate the FTPL tenet of an alternative between following a Ricardian or a Non-Ricardian Regime by conducting econometric estimates for European countries which cover the four decades from 1962 to 2000. In the first two decades, central banks of most countries deviated from the anti-inflationary behaviour, so that the strategy mix put forward by the interaction between the monetary and the fiscal authorities proved to be highly inefficient. In the subsequent two decades, European countries have experienced a smooth – albeit slow – downward trend of the inflation rate. We will test whether European governments have been adjusting period-by-period their fiscal stances, so as to establish a Ricardian Regime, or their fiscal stances failed to comply with the monetary stance implied by a credible monetary policy committed to low inflation, thus establishing a Non-Ricardian Regime.

The chapter is organized as follows: Section 6.2 casts the Ricardian and Non-Ricardian regimes in the IPBC equation; Section 6.3 analyses the institutional boundaries within which the behaviour of fiscal authorities was framed during the monetary integration process and provides the link between the FTPL and fiscal policy under Monetary Dominance; Section 6.4 introduces the empirical methodology; Section 6.5 presents the results, and Section 6.6 concludes.

6.2   Ricardian and Non-Ricardian Regimes

Let us write the flow government budget constraint as

$$B_t = B_{t-1}(1 + i_t) + P_t(G_t - T_t) - (M_t - M_{t-1}), \text{ for any } t \tag{6.1}$$

where B is the stock of public debt, i is the nominal interest rate, G are the public expenditures, T are the tax revenues, M is the money supply. In a steady state, $M_t/M_{t-1} = P_t/P_{t+1} = \mu = \Pi_{t+1} + 1$. Under a zero-inflation monetary rule $\mu = 1$, seignorage is ruled out $\Pi = \mu - 1$ and $\Pi = 0$ for any t. Therefore, the flow budget constraint becomes

$$b_t = b_{t-1}(i + r_t) + (\gamma_t - \tau_t) \tag{6.2}$$

where the real interest rate (r) is equal to the nominal, and lower case letters denote values of the income level normalized to the steady state. If fiscal authorities behave according to Monetary Dominance, the year-by-year equilibrium of this equation is sufficient for the IPBC to be satisfied.

Suppose now that expected inflation turns to be positive, the nominal interest rate lifts up, and new public bonds will then be issued in order to fund the increased amount of interest payments. To cope with this increase in public debt, fiscal sustainability asks fiscal authorities to set up the appropriate amount of current and future primary surpluses. In the case the government does not comply with this obligation, the discounted value of current and future primary surpluses will not match the stock of public debt, and seignorage will be endogenously determined. The price level change which is needed to satisfy the IPBC can be rationalized by assuming that the increase in the bond issuing determines a wealth effect. The consequent excess demand creates the appropriate increase of the price level, such that the real value of public debt is reduced and fiscal solvency is achieved.

In the scenario sketched above, in order to impose monetary stability in front of soaring inflationary expectations, a restrictive monetary stance will raise the nominal interest rate. Due to the permanent lift in the funding of the debt service, the stock of public debt will be posited on a rising dynamic path. The higher the accumulated stock of public debt, the more an increase in the interest rate engineered by monetary authorities will endanger Monetary Dominance, which in turn will affect fiscal sustainability (Chadha and Nolan, 2003). Since fiscal authorities are required to take responsibility for any exogenous change in the real interest rate impinging on the debt service, equation (6.2) does not adequately reflect the intertemporal constraint a government is facing after the upward lift of interest rates. Indeed, to verify whether or not fiscal sustainability will be preserved, the secondary deficit must be incorporated in the analysis of fiscal sustainability (McCallum, 1984).

Let us then define the total deficit (d_t) as

$$d_t = (\gamma_t - \tau_t) + r_{bt-1}/(1 + r). \tag{6.3}$$

To fulfil fiscal sustainability, in the case of a positive stock of public debt the future series of d_t must present a negative value. Let us then express the IPBC as

$$b_t = b_{t-1}(i + r) - v_t \tag{6.4}$$

where the surplus $v_t = \tau_t - \gamma_t - \mathrm{r}b_{t-1}/(1+r)$. By solving equation (6.4) for b_{t-1} and iterating for the subsequent periods, after k iterations we get

$$b_t = \sum_{i=0}^{k} (1+r)^{-i}(v_{t+i}) + (1+r)^{-k}b_{b+k} \tag{6.5}$$

where the first term on the right side is the present value of the planned future surpluses and the second term is the so-called transversality condition, which controls for the variation in the debt/GDP ratio not to exceed the difference between the interest rate and the GDP growth rate. In the case of a positive difference, fiscal solvency is still warranted, as the debt explosion could only happen under the inconsistent condition of tax revenues greater than the GDP (Bohn, 1998). When the 'transversality condition' is met, the second term converges to zero ($k \to \infty$):

$$\lim_{k \to \infty} (1+r)^{-k}b_{t+k} = 0. \tag{6.6}$$

The IPBC requires the public debt (b_t) to be equalized by the present value of future surpluses:

$$b_t \sum_{i=0}^{k} (1+r)^{-i}(v_{t+i}). \tag{6.7}$$

To assess whether equation 6.7 was satisfied by European governments as an identity according to the Ricardian Regime, or as an equilibrium condition according to the Non-Ricardian Regime, we have to tune the two regimes on the specific enforcement devices for Monetary Dominance which have been in place during the decades during which monetary integration has taken place.

6.3   The FTPL and the enforcement of Monetary Dominance

A largely shared view on the European monetary integration process holds that in many countries the monetary and fiscal policy interactions have been characterized by a lack of co-ordination between the two authorities. However, monetary authorities have resisted fiscal prodigality by not showing any disposition to co-ordinate with fiscal authorities and conduct an expansionary monetary policy. Neither during the years in which the Bundesbank's tight monetary policy was providing the nominal anchor of the fixed exchange rate regime (EMS), nor while accomplishing the tough task of complying with the Maastricht criteria and afterwards with the constraint put on public finances by the Stability and Growth Pact (SGP),[1] the European central banks have appeared to give in to fiscal authorities. By acting as Stackelberg leaders vis-à-vis their governments, the central banks of European countries were successful in obtaining low inflation, which was instrumental in eventually launching the monetary union.

The evolution of the European monetary integration amounts to a series of steps characterized by the fiscal authorities' obligation to comply with the monetary stability pursued by monetary policy. The degree of enforcement has progressively strengthened. The European governments' fiscal stances increasing coherence with the restrictive monetary policy was due to the commitment to defend the EMS bilateral parities, on which the success of the domestic disinflationary process was relying. The Maastricht criteria stated that a rapid process of public deficit and debt reduction was the inescapable condition for the prize of participation in the monetary union. In approaching the EMU, however, the enforcement device represented by the need to comply with the Maastricht criteria for public finances and be admitted in the eurozone was bound to the end. The concern that the commitment to fiscal restraint would have been jeopardized by the launch of the euro led to the decision to introduce a more stringent institutional straitjacket for fiscal authorities. The SGP constraints can be considered the enforcement device for the fiscal stances to comply with Monetary Dominance.[2]

Let us analytically describe the main requirement to obtain the fiscal restraint needed for Monetary Dominance; that is, to keep the public budget 'close to balance or in surplus' in structural terms (net of the operation of the automatic stabilizers) in the medium-term:[3]

$$d_s = d + \hat{s}(\hat{y}) \tag{6.8}$$

where (d_s) is the 'structural' (cyclically adjusted) total deficit/GDP ratio, ($\hat{s}$) is the cyclical sensitivity of the budget depending on the automatic stabilizers, and ($\hat{y}$) is the output gap. In the medium-term equilibrium, with the output gap equal to zero, the second term is nil, the total (d) equalizes the 'structural' total deficit/GDP ratio (d_s). Considering this medium-term equilibrium, tax revenues as a percentage of GDP (τ_t) could be devoted to discretionary fiscal policy – aimed at allowing the public expenditures not to be cut after a disturbance to the potential output (y_t^*); that is, $y_t^* < y_{t-1*}$ – and/or to debt decumulation, respectively:

$$\tau_t = \alpha(y_t^*) + \beta(b_{t-1}/p_t). \tag{6.9}$$

Under a R Regime, fiscal authorities abstain from discretionary interventions ($\alpha = 0$) as the Ricardian equivalence applies. The appropriate series of future surpluses are set, such that the public debt could be fastly paid back ($\beta = 1$). The IPBC of equation 6.7 is then met as an equilibrium condition.

The SGP requirement to bring the 'structural' total deficit/GDP ratio d_s down to zero is an attempt to avoid a deviation of the total deficit from its zero medium-term value which could hamper the fulfilment of the debt consolidation target. Suppose now an upward tendency of the total deficit, caused by a slowdown in the formation of tax revenues after a lowering of the GDP growth rate, or by an exogenous rise of the interest rate which increases the interest payments. In order for fiscal sustainability to be preserved, this exogenous shock to the medium-term zero total deficit should be counteracted by a correspondent fiscal restriction (granted that the tax rate is kept constant, according to the Tax Smoothing doctrine). Yet, in the case that fiscal authorities do not upwardly correct the stream of current and future surpluses, the R Regime does not establish, and the transversality condition is not met. This is just the case highlighted by the FTPL. Considering that in equation (6.5) $b_t = B/py$, the IPBC will be satisfied by a rise in the price level, such that the reduction in the real value of the public debt on the left side could offset the lack of zero convergence of the second term on the right side.

Therefore, the econometric assessment of the existence of a Ricardian or a Non-Ricardian Regime corresponds to verifying what happens when fiscal authorities are unwilling and/or unable to equalize the present value of current and future surpluses to the stock of public debt. Econometric tests of the FTPL often present ambiguous results (Afonso, 2002; Ballabriga and Martinez-Mongay, 2003; Favero and Monacelli, 2005; see also Wren-Lewis, 2003). Indeed, testing the FTPL is often doubted (Woodford, 1995), as the public sector budget constraint is a relationship consisting of equilibrium data in which no causality can be detected. The difficulty to assess the right causality link between surpluses and the debt dynamics requests not to interpret a correlation connecting the reduction of public liabilities to a positive innovation in the surplus (Canzoneri *et al.*, 2001) as an unambiguous proof of a 'passive' fiscal policy in a Ricardian Regime. This finding might also signal a Non-Ricardian Regime, whereby expectations of a future reduction in primary surpluses caused by an 'active' fiscal policy, such as expansionary discretionary interventions or an overturn in the trend of debt consolidation, brings about an increase in the price level downward adjusting the real value of government liabilities (see Cochrane, 1998).

Our investigation attempts to overcome this indeterminacy. Firstly we estimate the liabilities' response to an innovation in the primary surplus, and secondly the series of surpluses in the periods subsequent to an innovation in the primary surplus. A positive sign in the first correlation shall not be straightforwardly taken as a confirmation of the hypothesis of a Non-Ricardian Regime. One might also think of reverse causation; that is, a positive primary surplus responding to an increase in the real value of the public debt, which is a proof of an R Regime. In the literature, the label of Ricardian Regime has been assigned both to a negative response of public debt to the primary surplus (Canzoneri *et al.*, 2001) and to a fiscal surplus counteracting an increase in public debt (Bohn, 1998). Any negative relationship between fiscal surpluses and public liabilities is then exposed to the presence of reverse causation. Therefore, we control for the sequence of current and future surpluses in order to understand whether a government implementing an innovation in surplus, which was meant to ensure fiscal sustainability, was persistently maintained. When the series of future surpluses follow a stable path, we conclude in favour of an R Regime. When the sequence turns out to be stochastic – for instance, a rise in the primary surplus at time t is followed by a reduction in the surplus at time $t + 1$ – we think of a Non-Ricardian Regime. In this latter case, contrary to the presumption that a negative correlation between an innovation in surplus and public liabilities unambiguously designates a Ricardian Regime, the IPBC is met just because a positive innovation in surplus is followed by a hike in the price level, causing the real value of the public debt to fall down.

6.4 Model and data

We apply the methodology devised by Canzoneri *et al.* (2001). In an R Regime, the surplus at time t pays off some of the debt, and liabilities at $t + 1$ fall. In an NR Regime, there are three possibilities. First, an innovation in surplus is not correlated with the subsequent surpluses. In the case we are considering, liabilities at time $t + 1$ should not be affected by the innovation in surplus at time t. Second, an innovation in surplus at time t is positively correlated with future surpluses and discount factors. In this case, liabilities at time $t + 1$ should rise. In either of these cases, it should in principle be possible to differentiate between R and NR Regimes. For example, the impulse response function from a VAR in surplus and liabilities would tell us how liabilities respond to an innovation in surplus. If liabilities fall, we have an R Regime; if it does not, we have an NR Regime.

The first step of the analysis is the characterization of the stochastic properties of the series. As shown in the next section, the series involved in our analysis contain unit-roots, therefore we need to modify the empirical strategy undertaken by Canzoneri *et al.* (2001), who find that their series were stationary. The second step of our analysis involves cointegration between the variables included. Having assessed that the series are cointegrated, we can move to the impulse response analysis. In the I(0) case the effect of a shock can be seen in its moving average representation:

$$y_t = \Phi_0 u_t + \Phi_1 u_{t-1} + \Phi_2 u_{t-2}, \tag{6.10}$$

where $\Phi_0 = I_K$, and the

$$\Phi_s = \sum_{j=1}^{s} \Phi_{s-j} A_j, \quad s = 1, 2, \ldots \tag{6.11}$$

are computed recursively from the reduced-for of the VAR in levels. The coefficients of this representation may be interpreted as the responses to impulses hitting the system. In this case $\Phi_s \to 0$ as $s \to \infty$, and the effect of an impulse vanishes over time.

In the I(1) case, that our preliminary tests show being relevant to the variables involved in the analysis, although the Wold representation does not exist for non-stationary cointegrated processes, the Φ_s matrices can be computed in the same way as in standard VAR with in I(0) variables. In this case, the Φ_s may not converge to zero as $s \to \infty$, therefore some shocks may have permanent effects (Breitung *et al.*, 2004). From Johansen (1995) we know that if y_t is generated by a reduced-form VECM, it has the following moving average representation:

$$y_t = \Xi \sum_{i=1}^{t} u_i + \Xi^*(L) u_t + y_0^*, \tag{6.12}$$

where $\Xi = \beta_\perp (\alpha'_\perp (I_K - \sum_{i=1}^{p-1} \Gamma_i) \beta_\perp)^{-1} \alpha'_\perp$, $\Xi^*(L) = \sum_{j=0}^{\infty} \Xi_j^* L^j$ is an infinite-order polynomial in the lag operator with coefficients matrix Ξ_j^* that goes to zero as $j \rightarrow \infty$. y_0^* contains the initial values. The matrix Ξ_j^* has rank $K - r$ if the cointegrating rank of the system is r. It represents the long-run effects of the forecast impulse responses, whereas the Ξ_j^* contains the transitory effects.

To identify the shocks we can replace u_t by $A^{-1}B\varepsilon_t$, the orthogonalized short-run impulse response is obtained as $\Xi_j^* A^{-1}B$ as in the stationary VAR. The long-run effects of a shock are given by $\Xi A^{-1}B$. This matrix has rank $K - r$, and therefore can have at most r columns of zeros. Hence, there can be at most r shocks with no long-run impact, and at least $k^* = K - r$ shocks with permanent effects. Assuming $A = I_K$, we have just enough restrictions to identify B.

We consider eight European countries that have been involved in the process of monetary integration, though not all of them participate in the EMU. Two variables are considered: *LIAB* (defined as the sum of government outstanding debt and monetary base over GDP), and *SPL*, government surplus over GDP. Data are taken from the International Financial Statistics database of the International Monetary Fund. They cover the period ranging from 1960 to 2000, with the exception of Spain (1962–2000).[4]

6.5   Results

6.5.1 Unit-roots tests

The first step of the analysis is to study the stochastic properties of the series. To do so, we run two unit-roots tests: ADF1 and ADF2 (Fuller, 1976; Dickey and Fuller 1979; Said, 1991). For the former the null hypothesis is unit-root and the alternative is stationarity, for the latter the null is unit-root with drift and the alternative is trend stationarity. ADF1 specification includes a constant and ADF2 includes constant and trend. The lag-length is determined using the Schwarz Information Criterion. For all the countries and for both series we cannot reject the null hypothesis of a unit-root (Table 6.1).

6.5.2 Cointegration tests

Having established that our series are all characterized by unit-roots, the second step is to see whether they are cointegrated; that is, there exists a linear combination of the two series that is stationary. We employ the Johansen procedure (1988, 1991) by calculating two statistics: the λmax and the λtrace tests. Models include intercept and trend, with cointegrating restrictions on the time trend imposed. Again, the lag-length is determined by using the Schwarz Information Criterion.

In the Johansen tests we first test the null hypothesis that there are zero cointegrating vectors, and second we test the null that there is one cointegrating vector. For all countries but Germany (Table 6.2), we can reject the first null hypothesis, but we can never reject the second one.[5] Therefore, we proceed with the impulse response analysis for all countries with the exception of Germany.

Table 6.1 ADF tests results, 1960–2000

	LIAB		SPL	
	ADF1	*ADF2*	*ADF1*	*ADF2*
Belgium	−0.617 (1)	−2.270 (8.4)	−1.279 (1)	−0.699 (1)
Finland	−0.801 (6)	−0.172 (6)	−2.539 (1)	−3.179 (1)
France	−0.824 (1)	−2.017 (1)	−0.110 (1)	−3.002 (1)
Germany	−1.436 (1)	−1.725 (1)	−2.799 (1)	−3.101 (1)
Italy	−0.191 (1)	−1.663 (1)	−1.394 (1)	−0.896 (1)
Netherlands	−1.693 (1)	−2.283 (1)	−2.018 (1)	−1.646 (1)
Spain[1]	−0.726 (1)	−2.195 (1)	−2.248 (1)	−2.031 (1)
Sweden	−2.308 (1)	−3.392 (1)	−2.726 (1)	−2.209 (1)

Notes
Critical values at 5% and 1% are equal to −3.58 and −3.22, respectively for the ADF1 test, and −4.15 and −3.80 respectively for the ADF2 test for a sample size equal to 50. Number in parentheses indicate the lag-length determined using the Schwarz Information Criterion. ADF1 specification includes a constant and ADF2 includes constant and trend.[1] The time-span is 1962–2000.

Table 6.2 Cointegration results

Country	Lag length	r	λ_{max}	λ_{trace}
Belgium	1	0	28.3	38.4
		1	10.1	10.1
Finland	1	0	88.7	6.1
		1	6.1	94.8
France	1	0	45.5	55.0
		1	9.4	9.4
Germany	1	0	13.0	20.6
		1	7.6	7.6
Italy	1	0	23.4	31.4
		1	8.0	8.0
Netherlands	1	0	70.3	73.8
		1	3.5	3.5
Spain	1	0	32.8	40.0
		1	7.2	7.2
Sweden	2	0	24.2	40.3
		1	6.9	4.2

Notes
Critical values at 10 and 5% are equal to 16.9 and 19.2, respectively for 0 cointegrating vectors to 10.6 and 23.5, respectively for 1 cointegrating vector in the λ_{max} test, and 23.0 and 25.4 respectively for 0 cointegrating vectors and 10.6 and 12.5, respectively for 1 cointegrating vector for the λ_{trace} test. Models include intercept and trend, with cointegrating restrictions on the time trend imposed.

6.5.3 Impulse response functions in a non-stationary VAR

In Section 6.3 we have presented the framework of the impulse response analysis in the case of a non-stationary VAR. In small samples more reliable statistical inference can be obtained by constructing confidence intervals through bootstrapping than using asymptotic theory. Moreover, the analytical expressions of the asymptotic variances of the impulse response coefficients are rather complicated, and the use of bootstrapping avoids calculating these expressions explicitly (Kilian, 1998). Denote with $\phi, \hat{\phi}$, and $\hat{\phi}^*$ some impulse response coefficient, its estimator implied by the estimators of the model coefficients, and the corresponding boot-strap estimator, respectively. Hall (1992) states that the distribution of $(\hat{\phi} - \phi)$ is approximately equal to that of $(\hat{\phi}^* - \hat{\phi})$ in large samples. Therefore, the confidence interval

$$CI_H = \left\lfloor \hat{\phi} - t^*_{(1-\gamma/2)}, \hat{\phi} - t_{\gamma/2} \right\rfloor \tag{6.13}$$

can be derived. We constructed bootstrapping confidence intervals by using 2000 replications.

In Figures 6.1–6.7, we present the results of the analysis. In each graph, in the upper panels the order of causality is $LIAB \rightarrow SPL$, in the lower panels the VAR is based on the opposite order of causality. In each figure we report the lag-length of the VAR, obtained applying the Schwarz Information Criterion. In the figures bands represent 95% confidence levels of each response.

The general picture emerging from Figures 6.1–6.7 is not completely in line with the results found by Canzoneri *et al.* (2001), though it does not support an NR regime. In particular, we can summarize our findings along these lines:

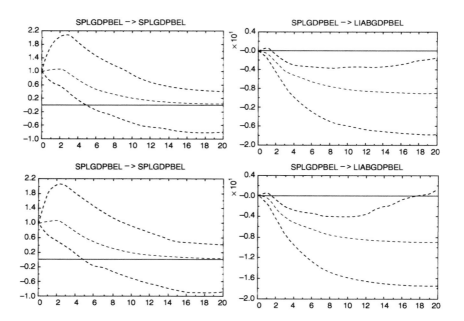

Figure 6.1 Belgium (p = 1).

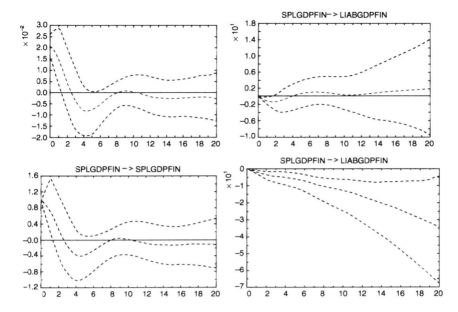

Figure 6.2 Finland (p = 2).

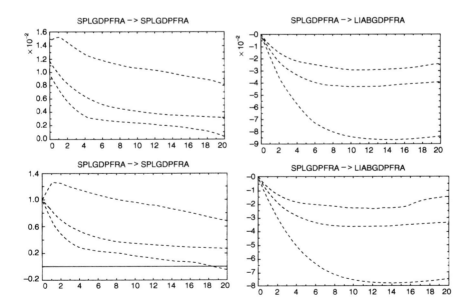

Figure 6.3 France (p = 1).

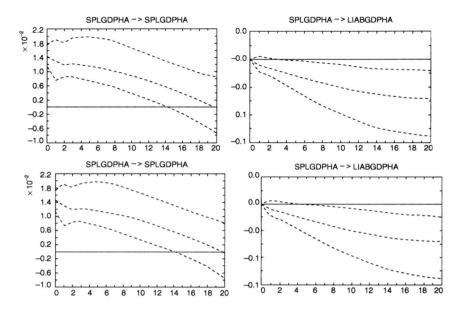

Figure 6.4 Italy (p = 2).

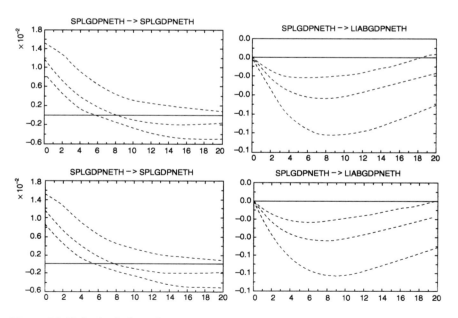

Figure 6.5 Netherlands (p = 1).

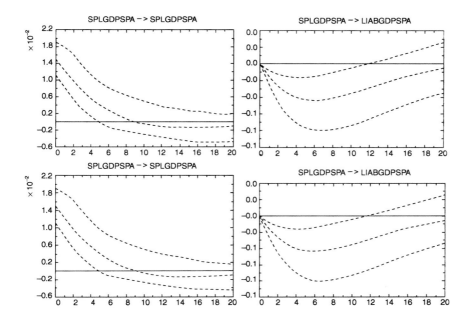

Figure 6.6 Spain (p = 1).

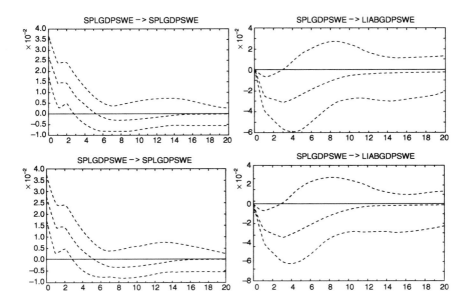

Figure 6.7 Sweden (p = 1).

1. a 1% shock on the surplus/GDP ratio has a temporary positive effect on the same variable, and eventually the ratio returns to its starting level within ten years. This can be interpreted as evidence of an R Regime;
2. a 1% shock on the surplus/GDP ratio has typically a negative effect on the liabilities/GDP ratio in the first few years, but it does not bring the liabilities/GDP ratio – as it instead happens in the case of the United States – to a level lower than the starting one in the majority of the countries. Indeed, this is the most important case to distinguish between an R and an NR Regime.

Results are similar for both orders of causality.

The contrast between finding 1 and finding 2, pointing to the presence of an R Regime and of an NR Regime, respectively, is difficult to solve. We might interpret it as a confirmation of exogenous shocks weakening the fiscal authorities' determination to comply with Monetary Dominance. A restrictive fiscal stance may have created a surplus in the primary budget, which has been lasting for several years. Yet, according to our hypothesis, this fiscal restraint proved insufficient whenever an exogenous shock made more severe the fiscal restriction which would have been required by fulfilment of the IPBC.

Looking more closely to individual countries, we can distinguish two groups. First, there are three countries that strictly behave as the R Regime predicts: Belgium, France and Italy (Figures 6.1, 6.3 and 6.4). However, France has a Ricardian behaviour more in the case of a shock of surplus on liabilities, than in the case of a shock of surplus on itself. Second, countries like Finland, The Netherlands, Spain and Sweden (Figures 6.2, 6.5, 6.6 and 6.7) bring the surplus/GDP ratio to its initial level, but fail to significantly reduce the liabilities/GDP ratio. In particular, The Netherlands and Spain experience an uprising trend in the liabilities/GDP ratio after an initial period in which this ratio is lowered. In the 20 years period this increase is significant for the former and insignificant for the latter. The difference between these groups of countries possibly lies in the fact that Belgium and Italy have the highest debt/GDP ratio in the European Union, whereas debt is not a significant issue for other countries. Belgium and Italy, therefore, needed to respond by reducing their debt because of their unsound financial stance. However, this explanation leaves aside France.[6]

6.6   Concluding remarks

In this chapter we analysed the fiscal theory of the price level in a number of European countries, applying the methodology devised by Canzoneri *et al.* (2001). Having assessed that the series involved in the analysis are cointegrated, we use a cointegrated VAR approach to test for the theory. We find that only Belgium and Italy show that a shock on the surplus/GDP ratio has a temporary positive effect on the same variable, and eventually the ratio returns to its starting level, and a shock on the surplus/GDP ratio has typically a negative effect on the liabilities/GDP ratio in the first few years, bringing the liabilities/GDP ratio – as in the case of the United States – to a level lower than the initial one. For most countries the second circumstance is not fulfilled, while France is closer to the two high-debt countries than the others.

What can we learn from these results on the debate over the SGP? Too expansionary fiscal stances are not the only threat to sound public budgets. Fiscal sustainability is constantly threatened by the need to cope with a worsening in the deficit/GDP ratio, after a rise in interest payments and/or a slowdown in the GDP growth rate. It is then striking that Belgium and Italy – the two countries which for the most of the 1980–2004 period experienced the highest figures for the stock of public debt – strictly fulfil the criteria for an R Regime. We may speculate that for the governments of these high-debt countries to leave the monetary authority to deal with monetary stability was not a solution. Accordingly, once an innovation in surplus had been implemented, these fiscal authorities did not let the fiscal stance revert from restriction, but a stable path of future surpluses was continuously followed. In other words, the proximity to an ultimate loss of fiscal sustainability forced these governments to set $\alpha = 0$ and $\beta = 1$ in equation 4. On the other hand, fiscal authorities that were not burdened by a high public debt do not appear to follow the prescription of an R Regime and to behave consistently with Monetary Dominance.

Our investigation has highlighted the absence of a common behaviour shared across European fiscal authorities. This finding suggests that heterogeneity across European countries has probably been the most important missing element in the enforcement mechanism for fiscal solvency. Yet, it should not be left unnoticed that the progressive strengthening in the enforcement of restrictive public stances has found most EMU countries – also those with an accumulation of public debt much lower than Belgium and Italy – unable to bring the liabilities/GDP ratio to a level lower than the starting one. The new design of the SGP, pointing to a lessening of obligations just for these countries, may then be doubted. It is likely that the whole philosophy of the SGP is worth being revised.

Notes

* We wish to thank Sebastian Rovira for useful research assistance. A previous version was presented at the First International Conference on 'Small Open Economies in a Globalized World' organised by the University of Bologna at Rimini in 2006. We wish to thank the audience for useful comments. Funding provided by MIUR under the research programme 'The European Economic Institutions and the new Keynesian dynamics with unionised labour markets' are gratefully acknowledged.
1 The SGP guidelines for the implementation of Art. 104 of the Maastricht Treaty have been integrated many times. The most important clarifications are the Resolution of the European Council and the two ECOFIN Council Regulations of 1997, that introduced the concept of 'close to balance or in surplus' and the Excess Deficit Procedure, and the 2002 Council Opinion whereby the 'cyclically adjusted' (structural) deficit has to be used to assess the budgetary position of a country. In March 2005, the so-called New GDP has opened to a discretionary evaluation the evolution of public finances, also lessening the constraints on fiscal stances. In particular, countries with a 'low' public debt are allowed a higher deficit/GDP ratio (3.5%) limit, a longer time spam within which an excessive

deficit is to be reversed with no sanctions, and growth-friendly public expenses are excluded from the computation of the 3.5% limit.

2 Some authors have found confirmation of this hypothesis in the upward trend experienced the public deficit and debt over GDP in many EMU countries at the inception of the EMU. They claim that, by the time in which the euro has provided the shield for public finances, fiscal authorities have been taken by a 'consolidation fatigue' (Huges-Hallett *et al.*, 2003).

3 The link between Monetary Dominance and the fiscal stances under the SGP constraints have been extensively analysed. See Buti *et al.* (2001); Farina and Tamborini (2001) and (2004); Andrés *et al.* (2002); Allsopp and Artis (2003); Hughes-Hallett *et al.* (2003).

4 The United Kingdom was excluded because data were available only for a shorter period (1970–2000).

5 For Germany the results are similar if we add a break in 1989 for the reunification.

6 These results are quite in line with Creel and Le Bihan (2006), which consider France, Germany, Italy and the United Kingdom. They use structural balance data to overcome the Cochrane (1998) critique but still along the Canzoneri *et al.* (2001) methodology, and do not find support for the FTPL.

References

Afonso, A. (2002), 'Disturbing the fiscal theory of the price level: can it fit the Eu-15?', Department of Economics, Lisbon University, Working Paper no. 2002/01.

Allsopp, C. and Azhs, M. (2003), "The assessment: Emu, four years old, in Oxford Review of Economic Policy, 19: 1–29.

Andrès, J., Ballabriga F., Vallès, J. (2002), 'Hou-Ricaronian fiscal policies is an Olzeu Woultary Union', European Commission, Economic Papers, no. 169.

Ballabriga, F. C. and Martinez-Mongay, C. (2003), 'Has EMU shifted fiscal policy?', in M. Buti (ed.), *Monetary and Fiscal Policies in EMU*, Cambridge: Cambridge University Press, 246–272.

Bohn, H. (1998), 'The behaviour of U.S. Public Debt and Deficits', *Quarterly Journal of Economics*, 113: 949–63.

Breitung, J., Brüggeman, R. and Lütkepohl, H. (2004), 'Structural vector autoregressive modeling and impulse response', in H. Lütkepohl and M. Krätzig (eds), *Applied Time Series Econometrics*, Cambridge: Cambridge University Press, 159–196.

Buiter, W. H. (2002), 'The fiscal theory of the price level: a critique', *Economic Journal*, 112: 459–80.

—— (2005), 'New developments in monetary economics: two ghosts, two eccentricities, a fallacy, a mirage and a mythos', *Economic Journal*, 115: C1–C31.

Buti, M., Roeger, W. and In't Veld, J. (2001), 'Monetary and fiscal policy interactions under a stability pact', *Journal of Common Market Studies*, 39: 801–24.

Canzoneri, M., Cumby, R. and Diba, B. (2001), 'Is the price level determined by the needs of fiscal solvency?', *American Economic Review*, 91: 1221–38.

Chadha, J. S. and Nolan, C. (2003), 'On the interaction of monetary and fiscal policy', in S. Altug, J. S. Chadha and C. Nolan (eds), *Dynamic Macroeconomic Analysis*, Cambridge: Cambridge University Press, 243–307.

Christiano, L. J. and Fitzgerald, T. J. (2000), 'Understanding the fiscal theory of the price level', *Economic Review*, 36: 2–38.

Cochrane, J. H. (1998), 'A frictionless view of U.S. inflation', in B. S. Bernanke and J. Rotemberg (eds), *NBER Macroeconomics Annual Cambridge*, Cambridge, MA: MIT Press, 323–384.

—— (2001), 'Long term debt and optimal policy in the fiscal theory of the price level', *Econometrica*, 69: 69–116.

Creel, J. and Le Bihan, H. (2006), 'Using structural balance data to test the fiscal theory of the price level: some international Evidence', *Journal of Macroeconomics*, 28: 338–60.

Dickey, D. A. and Fuller, W. A. (1979), 'Estimators for autoregressive time series with a unit root', *Journal of the American Statistical Association*, 74: 427–31.

Farina F. and Ricciuti, R. (2006), 'L'évaluation des politiques budgétaires en Europe: règles budgétaires et marges de manoeuvre des gouvernements', *Revue de l'OFCE*, 99: 275–301.

Farina F. and Tamborini, R. (2001), 'Macroeconomic stabilization policies in Europe under the new regime of monetary union', *Quaderni del Dipartimento di Economia Politica*, Università di Siena, no. 317.

—— (2004), ' "Set a sufficiently ambitious budget target and let automatic stabilizers work." Will it really work in the European Monetary Union?', *Open Economies Review*, 15: 143–68.

Favero, C. and Monacelli, T. (2005), 'Fiscal policy rules and regime (in)stability: evidence from the U.S.', IGIER Working Paper no. 282.

Fuller, W. A. (1976), *Introduction to Statistical Time Series*, New York: John Wiley.

Hall, P. (1992), *The Bootstrap and Edgeworth Expansion*, New York: Springer-Verlag.

Hughes Hallett, A., Lewis, J. and von Hagen, J. (2003), *Fiscal Policy in Europe, 1991–2003. An Evidence-based Analysis*, London: CEPR.

Johansen, S. (1988), 'Statistical analysis of cointegrating vectors', *Journal of Economic Dynamics and Control*, 12: 231–54.

—— (1991), 'Estimation and hypothesis testing of cointegrating vectors in Gaussian vector autoregressive models', *Econometrica*, 59: 1551–80.

Kilian, L. (1998), 'Small-sample confidence intervals for impulse response functions', *Review of Economics and Statistics*, 80: 218–30.

Leeper, E. (1991), 'Equilibria under active and passive monetary and fiscal policies', *Journal of Monetary Economics*, 27: 129–47.

Leith, C. and Wren-Lewis, S. (2000), 'Interactions between monetary and fiscal policy rules', *Economic Journal*, 110: C93–C108.

Said, S. E. (1991), 'Unit root test for time series data with a linear time trend', *Journal of Econometrics*, 47: 285–303.

Sargent, T. J. and Wallace, N. (1981), 'Some unpleasant monetarist arithmetic', Federal Reserve Bank of Minneapolis, *Quarterly Review*, 5: 1–17.

Woodford, M. (1995), 'Price level determinacy without control of a monetary aggregate', *Carnegie-Rochester Series on Public Policy*, 43: 1–46.

—— (1996), 'Control of the public debt: a requirement for price stability?', NBER Working Paper no. 5684.

—— (2001), 'Fiscal requirements for price stability', *Journal of Money, Credit and Banking*, 33: 669–728.

—— (2003), *Interest and Prices: Foundations of a Theory of Monetary Policy*, Princeton: Princeton University Press.

Wren-Lewis, S. (2003), 'The compatibility between monetary and fiscal policies in EMU: a perspective from the fiscal theory of the price level', in M. Buti (ed.), *Monetary and Fiscal Policies in EMU*, Cambridge: Cambridge University Press.

Part III

Fiscal policy and the EMU countries

Heterogeneity, Interdependence and Divergence

7 One size does not fit all

Country size and fiscal policy in a
monetary union[1]

J. Le Cacheux and F. Saraceno

7.1 Introduction

After the decision of the Ecofin Council, in November 2003, to waive the sanctions recommended against France and Germany by the European Commission, and then the decision by the Commission to take the Ecofin Council to court for not respecting the letter of the treaties with regard to fiscal policy rules in the euro zone, there has been widespread feelings that 'large' countries were somehow taking advantage of their size and power to violate the rules they themselves had imposed on others. This resentment was aired again by several governments of 'small' countries on the eve of the 23 March 2005 Council meeting when a some-what reformed Stability and Growth Pact eventually emerged from the discussions and gained unanimous support. Coming after several years of skirmishes between the Commission and a number of governments from fiscally 'virtuous' countries, on the one hand, and the governments of a small number of countries, mostly large ones, who were finding it difficult, if not impossible, to meet the stringent require-ments of the SGP as interpreted by the Commission, on the other, these episodes point to a number of difficulties and misunderstandings concerning the purpose and precise design of fiscal policy rules in a monetary union with decentralized fiscal authorities.

Newspaper and layman explanations of why violations of the SGP by large countries have tended to be more frequent and more protracted than those commit-ted by small countries have mostly been variations over the 'arrogance' argument: national governments of large countries tend to be more spiteful of rules, including the ones they have advocated and imposed on others. A related argument is some-times added; namely, the hypothesis that interest groups may be powerful, and may therefore be in a better position to get their way in large countries, effectively blocking politically painful fiscal consolidation policies.

These explanations do not really explain anything. Couldn't it be the case that country size matters for the choice of macroeconomic strategies in a monetary union? Shouldn't we pay more attention to the standard textbook arguments: (i) that multipliers are larger in less open economies; (ii) that spillovers are weighted by size? Even refurbished with proper micro-foundations in the spirit of the recent literature on fiscal–monetary policy interaction, these arguments appear still valid, and we contend that such an explanation is more appealing than the standard argument in terms of intrinsic differences in policy-makers' preferences or attitudes, that is, what we have termed earlier the 'arrogance factor'.

In order to support the argument that 'size matters', we explore a simple two-country model of a monetary union in the spirit of this recent literature in order to demonstrate that country size has an effect on the optimal level of public spending or public deficit in response to fiscal or demand shocks.

Sections 7.2 and 7.3 document the very significant degree of heterogeneity of national fiscal policies and macroeconomic performances and, more generally, the differences in responses of national economies to common shocks and policies. In Section 7.4, we propose a simple, two-country model showing that country size is a relevant dimension to consider when analysing the incentives facing national governments in a monetary union. Finally, Section 7.5 offers some tentative conclusions about the design of rules and institutions.

7.2   Heterogeneity in the euro zone

In spite of efforts during the transition phase to economic and monetary union, especially through the imposition of convergence criteria – the so-called Maastricht criteria – the economies of the euro zone have proven much more heterogeneous than what had been expected. In particular, they have tended to pursue divergent fiscal policies, with on average larger budget deficits in large countries (Table 7.1).

There has also been a great deal of heterogeneity in the standard macroeconomic performance indicators of economic growth (Table 7.2), price stability (Table 7.3), and hence – because nominal interest rates have tended to be very close within the monetary union – in short- and long-term real interest rates (Tables 7.4 and 7.5).[2] These persistent differences make macroeconomic policy-making in the euro zone more difficult, especially to the extent that national indicators are still published and widely regarded as more relevant than euro zone averages.

For monetary policy, the heterogeneity of monetary conditions and transmission mechanisms raises a number of serious problems: the better known ones relate to the decision-making rules in the ECB council, with the excessive weight of small countries, many of which happen to have inflation rates higher than average (see below). With regard to fiscal policies, the 'one-size-fits-all' character of the rules may also prove harmful in a number of contexts.

7.3   Small and large states: coping with differences in incentives

Although the equal treatment principle is deeply entrenched in the democratic ideals and widely regarded as the only fair organization rule in a democracy, the recent crises with the implementation of the SGP and the failed adoption of the constitutional treaty project have revealed a profound cleavage between small and large countries in the EU, a distinction that had never been that apparent before. For scholars of the history of federal states and institutions, especially of the United

Table 7.1 Fiscal deficit and public debt ratios, Euro zone countries, 1999–2005 (as percentages of GDP)

	1999	2000	2001	2002	2003	2004*	2005*
Belgium	−0.4	0.2	0.6	0.1	0.4	−0.1	−0.3
	114.8	109.1	108.0	105.4	100.0	95.8	94.4
Germany	−1.5	1.3	−2.8	−3.7	−3.8	−3.9	−3.4
	61.2	60.2	59.4	60.9	64.2	65.9	67.2
Greece	−4.0	−4.1	−3.7	−3.7	−4.6	−5.5	−3.6
	105.2	114.0	114.7	112.5	109.9	112.2	111.9
Spain	−1.2	−0.9	−0.4	0.1	0.4	−0.6	−0.1
	63.1	61.1	57.5	54.4	50.7	48.2	45.5
France	−1.8	−1.4	−1.5	−3.2	−4.1	−3.7	−3.0
	58.5	56.8	56.5	58.8	63.7	64.9	65.5
Ireland	2.4	4.4	0.9	−0.2	0.1	−0.2	−0.6
	48.6	38.3	35.9	32.7	32.1	30.4	30.7
Italy	−1.7	−0.6	−2.6	−2.3	−2.4	−3.0	−3.0
	115.5	111.2	110.6	107.9	106.2	106.0	104.6
Luxembourg	3.6	6.0	6.4	2.8	0.8	−0.8	−1.6
	6.0	5.5	5.5	5.7	5.3	4.9	4.8
Netherlands	0.7	2.2	−0.1	−1.9	−3.2	−2.9	−2.4
	63.1	55.9	52.9	52.6	54.1	55.7	58.6
Austria	−2.3	−1.5	0.3	−0.2	−1.1	−1.3	−2.0
	67.5	65.8	66.1	65.7	64.5	64.0	63.9
Portugal	−2.8	−2.8	−4.4	−2.7	−2.8	−2.9	−3.7
	54.3	53.3	55.8	58.4	60.3	60.8	62.0
Finland	2.2	7.1	5.2	4.3	2.3	2.3	2.1
	47.0	44.6	43.8	42.6	45.6	44.8	43.4
Euro area	−1.3	0.1	−1.7	−2.4	−2.7	−2.9	−2.5
	72.8	70.4	69.4	69.4	70.7	71.1	71.1

Source: European Commission, Autumn forecasts, November 2004.

Note
* Forecasts.

States of America, this should not come as a surprise (see Laurent and Le Cacheux, 2004).

Nor it is a surprise for economists, as it may easily be shown that the incentives facing a small open economy (e.g. Ireland) are not at all the same as the ones facing a medium-sized one, such as Germany or France, which may help explain the differences in performances and strategies that seem so systematic in the recent history of the euro zone (Le Cacheux, 2005).

In economic terms, the differences between large and small countries are real and far-reaching: they correspond, in a monetary union, to a strategic asymmetry that triggers distinct incentives for each group of countries and allow 'small' ones to make choices that large ones can not afford without negative consequences and costs for themselves as well as for the whole monetary zone.

No wonder then that their respective macroeconomic situations differ sharply and systematically, most of the 'small' member states displaying relatively higher inflation, less unemployment and sounder public finances.

Table 7.2 GDP annual growth rates, 2000–5

	2000	2001	2002	2003	2004*	2005**
Belgium	3.9	0.7	0.9	1.3	2.5	2.5
Germany	2.9	0.8	0.1	−0.1	1.9	1.5
Greece	4.5	4.3	3.6	4.5	3.8	3.3
Spain	4.4	2.8	2.2	2.5	2.6	2.6
France	3.8	2.1	1.2	0.5	2.4	2.2
Ireland	9.9	6.0	6.1	3.7	5.2	4.8
Italy	3.0	1.8	0.4	0.3	1.3	1.8
Luxembourg	9.0	1.5	2.5	2.9	4.0	3.5
Netherlands	3.5	1.4	0.6	−0.9	1.4	1.7
Austria	3.4	0.7	1.2	0.8	1.9	2.4
Portugal	3.4	1.6	0.4	−1.2	1.3	2.2
Finland	5.1	1.1	2.3	1.9	3.0	3.1
Euro Zone	3.5	1.6	0.9	0.6	2.1	2.0
EU 15	3.6	1.7	1.1	0.9	2.3	2.2
US	3.7	0.8	1.9	3.1	4.4	3.0

Source: EU Commission, Autumn forecasts, November 2004.

Notes
* Estimate, October 2004.
**Forecasts, October 2004.

Table 7.3 Annual inflation rates, 1999–2004 (harmonized consumer price index)

	1999	2000	2001	2002	2003	2004*
Belgium	1.1	2.7	2.4	1.6	1.5	2
Germany	0.6	1.4	1.9	1.3	1.0	1.7
Greece	2.1	2.9	3.7	3.9	3.4	3.0
Spain	2.2	3.5	2.8	3.6	3.1	3.1
France	0.6	1.8	1.8	1.9	2.2	2.3
Ireland	2.5	5.3	4.0	4.7	4.0	2.3
Italy	1.7	2.6	2.3	2.6	2.8	2.3
Luxembourg	1.0	3.8	2.4	2.1	2.5	3.0
The Netherlands	2.0	2.3	5.1	3.9	2.2	1.2
Austria	0.5	2.0	2.3	1.7	1.3	2.1
Portugal	2.2	2.8	4.4	3.7	3.3	2.4
Finland	1.3	3.0	2.7	2.0	1.3	0.2
Euro Zone	1.1	2.1	2.4	2.3	2.1	2.1
Denmark	2.1	2.7	2.3	2.4	2.0	1.1
Sweden	0.6	1.3	2.7	2.0	2.3	1.1
United Kingdom	1.3	0.8	1.2	1.3	1.4	1.4
United States	2.2	3.4	2.8	1.6	2.3	2.6

Source: EU Commission, Autumn forecasts, November 2004.

Note
*Forecasts, October 2004.

Table 7.4 Short-term real interest rates, 1999–2004

	1999	2000	2001	2002	2003	2004*
Belgium	1.9	1.7	1.9	1.7	0.8	0.1
Germany	2.4	3	2.4	2	1.3	0.4
Greece	8	4.8	0.6	−0.9	−1.1	−0.9
Spain	0.8	0.9	1.5	−0.3	−0.8	−1
France	2.4	2.6	2.5	1.4	0.1	−0.2
Ireland	0.5	−0.9	0.3	−1.4	−1.7	−0.2
Italy	1.3	1.8	2	0.7	−0.5	−0.2
The Netherlands	1	2.1	−0.8	−0.6	0.1	0.9
Austria	2.5	2.4	2	1.6	1	0
Portugal	0.8	1.6	−0.1	−0.4	−1	−0.3
Finland	1.7	1.4	1.6	1.3	1	1.9
Euro Zone	2	2.4	1.9	1	0.2	0
Denmark	1.3	2.3	2.4	1.1	0.4	1.1
Sweden	2.7	2.8	1.4	2.2	1	1.2
United Kingdom	4.2	5.4	3.8	2.8	2.4	3.2
United States	3.2	3.1	1	0.2	−1.1	−1

Source: EU Commission, Autumn forecasts, November 2004.

Table 7.5 Long-term real interest rates, 1999–2003

	1999	2000	2001	2002	2003	2004
Belgium	3.7	2.9	2.7	3.4	2.7	2.3
Germany	3.9	3.9	2.9	3.5	3.1	2.5
Greece	4.2	3.2	2.2	1.2	0.9	1.4
Spain	2.5	2.0	2.3	1.4	1.0	1.2
France	4.0	3.6	3.2	3.0	1.9	2.0
Ireland	2.2	0.2	0.9	0.2	0.1	2.0
Italy	3.0	3.0	2.9	2.4	1.5	2.1
The Netherlands	2.6	3.1	−0.1	1.0	1.9	3.1
Austria	4.2	3.6	2.8	3.3	2.9	2.3
Portugal	2.6	2.8	0.8	1.4	0.9	1.9
Finland	3.4	2.5	2.3	2.9	2.8	4.1
Euro zone	3.6	3.3	2.6	2.6	2.0	2.1
Denmark	2.8	2.9	2.8	2.6	2.3	3.4
Sweden	4.4	4.1	2.4	3.3	2.3	3.5
United Kingdom	3.7	4.5	3.7	3.6	3.2	3.7
United States	3.4	2.6	2.2	3.0	1.7	1.7

Source: EU Commission, Autumn forecasts, November 2004.

Indeed, for a small country, tools available to adjust to a negative macroeconomic shock (recession and rise of unemployment) are not of the same essence, and thus of the same effects, than for a large one. Because its economy is largely open, regarding goods and services as well as foreign direct investments and other capital flows fiscal policy will have little effect on domestic demand, since most of its impact will be absorbed through imports.

Hence, for a small open economy, traditional fiscal policy of the Keynesian kind will usually be of little efficiency, whereas all policies that improve the competitiveness of the national economy by lowering production costs of firms located in the domestic economy are relatively more powerful: this may explain why fiscal consolidations in small countries have been found to have 'non-Keynesian' effects (see Giavazzi and Pagano, 1996); it also suggests that tax competition, 'structural reforms' and wage moderation policies will all have very powerful, positive effects for a small open economy, both because exports represent a major fraction of demand to domestic firms and because the elasticity of the supply of external capital – in particular, foreign direct investments – is higher, the smaller and the more open the economy is. In addition, policies that lower production costs in a small economy do not harm domestic demand very much, and they have little incidence on domestic inflation, so that they do not raise real interest rates, as nominal rates in a monetary union tend to be uniform across countries and to be relatively little influenced by the policies of a single, small country.[3]

For large countries, on the contrary, free riding is impossible, and the various policy choices reviewed above tend to be more costly, or even counterproductive. Traditional, Keynesian-style demand-management policies, especially fiscal policies, are more efficient than for a small open economy, because demand spillovers are relatively less. On the other hand, all policies tending to lower production costs are less effective, and they all tend to lead to a lower domestic inflation, which then results in a higher real interest rate, so that they tend to be costly in terms of economic activity and growth. The fate of Germany over the past few years seems to be a perfect illustration of this difficulty of large countries in an economic and monetary union.

This helps explain why small countries may be tempted to free ride on large ones in the face of a common macroeconomic shock. Benefiting from the latter's expansionary policies, they do not bear the costs of them, not in fiscal nor in real interest terms. Furthermore, one should not be surprised that small countries undertake 'virtuous' fiscal consolidations and 'structural reforms' strongly advocated by the European Commission, while the large countries are apparently inherently 'vicious'. The debates, at times polemics, over the SGP reveal just this inescapable divide.

In the rapidly growing literature on international political economy, country size has indeed been emphasized as a major dimension of national strategic choices (Alesina and Spolaore, 2003; Alesina, Spolaore and Warcziac, 2005), though the rationale has often been in terms of optimal country size in the presence of both decentralization (centrifugal) forces – such as the necessity to better adhere to citizens' preferences in the provision of public goods – and centripetal forces – such as economies of scale in administration and fixed costs of governments. In the EU context, this distinction has also been shown to generate a genuine cleavage in terms of strategies for reforms and economic policies, as well as economic performance (Duval and Esmelkov, 2005; Creel and Le Cacheux, 2006; Laurent and Le Cacheux, 2006): in this strand of analyses, the rationale is closer to our analytical framework, the reasoning being squarely in terms of macroeconomic adjustments and policies.

7.4 The model

7.4.1 The economy

Our model is similar in spirit to Uhlig (2002). We have a monetary union with two countries and one central bank, which sets the unions' interest rate. The IS curve, for each of the two countries ($j = 1, 2$), is

$$x_j = -\phi \left(\bar{i} - \pi_j^e \right) + g_j + \gamma \frac{\psi_{-j}}{\psi_j} x_{-j}$$

where x_j is the output gap, π_j^e is expected inflation, and $\bar{i}$ is the union-wide interest rate. g_i is the government's decision variable, and represents government deficit. Our innovation with respect to the standard literature is the term $\gamma \frac{\psi_{-j}}{\psi_j} x_{-j}$, that captures the correlation of output gaps across the union ($-j$ denotes the country other than j), that depends on relative size ($\psi_1 + \psi_2 = 1$ are the weights). We assume that $0 \leq \gamma < 1$.

The supply side is modelled by a standard Phillips curve:

$$\pi_j = \lambda x_j + u_j$$

where u_j is a cost-push supply shock ($E(u_j) = 0$). The IS and the Phillips curve can be derived by a standard sticky-prices model, in the spirit of the Neo-Keynesian literature (Woodford, 2003). Uhlig (2002) shows how to derive this reduced form.

We have two fiscal authorities and a central bank; the objective function of the latter is

$$\max_{\bar{i}} \mathscr{L}_{CB} = -\frac{1}{2}(\alpha \bar{x}^2 + \bar{\pi}^2)$$

where union-wide values are weighted averages: $\bar{x} = \psi_1 x_1 + \psi_2 x_2$ and $\bar{\pi} = \psi_1 \pi_1 + \psi_2 \pi_2$.

The objective function of fiscal authorities

$$\max_{g_j} \mathscr{L}_j = -\frac{1}{2} \left[x_j^2 + \theta (g_j - \varepsilon_j)^2 \right]$$

that assumes national authorities to care about the output gap, but also about deviations of public expenditure from a random target value ε_j, that are weighted by θ. In fact, on average ($E(\varepsilon_j) = 0$), the government values a balanced budget, $g_j = 0$. A positive shock ε_j represents the additional slack that may be given by unexpected revenues, or unforeseen spending needs; conversely, a negative value of ε_j captures the *ex ante* unexpected need to tighten fiscal policy.

The sequence of events is standard:

- the public forms inflation expectations π_j^e, that are set rationally;
- shocks ε_j and u_j are drawn;

- fiscal authorities choose g_j;
- the monetary authority chooses $\bar{i}$.

7.4.2 The central bank's problem

The model is solved backwards, starting from the central bank problem. If we take union-wide averages, the output gap equation becomes

$$\bar{x} = \psi_1 x_1 + \psi_2 x_2 = -\phi(\bar{i} - \bar{\pi}^e) + \bar{g} + \gamma\bar{x}$$

$$\Rightarrow \bar{x} = \frac{\bar{g} - \phi(\bar{i} - \bar{\pi}^e)}{1 - \gamma}$$

The programme of the central bank is

$$\max_{\bar{i}} \mathscr{L}_{CB} = -\frac{1}{2}(\alpha\bar{x}^2 + \bar{\pi}^2)$$

$$s.t.$$

$$\bar{x} = \frac{\bar{g} - \phi(\bar{i} - \bar{\pi}^e)}{1 - \gamma}$$

$$\bar{\pi} = \lambda\bar{x} + \bar{u}$$

Maximizing with respect to $\bar{i}$ gives

$$\bar{i} = \frac{(\phi\bar{\pi}^e + \bar{g})}{\phi} + \frac{(1 - \gamma)\bar{u}\lambda}{\phi(\alpha + \lambda^2)};$$

substituting back into the equation for the output gap, we obtain

$$\bar{x} = -\frac{\bar{u}\lambda}{(\alpha + \lambda^2)} = -\lambda q\bar{u}$$

where $q \equiv (\lambda^2 + \alpha)^{-1}$. Then, it is straightforward to compute

$$\bar{\pi} = \lambda\bar{x} + \bar{u} = -\frac{\bar{u}\lambda}{(\alpha + \lambda^2)}\lambda + \bar{u}$$

$$= \alpha q\bar{u}$$

The interest rate rule is derived by substituting the value for inflation, and by noticing that $\bar{\pi}^e = E(\bar{\pi}) = \alpha q E(\bar{u}) = 0$. We can then obtain

$$\bar{i} = \frac{\bar{g}}{\phi} + \frac{(1 - \gamma)q\lambda}{\phi}\bar{u}.$$

Notice that, by moving after the governments, the central bank can adjust to their policies, and use the interest rate to attain its preferred inflation and output gap objective. As a consequence, the equilibrium output gap and inflation rates only depend on the cost-push shock; the interest rate is the only variable that depends on average deficit, precisely because it is set in order to undo the behaviour of fiscal authorities. In this model there is no role for fiscal policy in the union as a whole. We chose this setting to better emphasize our results.

7.4.3 The fiscal authorities

Proceeding backwards, we can analyse the fiscal authorities problem. The two governments have to solve the following programme:

$$\max_{g_j} \mathscr{L}_j = -\frac{1}{2}\left[x_j^2 + \theta(g_j - \varepsilon_j)^2\right]$$

s.t.

$$x_j = -\phi\left(\bar{i} - \pi_j^e\right) + g_j + \gamma\frac{\psi_{-j}}{\psi_j}x_{-j}+$$

$$\phi\bar{i} = \psi_1 g_1 + \psi_2 g_2 + (1 - \gamma)q\lambda\bar{u}$$

Take country one (country two is symmetric). The unconstrained maximization problem can be written as

$$\mathscr{L}_1 = -\frac{1}{2}(A_1 + \psi_2 g_1)^2 - \frac{1}{2}\theta(g_1 - \varepsilon_1)^2$$

where $A_1 \equiv -\psi_2 g_2 - (1 - \gamma)q\lambda\bar{u} + \phi\pi_1^e + \frac{\gamma\psi_2}{\psi_1}x_2$ collects all terms not depending on g_1. The First order condition (FOC) is

$$\frac{\partial L_1}{\partial g_1} = \theta\varepsilon_1 - \psi_2 A_1 - g_1(\psi_2^2 + \theta) = 0$$

that yields

$$g_1 = \frac{\theta\varepsilon_1 - \psi_2 A_1}{(\psi_2^2 + \theta)} = \frac{\theta\varepsilon_1 + \psi_2\left(\psi_2 g_2 + (1 - \gamma)q\lambda\bar{u} - \phi\pi_1^e - \gamma\frac{\psi_2}{\psi_1}x_2\right)}{(\psi_2^2 + \theta)}.$$

Thus, fiscal policy is positively correlated with own fiscal shocks, as well as with supply shocks; this sensitivity increases with the size of the country (a lower weight of the other member, ψ_2). Reactivity to the fiscal policy of the other members of the union, though positive, is positively related to $\psi_2 = 1 - \psi_1$, thus negatively correlated to own size.

Both fiscal policy and the interest rate are linear in the shocks, and thus inflation rates in individual countries will be given by (zero mean) deviations from the union average. As a consequence,

$$\pi_j^e = \bar{\pi}^e = 0.$$

Repeating the same steps for country 2, we obtain the following system:

$$g_1 = \frac{\theta\varepsilon_1 - (1 - \psi_1)\left(-(1 - \psi_1)g_2 - (1 - \gamma)q\lambda\bar{u} + \gamma\frac{1-\psi_1}{\psi_1}x_2\right)}{(1 - \psi_1)^2 + \theta}$$

$$g_2 = \frac{\theta\varepsilon_2 - \psi_1\left(-\psi_1 g_1 - (1 - \gamma)q\lambda\bar{u} + \gamma\frac{\psi_1}{1-\psi_1}x_1\right)}{\psi_1^2 + \theta} \tag{7.1}$$

$$x_1 = (1 - \psi_1)(g_1 - g_2) - (1 - \gamma)q\lambda\bar{u} + \gamma\frac{1 - \psi_1}{\psi_1}x_2$$

$$x_2 = \psi_1(g_2 - g_1) - (1 - \gamma)q\lambda\bar{u} + \gamma\frac{\psi_1}{1 - \psi_1}x_1$$

The solution to this system gives the equilibrium values of public expenditure (g_1 and g_2) and output gap (x_1 and x_2) as linear functions of demand and supply shocks. We focus on one country, the other being symmetrical, and we obtain the following expression for g_1:

$$
\begin{aligned}
g_1 &= \frac{\psi_1^2 + \theta(\gamma + 1)}{1 + \theta(\gamma + 1) - 2\psi_1(1 - \psi_1)}\varepsilon_1 \\
&\quad + \frac{(1 - \psi_1)^2}{1 + \theta(\gamma + 1) - 2\psi_1(1 - \psi_1)}\varepsilon_2 \\
&\quad + \frac{(1 - \psi_1)\left((\psi_1(1 - \gamma) + \gamma)\theta + \psi_1^2\right)}{\psi_1\theta\left(1 + \theta(\gamma + 1) - 2\psi_1(1 - \psi_1)\right)}q\lambda\bar{u} \\
&= A_{\varepsilon_1}\varepsilon_1 + A_{\varepsilon_2}\varepsilon_2 + A_u\bar{u}
\end{aligned}
$$

The sign of the reaction coefficients is unambiguous:

$$A_{\varepsilon_1} = \frac{\psi_1^2 + \theta(\gamma + 1)}{1 + \theta(\gamma + 1) - 2\psi_1(1 - \psi_1)} > 0$$

$$A_{\varepsilon_2} = \frac{(1 - \psi_1)^2}{1 + \theta(\gamma + 1) - 2\psi_1(1 - \psi_1)} > 0$$

$$A_u = \frac{(1 - \psi_1)\left((\psi_1(1 - \gamma) + \gamma)\theta + \psi_1^2\right)}{\psi_1\theta\left(1 + \theta(\gamma + 1) - 2\psi_1(1 - \psi_1)\right)}q\lambda > 0$$

This is intuitive in what concerns fiscal disturbances: fiscal policy reacts positively to the additional slack given by ε. Interestingly,

$$A_{\varepsilon_2} > A_{\varepsilon_1} \quad \Leftrightarrow \quad 1 > 2\psi_1 + \theta(\gamma + 1),$$

which means that for ψ_1 (i.e. country size) small enough, the country may react more to the shock hitting the partner than to its own. The spillover effects (γ) mitigate this feature of the model.

It is, on the other hand, interesting to notice that $A_u > 0$. The reason is that fiscal authorities rationally forecast a tightening of monetary policy in response to cost-push shocks, and hence react by increasing their deficit in order to compensate for the restrictive effect of $\bar{i}$ on the output gap (a result already found by Alesina and Tabellini, 1987). In fact, each country attempts to free ride on the others (Uhlig, 2002), and to increase its own level of activity.

7.4.4 Country size and optimal fiscal policy

We are now in a position to look into the main question of this chapter. The relationship between country size and fiscal policy is captured by $\frac{\partial A_{\varepsilon j}}{\partial \psi_1}$ ($j = 1, 2$), that we can easily sign as follows:

$$
\begin{aligned}
\frac{\partial A_{\varepsilon_1}}{\partial \psi_1} &= \frac{2(1 - \psi_1)(\psi_1 + \theta(\gamma + 1))}{(1 + \theta(\gamma + 1) - 2\psi_1(1 - \psi_1))^2} > 0 \\
\frac{\partial A_{\varepsilon_2}}{\partial \psi_1} &= -\frac{2(1 - \psi_1)(\theta(\gamma + 1) + \psi_1)}{(1 + \theta(\gamma + 1) - 2\psi_1(1 - \psi_1))^2} < 0
\end{aligned}
\tag{7.2}
$$

Thus, the simple model we presented delivers the result we argued for: the reaction of fiscal policy to shocks depends positively on country size: the optimal response to fiscal shocks of larger countries relies more on fiscal policy. Intuitively, the weight of external factors in the determination of the output gap is lower for larger countries that, as a consequence, have to rely more heavily on their own policy in order to deal with shocks. The same logic explains why large countries react less to shocks hitting their partners.

Notice furthermore that $\lim_{\psi_1 \to 1} A_u = \lim_{\psi_1 \to 1} A_{\varepsilon_2} = 0$, and $\lim_{\psi_1 \to 1} g_1 = \varepsilon_1$. When the union tends to a single country (and a single fiscal authority), we converge to a perfect division of labour, with the central bank that takes care of supply shocks u, while fiscal policy takes care of fiscal shocks ε. In fact, if there is only one country, the reaction of monetary policy to the deficit will be fully internalized by the fiscal authority, and there will be no incentive for attempting to free ride.

Finally, we need to analyse the role of the parameter γ, that captures the importance of spillovers in the output gap equation. In fact, the existence of spillovers is not necessary to establish our main result, as in equation (7.2) we have $\frac{\partial A_{\varepsilon_1}}{\partial \psi_1} > 0$ even when $\gamma = 0$. Thus, it is not spillovers *per se*, but rather the complementarity between fiscal policies in the union that yields our results. Nevertheless, the spillover amplifies this effect, as

$$
\begin{aligned}
\frac{\partial A_{\varepsilon_1}}{\partial \gamma} &= \theta \frac{1 - \psi_1(2 - \psi_1)}{(1 + \theta(\gamma + 1) - 2\psi_1(1 - \psi_1))^2} > 0 \\
\frac{\partial A_{\varepsilon_2}}{\partial \gamma} &= -\frac{(1 - \psi_1)^2 \theta}{(1 + \theta(\gamma + 1) - 2\psi_1(1 - \psi_1))^2} < 0
\end{aligned}
$$

We can derive the output gap, using the system (7.1) and some algebraic manipulation:

$$x_1 = \frac{(1 - \psi_1)\theta}{(1 + \theta(\gamma + 1) - 2\psi_1(1 - \psi_1))}(\varepsilon_1 - \varepsilon_2)$$
$$- \frac{\psi_1\theta(1 - \gamma) + \psi_1^2 + \gamma\theta}{\psi_1(1 + \theta(\gamma + 1) - 2\psi_1(1 - \psi_1))}q\lambda\bar{u}$$

The first term is positive if $\varepsilon_1 > \varepsilon_2$, as it is to be expected (more slack for fiscal policy yields higher deficit and higher positive output gap). What is interesting is that, as long as $\theta(\gamma + 1) > 1$, this positive effect is decreasing with country size:

$$\theta(\gamma + 1) > 1 \Rightarrow \frac{\partial\left(\frac{(1 - \psi_1)\theta}{(1 + \theta(\gamma + 1) - 2\psi_1(1 - \psi_1))}\right)}{\partial\psi_1}$$
$$= \theta\frac{2\psi_1(\psi_1 - 2) - \theta(\gamma + 1) + 1}{(1 + \theta(\gamma + 1) - 2\psi_1(1 - \psi_1))^2} < 0.$$

This result is in line with our previous finding: small countries are more able to exploit the slack given by fiscal shocks than large countries; this happens if sufficient weight is given to budget discipline (high θ) and/or if the externality γ is large enough. For large ψ_1 the effect is even more evident.

The effect of country size on the supply shock 'multiplier' is instead impossible to sign. In this respect, the effect of γ becomes crucial. Assuming $\theta = 1$, we can plot (Figure 7.1) the value of the multiplier for different values of γ. Except for the solid line that corresponds to $\gamma = 0$, the shape of the lines is similar:

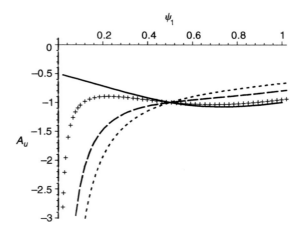

Figure 7.1 Supply shock multiplier for $\theta = 1$ and different values of γ ($\gamma = 0$, solid line; $\gamma = 0.1$, crosses; $\gamma = 0.5$; dashes; $\gamma = 0.99$, dots).

an increase in country size reduces the absolute value of the supply shock multiplier. Furthermore, the larger γ, the larger the change of the multiplier.

This admittedly simple model, in which countries interact strategically in deciding their deficit level, shows how country size and the type of shock hitting the economy affect the reaction of fiscal authorities. Demand shocks require a more important reaction of larger countries, and the existence of demand spillovers emphasizes this result.

7.5 Conclusion and policy implications

This chapter suggests that the present institutional design of the EU regarding macroeconomic policies might not be suited to allow for high levels of growth and foster integration and solidarity between member states involved in the EMU. The major reason for this unfitness could be that the criterion of size (determining economic constraints and incentives) of the different yet interdependent countries, while prominent in the new context created by the Eastward enlargement of May 2004, has never been taken into account by European officials and national governments while implementing and enforcing the 'rules of the game' of the EU. The provisions regarding economic governance contained in Part III of the project of Constitutional Treaty submitted to the approval of the member states is unfortunately no exception to this failure. Time should thus come to thoroughly discuss the EMU rules on the basis of the size criteria, starting with the SGP. Unfortunately, also, the re-interpretation of the Pact decided upon at the Brussels Council meeting of 23 March 2005, although it may end up introducing more judgement and hence more 'political' reasoning in the implementation of fiscal rules, has not taken this criterion explicitly into account.

Notes

1 Research collaboration with economists of OFCE, especially Jean-Paul Fitoussi, Jérôme Creel and Eloi Laurent, as well as long-standing exchanges with members of the GOVECOR research network have been important in feeding our reflection. We also thank Anton Granik for comments and suggestions.
2 See also Creel and Le Cacheux in this volume.
3 The notion of 'small, open economy' also refers to the idea that it has no influence on its environment, therefore is a 'price taker' and, in game theory terms, chooses strategies without caring about possible reactions or retaliation from partners. Our arguments are also somewhat reminiscent of, though different from the well known result of trade theory, namely that small countries gain from a unilateral tariff reduction, whereas larger countries are likely to lose.

References

Alesina, A. and Spolaore, E. (2003), *The Size of Nations*, Cambridge, MA: MIT Press.
Alesina, A. and Tabellini, G. (1987), 'Rules and discretion with non-coordinated monetary and fiscal policies', *Economic Inquiry*, 25: 619–30.

Alesina, A., Spolaore, E. and Warcziarg, R. (2005), 'Trade, growth and the size of countries', in P. Aghion and S. Durlauf (eds), *Handbook of Economic Growth*, Amsterdam: North Holland, pp. 1499–542.

Creel, J., Latreille, T. and Le Cacheux, J. (2002), 'Le Pacte de stabilité et les politiques budgétaires dans l'Union européenne', *Revue de l'OFCE*, Hors série, mars.

Duval, R. and Elmeskov, J. (2005), 'The effects of EMU on structural reforms in labour and product markets', OECD Economics Department Working Paper no. 438.

Fitoussi, J.-P. (2002), *La règle et le choix – De la souveraineté économique en Europe. Coll. La République des idées*, Paris: Seuil.

Fitoussi, J.-P. and Le Cacheux, J. (eds) (2003), *Rapport sur l'état de l'Union européenne 2004*, Paris: Fayard and Presses de Sciences Po.

—— (eds) (2005), *L'état de l'Union européenne 2005*, Paris: Fayard and Presses de Sciences Po.

Giavazzi, F. and Pagano, M. (1996), 'Non-Keynesian effects of fiscal policy changes: international evidence and the Swedish experience', NBER Working Paper no. 2082.

Laurent, E. and Le Cacheux, J. (2004), 'L'Europe boucles d'or: trois maximes pour sortir d'une impasse', *Lettre de l'OFCE*, 246.

—— (2006), 'Integrity and efficiency in the EU: the case against the European Economic Constitution', Center for European Studies, Harvard University, CES Working Paper no. 130

Le Cacheux, J. (2000), 'Les dangers de la concurrence fiscale et sociale en Europe', in Questions européennes, *Les Rapports du CAE*, 27.

—— (2005), 'Politiques de croissance en Europe: un problème d'action collective', *Revue Économique*, May 2005, 56(3): 705–13.

Lucas, R. E. Jr (2003), 'Macroeconomic priorities', *American Economic Review*, 93(1): 1–14.

OECD (1998), *Harmful Tax Competition: An Emerging Global Issue*, Paris: Organization for Economic Cooperation and Development.

OFCE (1999), 'Etude sur la concurrence fiscale en Europe', in Marini (Rapp.) 'La concurrence fiscale en Europe: une contribution au débat', *Les Rapport du Sénat*, no. 483, Paris. http://www.senat.fr/rap/r98-483/r98-483.html

Olson, M. (1965), *The Logic of Collective Action*, Cambridge, MA: Harvard University Press.

Sapir, A., Aghion, P., Bertola, G., Hellwig, M., Pisani-Ferry, J., Rosati, D., Vinals J. and Wallace H. (2004), *An agenda for a growing Europe -The Sapir Report*, Oxford: Oxford University Press.

Uhlig, H. (2002), 'One money, but many fiscal policies in Europe: what are the consequences?', CEPR Discussion Paper no. 3296.

8   Euro bonds

In search of financial spillovers[1]

S. Schiavo

8.1   Introduction

This paper investigates the empirical relevance of *negative financial spillovers* among EMU member countries. The integration of national bond markets that resulted from the inception of the euro and the consequent elimination of exchange rate risk has rendered securities issued by different EMU governments closer substitute. In a recent survey on financial integration in the euro area, Baele *et al.* (2004) show that in the last few years movements in government bond yields are increasingly explained by the behaviour of the benchmark asset. Out of finance jargon, one can interpret this as evidence that security returns are now driven more by international factors and less by purely domestic news. Building on this notion, the financial spillovers hypothesis questions the ability of financial markets to correctly price risk and to discriminate among different issuers. More in detail, this hypothesis postulates a link between the fiscal imbalances run by each government in the euro zone and the borrowing costs faced by all other countries participating in the currency area. Such an externality in turn entails a redistribution of costs through the common monetary policy and results in crowding out of productive investments in economies where the interest rate would otherwise be lower.

The negative financial spillover hypothesis is often regarded as one of the (few) theoretical foundations of the SGP: yet, as it will become apparent below, economic theory does not establish a clear-cut link between fiscal variables and the rate of interest.

Beside the relevance for European economic policy – the recent debate about the opportunity and costs of having binding fiscal rules witnesses for that – the topic is also interesting on purely academic grounds, as it rests on two broader unresolved issues in modern macroeconomics: the impact of the fiscal stance on interest rates, and whether the latter are determined by stock or by flow variables. The first contribution to the existing literature therefore consists on an analysis of different classes of models that reach opposite conclusions on both the aforementioned issues. Hence, we show that – contrary to what is usually claimed – theory offers only limited support to the negative financial spillover hypothesis.

Despite the fact that the issue remains an empirical question, the phenomenon has never been tested explicitly so far. This represents the second contribution of the paper. In particular, the presence and relevance of spillover effects is investigated from different angles and using a wide array of techniques.

The paper is organized as follows: Section 8.2 contextualizes the financial spillover hypothesis in the recent debate over fiscal rules and the SGP. Section 8.3 shows that economic theory offers little guidance as not only different models present different implications, but the same model may lead to opposite conclusions when a single assumption is modified. The paper then takes a step backwards and Section 8.4 analyses German unification as an episode where spillovers from fiscal variables to bond yields may have occurred. Moving to more formal empirical analysis, Section 8.5 investigates the impact of a European-wide fiscal indicator on the average yield on government bonds, while Section 8.6 narrows the focus on a subset of EMU member countries and estimates the effect of fiscal variables on domestic and foreign interest rates. Section 8.7 concludes.

8.2 Negative financial spillovers and the SGP

The whole process of European integration is based not only on the belief that fiscal discipline is necessary for the correct functioning of a monetary union, but also on the conviction that such discipline must be imposed onto member states from above (i.e. from European institutions). By joining a monetary union, in fact, countries are thought to incur a bias towards excessive deficit since the common monetary policy -tailored to serve the 'representative country' – redistributes costs onto all economies, thus generating an incentive to free ride (Afonso and Strauch, 2004: 6). Moreover, easier access to international markets (granted by the EMU) reduces the financial constraint on national governments and thus spurs fiscal laxity.

Three sets of mechanisms have been devised to limit this perverse outcome: the first aims at furnishing the ECB with the highest degree of independence and credibility, the second limits the ability of governments to run fiscal deficits, the third explicitly states that no co-responsibility exists among member states with respect to national debts (no-bail-out clause). To gain some insight, assess the relevance of the hypotheses formulated to support and rationalize the Pact, and weight pros and cons of such an institutional framework, it is useful to analyse the reasons that lead to the creation of the SGP.

In the road towards the single currency, at the beginning of the 1990s, European countries decided to give themselves a set of conditions to fulfil before joining the monetary union. This was done in order to make the monetary reform as smooth as possible. As is well known, the famous Maastricht criteria required a certain degree of convergence in terms of inflation and interest rates; moreover, candidate countries were committed to adopt measures of fiscal consolidation apt to assure low-budget deficits and decreasing debt burdens. On the basis of the conditions contained in the Maastricht Treaty, in May 1998 the European Council admitted 11 countries to join the EMU.

The rationale behind these rules was to give a solid fiscal backing to the newly established single currency, limit pressures to monetize fiscal imbalances on the ECB, and give the latter a jump start in terms of anti-inflationary credibility. The Maastricht Treaty, however, only served to judge potential entrants at one moment in time while having no power to restrain future fiscal stances. Arguably, once admitted, a government could start cumulating fiscal deficits, piling up public debt and so on and so forth.

The subsequent debate generated the SGP, which basically gives a permanent status to the fiscal rules contained in the Maastricht Treaty. This agreement (much more concerned with stability than with growth) establishes an institutional framework whereby member countries are required to achieve balanced or surplus budgets on average over the business cycle, while imposing an upper limit to deficits (no larger than 3% of GDP) in bad years. This ceiling to the deficit/GDP ratio is not binding in the (rather unlikely) event of a downturn in real GDP larger than 2%. All the criticisms of the SGP directly or indirectly question its foundations and the reasons that lead to its creation. Many of the contributions to the debate, however, fail to distinguish between two separate issues: the need for *a pact* and the rationale behind *this Pact*.

In one of the contributions contained in the famous Delors Report, Lamfalussy (1989) suggests that default in one country may force other members to intervene since part of the defaulted debt would be held by their citizens. However, even when no default occurs, in a deeply integrated market negative financial spillovers can take place. In this case, crowding out of more useful/profitable investments results in countries where the interest rate would otherwise be lower.

The basic question is then whether markets are able to discriminate among different issuers. Evidence from US states and Canadian provinces suggests this is indeed the case (see, among others, Bayoumi *et al.*, 1993; Cheung, 1996).[2] On the other hand, Thygesen (1999) reports that, in the mid-1990s, the premium paid by Italian 10-year government bonds over German *Bunds* narrowed to 30 basis points well ahead of debt reduction.

Restoy (1996) claims that three conditions have to hold for markets to be efficient in pricing risk: (i) free capital mobility, (ii) availability of complete and up-to-date information about member countries' public finance, (iii) credibility of the no-bail-out clause. Bayoumi *et al.* (1993) add a fourth condition, that is, (iv) resiliency of the financial system to potential failure of a large borrower.

Tamborini (2002) correctly points out that for fiscal rules to be sensible one needs to assume fiscal stimuli to be expansionary in the home country and contractionary abroad. Otherwise, there is incentive neither to run a budget deficit nor to limit this ability. In his paper, there exist two separate channels through which public spending in one country spills over: a trade channel linking domestic to foreign aggregate demand and production, and a financial channel working via the impact of budget deficits on the common interest and exchange rate. The strength of this latter channel depends crucially on the elasticity of aggregate demand to changes in the interest rate and on money/bond substitutability, that is, the elasticity of money demand to changes in the interest rate. When the latter is low, a larger movement in the interest rate is required to accommodate the excess demand of money generated by increased production (in turn due to the fiscal expansion). Deeper financial markets integration spurred by the introduction of the single currency should favour money/bond substitutability and hence reduce the strength of this financial channel.

Artis and Winkler (1999) as well identify three ways through which an increase in the interest rate can affect the real economy: crowding out of private investments, appreciation of the exchange rate and consequent decrease of exports, contagion in presence of a crisis. Buiter *et al.* (1993) elaborate on this contagion effect, suggesting that to avoid a credit crunch the ECB would need to inject liquidity into the system, thus raising inflation expectations. This in turn would severely damage the goal of price stability. From an empirical point of view, this kind of spillovers working through money demand and the common monetary policy of the ECB should have an impact mainly on short-term rates, that is, on monetary policy instruments.

Kenen (1995) stresses an absorption effect that is more relevant to our work: by issuing more debt, each country runs the risk of saturating the market by absorbing a large share of European saving.[3] Such demand/supply imbalances would result in a lower price (higher interest rate) for bonds. Again, this channel rests on the assumption that markets do not fully discriminate among different issuers, that is, that a monetary union makes bonds of different countries (almost) perfect substitutes. If this is not the case, this supply effect would be limited by the fact that securities issued by different countries span separate segments of the bond market; increased supply of one bond, then, would only raise the interest rate paid in that particular segment, with low or no repercusions on other 'goods'. For this 'loanable funds' hypothesis to work we need an additional condition to hold; namely, that after the introduction of a single currency (and the subsequent elimination of exchange rate risk) European financial markets have become so integrated that they represent a single pool of saving. At this point it is worth noting that according to Hartman *et al.* (2003) quantity based indicators show that a significant home bias still remains in European portfolios. The resulting segmentation in asset markets makes Kenen's hypothesis about financial spillovers less likely.

Fiscal events in one country should affect bond yields at the maturity for which the new issue has occurred. Hence, if Italian deficit is financed by means of 10-year bonds, yields on long-term bonds for all other countries should go up. If fiscal imbalances are covered by a mixture of debt instruments spanning the entire maturity spectrum, then the entire yield curve should shift upwards.

The present discussion has placed the issue of negative financial spillovers within the broader frame of the SGP and has shown that it represents one of the main justifications for having binding fiscal rules. In the next section we will go beyond this policy-oriented approach with the aim of investigating whether economic theory offers any support to the idea that a loose fiscal stance in one country may push upwards the world rate of interest.

8.3 The theoretical background

The debate about the existence and the relevance of negative financial spillovers rests on two broader theoretical issues in modern macroeconomics: whether fiscal policy has any impact on interest rates and whether the latter are determined by stock or flow variables. This section presents an overview of selected contributions that – far from constituting a comprehensive review of the endless literature on the topic – serves the purpose of providing us with a theoretical framework for subsequent analysis and with a context for our discussion.

All models presented here (with the exception of Branson, 1988) assume solvency is not at stake: therefore, changes in bond yields do not affect debt sustainability. The reason for so doing is multifaceted: first of all, default should be taken care of by the no-bail-out clause and has in principle little to do with the SGP. On a more practical ground, given current credit ratings the likelihood of default is extremely limited for all EMU member countries. Therefore, we will not cover the part of the literature that deals with debt repudiation and default and focus our attention on negative financial spillovers in their narrow meaning, that is, public spending resulting in crowding out of private expenditure via its effect on the common interest rate.

This section presents a taxonomy based on the distinction between models where the stock of government debt matters and models emphasizing the role of flow variables (budget deficits). We have chosen to concentrate on works that address the role of fiscal policy in an open economy with a fixed exchange rate regime, as this is the natural benchmark for EMU member countries. As will become apparent, not always clear-cut results emerge and different model specifications lead to different results. Thus, we will see under which conditions the theory predicts fiscal policy to have international spillover effects, in particular by affecting the world interest rate.

8.3.1 Flow models

We open our review with the classic Mundell–Fleming (MF) framework that has for long constituted the main workhorse of open economy macroeconomics.[4] Despite its limitations, among which there are the lack of microfoundations and its failure to distinguish among government consumption and investment (which makes it ill-suited to study the effects of fiscal policy (Obstfeld and Rogoff, 1996: 700)), the MF model is still regarded as a benchmark reference among professionals and academics. The MF framework postulates a simple income–expenditure Keynesian model with interest-bearing public bonds, fixed prices and demand-determined output. One consequence of the lack of any forward-looking behaviour is that no attention is given to intertemporal budget constraints and therefore to sustainability issues: hence, there is no role for stock variables.

As is often the case for open economy macroeconomic models, a distinction is drawn between the small country case and the fully-fledged two-country model.

The former assumes an economic system too small to affect world markets, so that prices and the interest rates are taken as given: fiscal policy then has no chance to impact on the these variables. This feature is not peculiar to the MF framework but rather spans the whole literature, irrespective of other basic assumptions: in the rest of the section therefore we will focus only on two-country versions of all models presented.

In the MF model, a debt-financed increase in public spending bids the interest rate up independently of the direction of output changes (which can be positive or negative depending on the effect of the interest rate on world demand for domestic and foreign products).

The second class of models consists of the neoclassical (intertemporal) ones:[5] here, a representative agent with infinite horizon and perfect foresight maximizes utility subject to a budget constraint. Perfect credit markets allow households to borrow and lend at the same interest rate as the government, which in turn levies lump-sum taxes and engages in public expenditures whose path is exogenously given. Under this set of strict conditions the interest rate, investment and consumption are invariant with respect to the way the government finances its expenditures: all that matters is the present value of government spending.[6] This result easily translates into an open economy framework: yet, while the irrelevance of the timing of taxes does not depend on size, size does matter for the timing of public expenditure G_t. Since the world economy cannot offset shifts of G_t towards, say, the present by borrowing and lending (even though the present value of the infinite stream of government spending does not change), such a shift will put upward pressure on the interest rate as in the traditional Keynesian model.

So far the government has not played any active role: by explicitly introducing government spending as a choice variable subject to an intertemporal budget constraint, one can actually study the effect of fiscal policy. Frenkel and Razin (1992) stress that there are two channels though which G_t influences the equilibrium of the model: the absorption of resources that affects consumption and wealth, and the consumption tilting that depends on the intra- and intertemporal complementarity/substitutability between public and private consumption. Assuming that G_t enters the utility function separately, one gets an intertemporal marginal rate of substitution independent of government spending and therefore shuts the second channel.

The absorption effect may produce different results according to the model setup: in case of a temporary increase in government spending the interest rate goes up as there is an excess demand for current goods; on the other hand, a permanent shift in G_t may lead to lower or higher interest rates depending on the marginal saving propensities of domestic versus foreign agents.

When we incorporate into the picture the distinction between tradeable and non-tradeable goods, we get that the effects of government spending depend on two aspects: the intertemporal allocation of public versus private consumption and their commodity composition. In particular, if public expenditures are biased towards non-tradeables (as one would expect), the effects on the interest rate depend on the marginal saving propensities of the government and households, plus on the intertemporal elasticity of substitution of the latter.

Another way to break Ricardian equivalence is introduced by the third 'family' presented here: overlapping generation (OG) models *à la* Diamond (1965) and Blanchard (1985). The presence of individuals characterized by a finite horizon together with an infinitely lived society results in households using a different interest rate than the government to discount future events: therefore, budget deficits do have a wealth effect. Frenkel and Razin (1992, chapter 11) present a two-period, two-country OG model where a budget deficit results from a decrease in taxes, holding the path of G_t given. As anticipated, in this setup the timing of taxes does have an effect on the world interest rate, but while current deficits undoubtedly push it up, the impact of current and future deficits is less clear-cut and depends on the comparison between the public and private saving propensities.

By introducing a third period into the model it is possible to study the impact of a budget deficit on the term structure of interest rates. Frenkel and Razin show that as long as the present value of government spending is held constant, expected future tax cuts increase the interest rate in the period of the deficit, while the short-term (current) rate of interest will be affected only if domestic and foreign marginal saving propensities are different. Shifting now to the effect of changes in government spending, transitory variations in current G_t bid up the interest rate along the entire maturity spectrum, while in the case of both transitory and permanent expected future changes, the direction of the interest rate shift depends once again on marginal saving propensities.

The last part of this section is dedicated to the new standard model in open economy macroeconomics, namely the Obstfeld and Rogoff (1996) (OR) framework. This is basically a sticky-price intertemporal model that combines Keynesian features into a fully microfounded framework based on utility maximization. In the simplest case, government expenditure is considered pure waste (it affects neither productivity nor private utility) and displays no home-bias. While a temporary rise in G_t has no effect on the interest rate, a permanent rise in world government spending actually reduces the short-term interest rates, thus reaching the opposite conclusion to the older MF model.[7] The authors, however, warn that different ways to model public expenditure would lead to different predictions about the interest rate. Corsetti and Pesenti (2001), for instance, assume that government spending enters households' utility function and obtains the standard MF result whereby a fiscal expansion (domestic or foreign) bids up the world interest rate.

8.3.2 Stock models

There are a number of models predicting an active role for the stock of government debt: the first and foremost example that comes to mind is portfolio models, where asset demand for bonds results from the maximization of a utility function subject to a wealth constraint. Tamborini (1997) provides an example referred to EMU member countries: investors allocate their wealth among two bonds issued by different countries in order to maximize an exponential utility function with constant absolute risk aversion. Despite securities having symmetric statistical properties, Tamborini (1997) shows that in presence of different stocks of outstanding debt, an interest rate differential may develop as a result of the *relative supply effect* typical of portfolio analysis. This kind of model, however, determines interest-rate differentials, not their absolute values and therefore is ill-suited to guide our empirical analysis.

Branson (1988) addresses the shift in the external position that characterized the United States in the 1980s (and then Germany after unification): in so doing, the author presents a two-country 'fundamental' model in the Keynesian tradition where the domestic interest rate is determined via uncovered interest parity, adjusted by a risk premium. The latter depends on the relative size of domestic to foreign debt and so any fiscal deficit, by adding to the outstanding stock of debt, modifies the risk premium and hence the interest rate. Branson (1988) considers a floating exchange-rate regime and the impact of foreign deficits on the domestic interest rate depends on the sensitivity of the current account to the exchange rate. As this would be zero in the case of a monetary union, it is not clear whether the specification would produce the same outcome with a different exchange-rate regime.

Branson (1988) introduces for the first time default risk into the picture: when that is taken into consideration, it is clear that the stock of debt matters. As we have anticipated above, however, credit risk will not be considered here on the ground that it is extremely unlikely that any European country defaults on its debt. Moreover, unless a country nosedives into debt, markets will not impose severe restrictions on its borrowing ability (including risk premia on bond yields).[8] As will become apparent by the rest of this brief literature review, however, there exists models in which default is not taken into consideration, yet the stock of debt does play a role of some sort.

First of all, Barro (1989) notes that, in open economy, invariance of equilibrium with respect to initial debt B_0 vanishes if foreigners hold part of it. This is because they are not subject to future taxes levied to pay back initial debt, which therefore represents a free lunch for them. A related issue is the so-called *transfer problem*: in a neoclassic intertemporal model, initial debt positions (stocks) may affect the equilibrium world interest rate if the two countries display different marginal saving propensities. Yet this example holds the stock of initial world debt fixed and deals just with a redistribution of shares, so there is no role for an active policy.

In the two-country OG model presented in Frenkel and Razin (1992, chapter 11), higher levels of past public expenditure means a larger stock of initial debt for the current generation. The result is reminiscent of the transfer problem and the effect on the interest rate depends on the comparison between domestic and foreign marginal propensity to save.

Within the OG framework, Obstfeld and Rogoff (1996, chapter 3) describe a government that, starting from a zero net asset position, issues a given amount of debt and distributes it to the current old. Current and future young are then subject to taxes in order to keep the ratio of debt to the labour force constant. Savers must now acquire government debt as well as productive capital, with the result that the steady state capital stock will be lower (and the interest rate higher) than without debt.

Leith and Wren-Lewis (2001) introduce an OG structure in a new Keynesian open economy model *à la* Obstfeld and Rogoff (1996). Since consumers are not infinitely lived, the rate of interest is different from their rate of time preference and it will be affected by the outstanding stock of government debt, which produces wealth effects.

In a recent contribution, Beetsma and Vermeylen (2005) present another OG model where – after monetary unification – countries exert interest-rate externalities on each other. The paper concentrates on the supply side of the public debt and makes the assumption that debt of all members in a monetary union is perfectly substitutable and the bond yields become perfectly correlated. This in turn increases the risk of the investors' portfolio, who therefore require a higher return. Two main results are of interest for us: first, the relative importance of interest-rate externalities depends on relative debt levels; second, while the average expected real return increases as a result of monetary unification, individual countries may experience a fall in the cost of finance.

Our review of flow models ended by noting that different ways to model government expenditure may lead to very different results. An interesting example is the paper by Aoki and Leijonhufvud (1987), where the authors present a characterization of investment whereby the return on capital (defined as the present value of the income stream resulting from the investment) depends on the stock of capital inherited from the past as well as on the rate of accumulation of new machinery. This is because a higher rate of investment and a larger stock of capital generate an increase of future production, which in turn implies an increase in future supply that is likely to drive down prices and revenues with them. Of course, to adapt this model to government consumption one needs to assume it (at least partly) to be constituted of investment goods and that such goods are substitutes rather than complements to private investment. This represents a further example of how much modelling choices can affect final results and hence the policy implications of economic theory.

We conclude this section by discussing one last channel through which stocks may influence bond yields, namely liquidity. The marketability of a security in the secondary market may in fact be an important determinant of bond yields and one expects diffusion to be closely related to the amount of outstanding assets. In a more sophisticated fashion, Gravelle (1999) calls this the 'effective supply hypothesis'. Effective supply represents the amount of bonds in the hands of active market participants, that is, investors that do not buy securities to hold them to maturity (the so-called buy-and-hold investors). The author assumes a link between the stock of outstanding securities and liquidity via effective supply and trading activity. Empirical evidence presented in the paper supports this intuition: in the case of US government T-bills, in fact, turnover appears to be correlated with the outstanding stock of assets. The paper goes on claiming that when liquidity is proxied by the bond turnover ratio, there is evidence supporting the idea that 'an increase in the size of the benchmark issue increases its liquidity' (Gravelle, 1999:29).

To reconcile the opposed forces of absorption and liquidity we have to assume that while the negative impact on interest rates dominates in the case of the issuer country (i.e. the interest rate fall due to a larger issue more than compensates its increase due to the excess supply effect), the opposite holds for the foreign country. In other words, while the saturation effect spills over to all economies drawing from the same pool of saving (and so generates a generalized rise in interest rates), the liquidity effect is a local phenomenon.[9]

8.4   Historical perspective: German unification

In our quest for financial spillovers it is useful to turn back to the past and analyse instances in recent European history when fiscal variables in one country moved in a significant way. By focusing on such large swings, and by observing the concurrent movement in European bond yields, we can establish a sort of benchmark episode to which subsequent, more ordinary dynamics can be compared.

Here we will analyse German unification: the magnitude and persistence of the shock is such that strong negative financial spillovers are expected to emerge and hit all European countries. In other words, if externalities exist, this is one place where we trust them to show up.

At the end of the 1980s, Germany represented the third economy in the world and played a pivotal role in the process of European integration. The European Monetary System had been established a decade before (1979), was basically centred on the DM, and was used by many countries as a device to import monetary credibility from the Bundesbank (Giavazzi and Pagano, 1988). Sound macroeconomic fundamentals made the yield on German long-term government bond the benchmark 'safe' asset for European investors.

For what concerns possible spillover effects, uncover interest parity (UIP) tells us that an interest-rate differential is explained by expectations about future exchange-rate movements (or by country-specific risk): in short, we can write

$$i_t - i_t^* = E_t \left[\dot{e}_{t+1} \right] + \rho \tag{8.1a}$$

where i_t and i_t^* are the domestic and foreign interest rates, $E_t \left[\dot{e}_{t+1} \right]$ the expectation about future movements in the exchange rate (price of foreign currency in terms of domestic currency) and ρ is a country-specific risk factor. Let us now take the vantage point of Italian investors and observe some of the consequences of German unification. Assuming that capital is freely mobile and that an increase in German deficit and debt puts upward pressure to the domestic interest rate, one should witness capital flows from Italy to Germany, as Italian investors are attracted by the higher interest rate paid on German bonds. We can further imagine that a risk coefficient is attached to Italian government bonds, so that ρ is larger than zero. Starting from an equilibrium characterized by a balanced Current account (CA), such financial flows will put upward pressure on the exchange rate, calling for an appreciation of the mark (and a consequent depreciation of the lira). Had this to actually occur, Italian investors holding German securities would experience a capital gain generated by the increased price of the foreign currency. To restore the equilibrium, the Italian interest rate not only has to reach German levels, but has to climb even further in order to compensate the expected devaluation:

$$i_t^{ita} = i_t^{ger} + E_t\left[\dot{e}_{t+1}\right] + \rho. \tag{8.1b}$$

This latter mechanism based on exchange-rate expectation is obviously eliminated by a currency union: hence, on purely theoretical ground, once a single currency circulates in a different economic system, the chances for financial spillovers should be – *ceteris paribus* – lower.

In the second part of the section we will describe the developments in German public finances, external position and interest rates, while at the same time investigating the impact on interest rates of other European countries. The discussion is based on data from the IMF *International Financial Statistics* and the Deutsche Bundesbank *Time Series Database*.

There is little doubt that German unification required a massive disbursement on part of the Federal Government: although part of the required funds were collected by rising taxes and cutting expenditures in other sectors, integration of new Länder into market economy resulted in a surge of public deficit and debt. The Bundesbank (1997: 18) claims that this was partly due to the fact that 'not only was the fiscal policy challenge associated with this [the unification process] unforeseen, its magnitude was also underestimated at first.'

From the same source we learn that the ratio of debt/GDP jumped from under 42% in 1989 to over 60% in 1996, despite the positive impulse to production generated by unification itself;[10] in fact, while between 1991 and 1993 nominal GDP grew at an average rate of 4.94%, in the following three years growth was 'only' 2.78%. The same applies to the deficit/GDP ratio that, thanks to robust production growth, never overcame 3%.

To get a feeling of the magnitude of the amount of resources drained by unification we can look at a few summary statistics: between 1985 and 1989, the average growth rate of public debt was 5.88%, while the average deficit of the public sector amounted to less then 20 DM billion. Over the years 1990–94, the stock of debt grew at an average rate above 15% and excessive spending amounted to almost 60 DM billion on average. Table 8.1 displays information about some key macroeconomic variables before and after 1990: one important aspect that emerges clearly from the data is not only the magnitude, but also the length of the fiscal effort required by unification.

As we can infer from columns (4) and (5) of Table 8.1, financing needs were met quite easily since foreign capital flew heavily into the country and kept coming for a long time after unification. This was facilitated by the increase in bond yields and by expectations about exchange-rate dynamics (which would in fact be fulfilled in September 1992 with the EMS crisis). A glance at Figure 8.1 gives an immediate idea of the dramatic turnaround in the external position of Germany: in the five

Table 8.1 German fiscal position: summary statistics

	Period averages			
	Debt growth rate	Deficit	Current account	Financial account
1985–9	5.88%	19.66	40.16	−41.73
1986–90	8.46%	23.56	46.08	−48.97
1989–94	15.07%	59.77	−7.92	9.46
1991–5	16.57%	64.23	−22.25	29.19

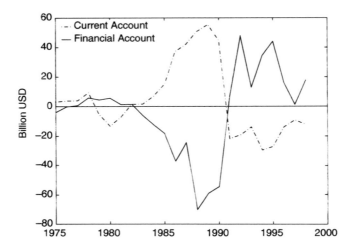

Figure 8.1 Current and financial account for Germany 1971–98.

Source: International Financial Statistics (IFS).
Note
Figures in billion USD.

years following unification, the country imported capital at an average rate of almost 30 billion dollars per year, for a cumulated financial inflow of roughly 150 billion. This stands in sharp contrast with what happened in the previous decade when German investors had exported an average of 48 USD billion each year.

So far, we have repeatedly claimed that the process of integrating East Germany implied an impressive and prolonged injection of resources on the part of the public sector. Moreover, BoP data suggest that Germany absorbed resources from abroad and in particular from European countries that constituted Germany's main trading partners. Table 8.2 reports the ratios of the German deficit to European GDP and to a European-wide stock of debt. These figures provide us with some information on the incidence of the German fiscal shock on continental asset markets.

While the deficit/GDP ratio has become a sort of benchmark measure of fiscal imbalances, the outstanding stock of debt proxies for market depth should therefore indicate the ability of the market to absorb a given amount of bonds. Of course,

Table 8.2 Impact of German unification on European-wide variables

	$deficit_{Ger}/debt_{EU}$ †	$deficit_{Ger}/GDP_{EU}$ ‡
1989	0.35%	0.05%
1990	4.03%	0.47%
1991	4.22%	0.67%
1992	4.05%	0.76%
1993	3.68%	0.84%
1994	2.03%	0.46%
1995	2.47%	0.62%
notional limits implied by Maastricht criteria		
	1.00%	1.00%

Note
†EMU 11 save for Ireland and Portugal; ‡EMU 11.

we expect a larger impact to cause a larger movement in European interest rates and, hence, a larger negative financial spillover. To get a clearer picture we can use the Maastricht criteria to compute the notional limits on the ratios displayed in Table 8.2. Using some elementary algebra, we can write

$$\frac{deficit_{Ger}}{debt_{Ger}} = \frac{deficit_{Ger}}{GDP_{Ger}} \cdot \frac{GDP_{Ger}}{debt_{Ger}} \cdot \frac{debt_{Ger}}{debt_{EU}}$$

and

$$\frac{deficit_{Ger}}{GDP_{EU}} = \frac{deficit_{Ger}}{GDP_{Ger}} \cdot \frac{GDP_{Ger}}{GDP_{EU}}$$

where the first term on the right-hand side of both equations is the deficit ceiling of 3%, and $GDP_{Ger}/debt_{Ger}$ is the inverse of the debt limit of 60%. For $debt_{Ger}/debt_{EU}$ and GDP_{Ger}/GDP_{EU} we use long-term averages of the German to European debt and GDP, which for the period 1970–1995 are 19.41% and 31.67%, respectively. In both cases we obtain threshold values that are just below 1%.[11]

Let us now focus on the behaviour of long-term interest rates in Germany and in the other European countries. We expect the yield on German bonds to go up under the pressure of the fiscal shock determined by unification. The first rows of Table 8.3 show the monthly yield on long-term German bonds between 1 and 36 months before and after unification: we take June 1990 – when the DM was formally introduced in the former GDR as the legal tender – as the origin of our imaginary time line. One thing to notice is that unification came at the end of an expansionary period and hence it contributed to overheating the economy: the Bundesbank raised interest rates sharply in order to control domestic inflation (Dornbusch and Wolf, 1992), and high demand resulted in full capacity utilization and spurred new investment. From Table 8.3 it emerges that German rates did not react immediately to the shock (one month after unification the yield on long-term bond is 30bp lower than one month before), but then the upswing is rather persistent: the average yield

Table 8.3 Yields on German and European bonds

		Months before and after unification						
		1	3	6	12	18	24	36
Germany	before	8.96	8.73	7.60	6.90	6.35	6.21	5.60
	after	8.64	9.21	8.95	8.50	8.51	8.28	6.62
Europe[†]: GDP weighted	before	11.18	11.35	10.53	9.98	9.44	9.38	9.47
	after	10.96	11.47	11.07	10.71	10.37	10.22	8.77
Europe[†]: trade weighted	before	10.67	10.82	10.01	9.37	8.83	8.82	8.86
	after	10.46	10.99	10.61	10.23	9.96	9.79	8.25

Note
†Austria, Belgium, Denmark, France, Ireland, Italy, Luxembourg, Netherlands, Portugal, Spain, Sweden, UK.

in the 18 months that followed unification is 124bp higher than the average yield prevailing in the 18 months that preceded June 1990. These two facts suggest the presence of rigidities that may have hindered the adjustment and that unification was perceived as a permanent rather than a transitory shock.

Turning now to the other European countries, the bottom part of Table 8.3 reports the yield on a weighted average of government bonds of European countries. Due to data availability, the basket of countries that constitute our European sample is slightly different from previous analysis, where we used the first 11 countries to join EMU, and takes into consideration also non-EMU countries like Denmark and the United Kingdom. Yields of different governments are weighted according to two different criteria: nominal GDP and a measure of trade linkages with Germany (imports on the part of Germany). While the former represents a natural choice to determine the importance of different economic systems in a European-wide context (Sinn, 1996, uses weights based on 1980 GDP figures), the latter method – giving more weight to countries more closely linked to Germany – should produce a European rate more prone to financial spillovers.

What emerges from Table 8.3 is that the European rate as well reacted with a lag to the shock of unification, but this time the upward pressure fades rapidly as the yield is back to pre-unification levels within six months of the event. Different weighting methods do not result in any difference in the behaviour of the European rate. Figure 8.2 plots the difference between the German and the European yields over the years 1988–92 and gives therefore a pictorial description of the phenomena analysed so far. Between June 1990 and September 1992, when speculators drove the lira and the pound out of the EMS, the spread shows a small tendency to decline and only on the verge of the crisis does it jump back to the levels of the beginning of the 1990s.

To better understand the issue of spillovers from Germany to other European countries we analyse spreads vis-à-vis the German bond yield. As anticipated above, the latter have long since been playing a pivotal role in the market for

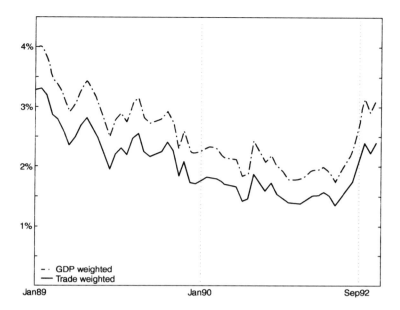

Figure 8.2 EU†– Germany long-term interest rate differential.

Note:

†Austria, Belgium, Denmark, France, Ireland, Italy, Luxembourg, Netherlands, Portugal, Spain, Sweden, UK. Dot-dashed line represents the difference between the German rate and an average European rate obtained weighting countries' yield by relative GDP shares; solid line repeats the exercise weighting yields by German import shares.

government securities and most debt instruments issued by other European countries pay a premium over it. Table 8.4 presents average-yield spreads of selected European countries: we consider not only future EMU members, but also the United Kingdom (one of the EU members that opted out of EMU) and Switzerland (which is neither member of the EMU nor of the EU). We expect that looser linkages with Germany result in smaller spillover effects. These in turn should provoke the spread to change only slightly as an increase in the German rate is closely followed by an analogous movement in foreign interest rates. In the limit, with a one-to-one spillover effect, the spread should not change at all. On the contrary, if national economies are insulated from external fiscal shocks, then the spread should decline (or increase, depending on whether it is a positive or a negative spread) in response to the increase in German rates caused by unification.

The picture that emerges from Table 8.4 is not homogeneous for all the countries examined. Grouping them according to the behaviour of their spread, we can say that Belgium, Ireland, Spain and, to a lesser extent, France display a marked decline of the premium paid over German rates. The same applies to Italy in the early aftermath of unification, while later on the Italian spread moves up again in response to the particularly weak fiscal position of the country, the latent fiscal crisis that was mounting, and the speculative attack that hit the lira in September 1992.

Table 8.4 Spread vis-à-vis German yields

		Months before and after unification						
		1	3	6	12	18	24	36
Austria	before	−0.15	0.02	0.25	0.27	0.18	0.41	1.02
	after	0.07	−0.23	−0.15	0.03	0.14	0.32	0.28
Belgium	before	0.89	1.18	2.07	1.50	1.70	1.63	2.22
	after	0.96	1.34	1.03	0.87	0.51	0.62	0.37
France	before	0.66	1.24	1.54	1.79	2.27	2.73	3.72
	after	0.97	1.31	0.98	0.65	0.28	0.46	0.50
Ireland	before	0.98	1.70	1.68	2.06	2.06	3.40	5.33
	after	0.88	1.35	0.94	0.74	0.34	0.59	0.87
Italy	before	2.57	2.82	3.84	3.94	3.67	3.91	3.89
	after	2.69	2.22	2.86	4.59	4.45	4.83	5.26
Luxembourg	before	−0.45	−0.24	0.74	0.38	−0.21	0.23	2.54
	after	−0.22	−0.64	−0.42	−0.28	−0.41	−0.36	0.37
Netherlands	before	−0.01	0.25	0.15	0.30	0.15	0.31	0.68
	after	0.10	−0.05	0.11	0.14	0.21	0.02	−0.03
Portugal	before	9.51	9.65	10.23	8.27	7.60	7.53	9.64
	after	9.90	9.65	9.83	9.87	8.62	6.82	7.90
Spain	before	5.67	6.13	6.89	6.88	6.47	4.65	7.60
	after	5.81	5.93	5.59	3.42	3.36	3.42	3.72
		non EMU members						
Switzerland	before	−2.64	−2.15	−1.85	−1.78	−2.12	−2.07	−1.49
	after	−2.56	−2.67	−2.27	−2.52	−2.16	−1.30	−2.08
UK	before	2.53	2.73	2.36	2.98	3.10	3.11	3.30
	after	2.39	2.11	1.47	1.84	1.05	0.74	1.77

Note
Data for Finland not available.

Luxembourg increased its margin over the German rate and 2 years after unification its (negative) spread was still larger than the value of March 1990. This date is taken as reference in order to shield from the possibility that markets had somehow anticipated unification and therefore bond yields prevailing one month before the formal introduction of the DM into former GDR were already uncommonly high.

The Austrian spread became negative after unification, then it climbed back to the values prevailing three months before unification. Dutch figures as well underwent only minor shifts: yet two years after unification the German-Dutch spread is nil, while two years before it amounted to 30bp. Portugal exhibits a puzzling dynamic that pushed up the interest rate spread vis-à-vis Germany; this tendency is only reversed at longer horizons, but it is nevertheless difficult to reconcile it with our analysis.

Turning now to the United Kingdom, we again observe that the spread is sensibly reduced, both in absolute terms (along the time line) and in comparison to average values before German unification; the oddity here is represented by the fact that, while the pound underwent in September 1992 a speculative attack that forced its exit from the EMS, no sign of upward pressure on the British rates emerges from the data. This behaviour can be rationalized by observing that having followed a policy of high interest rates for more than two years (in order to comply with the narrow fluctuation bands imposed by the EMS), the Bank of England cut its discount rate in half as soon as it was driven out of the EMS. The marked difference with respect to Italy may be justified by the stronger macroeconomic fundamentals that characterized the British economy at that time and that resulted in the currency crises not to impact on long-term interest rates.

The last country, Switzerland, constitutes a sort of 'control group': given its historical neutrality and its peculiar role in international capital markets, we expect German unification to have no effects on Swiss yields. In fact, the negative spread between the latter and German ones became even larger and it takes 18 months for it to go back to the levels observed three months before unification. Hence, the increase in German rates did not produce any comparable movement in Swiss yields.

All in all, there seems not to be much evidence in support of the negative financial spillovers hypothesis. While it is rather clear that the German rates were shifted up by the fiscal shock due to unification, yield on long-term securities issued by other European countries do not display any marked tendency towards an increase. Spreads vis-à-vis German rates declined for most countries considered. To support this interpretation one can integrate exchange-rate expectations into the picture and note that, in presence of an expected appreciation of the DM, not only should European rates have moved upwards, but they should have jumped higher than German ones as predicted by the UIP condition (1b). Hence, in presence of an expected appreciation of the DM, financial spillovers would not be the only determinant of any upward movement in other European interest rates. Despite a generalized consensus existing on the fact that the EMS crisis of 1992 was not anticipated by the market,[12] the realignment proposed by Germany as early as 1989 and the flexibility (albeit very limited) granted by EMS fluctuation bands suggest that the expected change in exchange rates could not realistically be set at zero and thereafter the limited upward movement of European rates is at least partially to be ascribed to exchange-rate movements, thus giving even less support to the spillover hypothesis.

Moreover, many authors (see, for instance, Rose and Svensson, 1994; Sinn, 1996, and the references therein) claim that the EMS crisis of September 1992 was caused by German unification itself: in particular, the upward swing in German rates and the consequent flow of financial resources into the central European country called for a revaluation of the DM. Once France, the United Kingdom and Italy opposed to the realignment in fear of undermining the anti-inflationary credibility they were importing through the pegged rate, real appreciation of the DM had to arrive through price changes. The liberalization of capital flows mandated by the Single European Act and implemented in most countries by the beginning of 1990 made it impossible to reconcile fixed exchange rates and independent monetary policies. Thus, a conflict emerged between the Bundesbank commitment to control domestic inflationary pressures, the sluggish economic performance of partner countries and their unwillingness to realign. This tension opened the door to a speculative attack and hence to the crisis with the resulting redefinition of central parities. This chain of events excludes any strong role for spillover effects on European interest rates: had they occurred, in fact, the flow of capital to Germany would have been limited, the need for revaluation not emerged and EMS band would have likely granted the system enough flexibility to face the shock.

It is probably fair to say that German unification is not the only culprit for the EMS crisis. In a classic contribution of the topic, Eichengreen and Wyplosz (1993) review four different explanations, do not find a great deal of support for the view that unification played a leading role, but nonetheless present some evidence in this direction. Their conclusion privileges the explanation based on self-fulfilling expectations but still acknowledges that several other factors contributed in building-up favourable conditions for speculators to succeed.[13]

8.5   Empirical analysis: aggregate behaviour in the euro area

Turning now to more formal empirical analysis, the search for potential spillovers of fiscal policies on the European interest rate crosses with tests of the 'Ricardian equivalence' hypothesis. One of the traditional means used for the purpose addresses the relation between fiscal deficits and interest rates.[14] The amount of research devoted to the issue is extremely vast, though empirical evidence is confused and gives mixed results.[15]

Recently, some authors have taken a slightly different route and have investigated the impact of world fiscal variables on interest rates. The parallelism with the issue of financial spillovers is straightforward. Indeed, Ford and Laxton (1999: 77–8) explicitly claim that with globally integrated capital markets it is world debt that matters for the determination of country-specific interest rates. Hence, they continue, 'countries with high levels of government debt may be imposing negative externalities on others.' The fundamental hypothesis at work here is that a euro cent of debt has the same impact on world markets regardless of the issuer. The conclusion of the two authors is that the ratio of OECD public debt to world GDP has had a substantial effect on the interest rates of nine industrial countries over the period 1977–97. Local developments, on the other hand, are only relevant to explain persistent *spreads*, though their effect is not significant on interest rate *levels*.

Breedon *et al.* (1999), who study G-3 economies over period 1975–88 using *ex-post* 10-year real interest rates, present similar results, even if they find a more relevant role for domestic factors that – they claim – are at least as important as international ones. The three authors interpret their result as evidence against financial markets integration.

Chinn and Frankel (2003) repeat the exercise, investigating the impact of G7 debt on the interest rates of Germany, France, Italy and Spain over the period 1988–2002, but find no significant effect.

Ardagna *et al.* (2004) investigate the relation between fiscal variables and long-term interest rates using a panel of 16 OECD countries over the last 40 years. Their findings support the idea international factors are relevant (so that negative financial spillovers do occur), yet to a much lesser extent than domestic ones. Again, this evidence points towards a lack of integration in capital markets. Closely related to our work is the finding by the authors that EMU does not constitute a breakpoint for European countries: the introduction of the single currency in fact seems not to have resulted in international variables to be more relevant and/or domestic ones to lose importance in the determination of bond yields. In sum, this work suggests that while there is an effect of international fiscal variables on interest rates, the inception of EMU has not provoked any structural change in the relation between deficit, debt and bond yields.

Following Chinn and Frankel (2003), we test the hypothesis that European capital market can be considered as a single pool of funds from which all countries draw and for which they all compete. Once confirmed by the data, this theory would back the idea that by absorbing a significant share of European saving, the fiscal imbalances in one country can affect the common interest rate and thus impose negative externalities on economic partners. Yet, the budget limits incorporated into the SGP are not aimed at limiting European-wide fiscal expansions, but rather the behaviour of single states. The relevant hypothesis is therefore more stringent than the one tested here. In other words, a failure to reject our null hypothesis does not immediately lend support to the existence of negative financial spillovers as postulated in the SGP.

In this first empirical exercise we consider the euro area as a single economic entity and look for a relation among aggregate measures of the fiscal stance and a weighted average of different bond yields. We exploit two sets of data, both of which report figures for the 12 EMU countries as a whole: first, we use quarterly data on the EMU published in the OECD *Economic Outlook* for the period 1980Q1 to 2004Q2, then – in order to isolate the effect of EMU – we turn to monthly data taken from the ECB *Monthly Bulletin* that range from January 1999 to April 2004.[16]

8.5.1 Quarterly data

In this first part of the analysis we exploit quarterly data for the EMU area as a whole published by the OECD. We have opted for the simplest possible specification, and therefore the basic estimating equation takes the form:

$$YLD_t = \varphi_0 + \varphi_1 t + \varphi_2 \frac{surplus_t}{GDP_t} + \varphi_3 \frac{debt_t}{GDP_t} + \varepsilon_t \tag{8.2}$$

where *YLD* is an average real yield on long-term bonds issued by EMU area governments, *t* is a time trend and *surplus* the primary balance.[17] As a robustness check, we introduce a second measure of the fiscal position specifically aimed at capturing the non-anticipated part of the fiscal stance. This variable, which appears as *fiscal* in the tables, is constructed following Blanchard (1990); Brunila *et al.* (1999);

and Farina and Tamborini (2002), and basically reports the fiscal stance net of cyclical effects: it is therefore an indicator of discretionary fiscal policy. Its construction is fairly easy: the first step is running a regression of the primary balance/GDP ratio (*PB*) on a constant, a time trend and GDP growth ($G\dot{D}P$)

$$PB_t = \lambda_0 + \lambda_2 t + \lambda_3 G\dot{D}P_t \; ; \tag{8.3}$$

then estimated coefficients are used to build a *growth-adjusted primary balance* (*GAPB*), which is obtained by inserting the previous period GDP growth rate into the estimated equation. This variable represents the primary balance that would have prevailed in period t, had the GDP grown at the same rate as in period $t - 1$. This is computed as

$$GAPB_t = \hat{\lambda}_0 + \hat{\lambda}_1 t + \hat{\lambda}_2 G\dot{D}P_{t-1} \tag{8.4}$$

while our fiscal stance indicator is simply given by the difference between the growth-adjusted measure and the observed value of the primary balance

$$fiscal_t = GAPB_t - PB_{t-1} \; . \tag{8.5}$$

As it is for *surplus*, a positive value of *fiscal* implies a fiscal restriction.

Columns (1)–(3) of Table 8.5 present results for estimation of equation (8.2) in levels. We find that fiscal imbalances do not have any impact on real bond yields, regardless of the variable used (either the primary surplus or the measure of discretionary policy *à la* Blanchard), whilst the stock of outstanding debt has a significant effect on the cost of borrowing, most probably via risk premia (columns (1) and (2)). Column (3) reports results for a new specification whereby a dummy for the EMU is included and interacted with fiscal variables, to check the hypothesis that the introduction of the single currency marks a break in the data so that after 1999 deeper integration of European capital market results in EMU fiscal variables having a larger impact on bond yields. Interaction terms are significant at 8% and 1% and suggest that monetary integration may in fact have increased the importance of euro-area variables in determining interest rates. In particular, the primary balance/GDP ratio (interacted with the EMU dummy) is positive, contrary to what theory suggests, while the stock of debt is negative. The latter interesting result tells that after 1999 liquidity effects dominate default risk consideration: financial markets cease to discriminate among EMU members' sovereign issuers and as the amount of outstanding debt increases, bond yields are pushed down by the increased liquidity of the securities.

One major caveat applies to these estimates: as unit-root tests cannot reject a null of non-stationarity for most of the variables involved in the regression, results may be spurious. This suspicion is confirmed by residual-based tests for cointegration:[18] regression residuals from equation (8.2) – considered as the cointegrating relation – are not stationary and therefore point towards the lack of any long-run equilibrium relation.

Table 8.5 Impact of fiscal variables on real long-term yields: quarterly data

	Levels			Differences		
	(1)	*(2)*	*(3)*	*(4)*	*(5)*	*(6)*
Surplus/GDP	−0.051		−0.229	−0.149		−0.380
	(0.20)		(0.39)	(0.49)		(0.75)
Fiscal/GDP		−0.094			−0.267	
		(0.36)			(0.74)	
Debt/GDP	0.153	0.134	−0.068	−0.203	−0.208	−0.268
	(2.50)*	(2.29)*	(0.58)	(1.43)	(1.55)	(1.34)
EMU • surplus/GDP			1.136			0.582
			(1.78)			(1.08)
EMU • debt/GDP			−0.079			0.303
			(−2.79)**			(1.14)
Observations	98	97	98	97	96	97
Adjusted R^2	0.26	0.28	0.39	0.06	0.07	0.06

Notes
Absolute value of HAC robust t-statistics in parentheses; * significant at 5%; ** significant at 1%;
constant and time trend not included.

We therefore run the same regression in first differences and display the results in
columns (4)–(6). Estimated coefficients lose significance and, more importantly,
the ratio of debt/GDP now changes sign and becomes negative; albeit it is not
significant at 10%. Again, the situation does not improve if we substitute *fiscal*
for *surplus*. Interacting fiscal variables with the EMU dummy does not change the
overall picture: coefficients are positive, but not significant, so the inception of
the monetary union seems not to have had any strong impact. Table 8.5 tells that
bond yields are not determined by fiscal variables.[19]

8.5.2 Monthly data

In order to focus on the impact of EMU, we now restrict our attention to the period
that followed the introduction of the single currency: to cope with this short time
span we have to resort to monthly observations compiled by the ECB and therefore,
instead of analysing the impact of public deficits on bond yields, we concentrate
on the issuing activity on part of the public sector (data on fiscal variables only
exist at lower frequencies). This 'restriction' has the additional benefit of allowing
for a direct test of the hypothesis that the absorption of saving by the pubic sector –
rather than fiscal variables *per se* – is what really matters for the determination of
bond yields.

Our baseline specification for the real interest rate is

$$\Delta YLD_t = \gamma_0 + \gamma_1 t + \gamma_2 \frac{issue_t^g}{GDP_t} + \gamma_3 \frac{issue_t^p}{GDP_t} + \gamma_4 \Delta \frac{stock_t^g}{GDP_t} + \gamma_5 \Delta \frac{stock_t^p}{GDP_t} + \varepsilon_t$$

$$(8.6)$$

where *YLD* is the real yield on government benchmark bonds and the superscripts *g* and *p* identify the public and private sector, respectively.

Many variables are non-stationary and thus enter the estimating equation in first differences. Euro-area yields are calculated on the basis of weights corresponding to nominal outstanding amounts of bonds in each maturity, and are deflated *ex post* using the harmonized consumer price index. Our dataset consists of monthly observations from January 1999 to April 2004 for a total of 64 observations.[20] We do not focus on a single maturity but use both 3- and 10-year bonds in order to span the yield curve. This is intended to give some information on the nature of spillovers: while in fact, according to the absorption hypothesis, bonds of all maturities should be affected by an increase in the issuing activity of the public sector, the spillover would occur only at longer time horizons were the driving force credit risk.

Interpretation of equation (8.6) is straightforward: under the 'standard' view the real rate should be affected by the absorption of resources by the public and the private sector. In addition, the basic equation is augmented with the introduction of GDP growth, which should capture responses of the interest rate to the business cycle.

Table 8.6 reports results for real yields on 3- and 10-year benchmark government bonds. Durbin–Watson statistics suggest the presence of autocorrelation among the residuals: this is confirmed by Ljung-Box Q test and leads us to compute Newey–West heteroskedasticy and autocorrelation consistent (HAC) standard errors from which t-statistics are computed. As one would expect, the short-term yield is more sensitive to business cycle fluctuations represented by GDP growth; interestingly, something similar occurs to the stock of private debt which also has a positive impact on bond yields once GDP growth is included. During economic upturns, interest rates go up and as the private sector increases its stock of debt, corporate bonds will bear a higher risk premium that pushes up returns. This, combined with return-seeking behaviour on the part of investors (typical of economic growth phases) may explain why a higher stock of private debt spills over to government benchmark bonds: in order to attract savers, public securities have to offer a higher return. In sum, Table 8.6 suggests that at shorter maturities it is as if private and public debt are less segmented due to the risk-seeking behaviour of investors. This effect is much less pronounced at longer horizons: columns (3) and (4) in fact show that neither GDP growth nor the stock of private debt are significant at 5%. Bond issue to GDP as well is not significantly different from zero at all maturities.

Overall, the empirical analysis does not provide much credit to the hypothesis that the fiscal position of the euro area as a whole affects either bond yields or the current account. This is consistent with recent evidence put forward by Breedon *et al.* (1999); Chinn and Frankel (2003); Ardagna *et al.* (2004); and Kormendi and Protopapadakis (2004). On the other hand, the results obtained in the case of 10-year bonds (and shown in Table 8.6) may be read as a sign that at longer maturities some sort of linkage exists between public finances and real interest rates: in this case, the relevant transmission channel would be credit risk.

Table 8.6 Impact of fiscal variables on real yields: monthly data

	3-year rate		10-year rate	
	(1)	*(2)*	*(3)*	*(4)*
Δ (issue/GDP)$_{gov}$	0.039	0.018	0.059	0.048
	(0.82)	(0.38)	(1.16)	(0.91)
Δ (issue/GDP)$_{pvt}$	0.024	0.014	0.033	0.028
	(0.38)	(0.26)	(0.60)	(0.57)
Δ (stock/GDP)$_{gov}$	−0.041	−0.024	−0.038	−0.028
	(0.67)	(0.48)	(0.59)	(0.48)
Δ (stock/GDP)$_{pvt}$	0.054	0.079	0.034	0.048
	(1.46)	(2.47)*	(0.97)	(1.73)
GDP growth		0.051		0.029
		(2.78)**		(1.38)
Observations	63	63	63	63
Adjusted R^2	0.01	0.08	0.02	0.03

Notes
1st difference of dependent variable; absolute value of HAC robust t-statistics in parentheses;
* significant at 5%; ** significant at 1%; constant and time trend not shown.

8.6 Linkages among EMU member states

This section goes deeper in the empirical analysis by narrowing the focus on the linkages among government bonds issued by EMU members. Recently, there has been a surge of interest on European government bonds market.[21] The latter is often regarded as the most important financial market, as government securities represent the dominant financial instrument in European portfolios (Perée and Steinherr, 2001). Moreover, different authors agree in identifying the bond market as the segment that has more promptly reacted to the inception of the EMU and that has most remarkably integrated to form a single pan-European market.

Most studies focus on spreads among securities issued by different European states, trying to detect their main determinants now that, with the elimination of exchange-rate risk, segmentation should decline and assets become closer substitutes. In presence of spillovers, however, it is not possible to assess whether spreads reflect correctly priced risks and so the strategy has to be adjusted.[22]

Codogno *et al.* (2003) investigate the behaviour of relative asset swap spreads (RAS) with respect to Germany; RAS – the difference between the bond yield spread and the spread on swap rates of the same maturity – represent the component of the yield differential not related to exchange-rate factors and thus allow the authors to pool together data collected before and after 1999. Empirical evidence suggests that international risk factors dominate liquidity, while no role is played by different debt/GDP ratios.

Hartman *et al.* (2003) agree on the point that remaining spreads cannot be explained by credit risk differentials and judge the fact that prices of bonds with identical ratings have not fully converged as a legacy of market segmentation.

According to their view, this hypothesis is backed up by the fact that quantity-based indicators still show a significant home-bias in European portfolios (though it has diminished after the introduction of the single currency).

Afonso and Strauch (2004) study the impact of 2002 fiscal policy events on default risk (measured by the spread between the swap rate and the yield on bonds of the same maturity). They use daily data for the same year and their findings witness to the lack of a strong reaction. This is consistent with the interpretation that with current credit ratings default risk is negligible for almost all EMU member countries.

Dunne *et al.* (2003) analyse interactions among German, French and Italian bonds in order to find the benchmark asset. Using cointegration analysis, they find that German bonds are the financial instrument to which the price of other securities react (the benchmark).

8.6.1 *Linkages across bond yields*

Figure 8.3 plots the yields on 10-year government bonds for the 11 countries that joined EMU in 1999: the graph spans the period between January 1990 and June 2004 and displays monthly averages of long-term bond yields. Two facts emerge: first, a dramatic convergence process took place between 1995 and 1997 and was almost completed before the actual introduction of the single currency; second, it is clear that yields on bonds issued by different European countries move together. This is striking since 1999, but even at the beginning of the sample there was a marked tendency to co-move.

Does this imply the existence of financial spillovers? Not necessarily: according to Dunne *et al.* (2003) and their definition of the benchmark asset, we need to distinguish financial spillovers from long-term equilibrium relations that link different

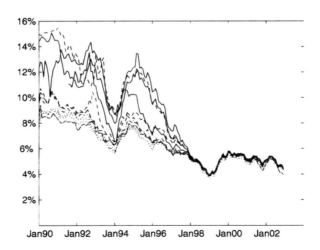

Figure 8.3 Yield on 10-year government bonds: EMU 11 countries.

financial instruments in the same market. Empirically, this entails addressing short-term dynamics rather than long-term analysis, that is, taking the opposite route from Dunne *et al.* (2003). This is consistent with what was suggested by Favero (2001), who notes that in recent research VARs in levels rather than Vector Error Correction Models are used when the focus is on short-run dynamics, regardless of the presence of non-stationary variables and cointegrating relations.

The first halt in our search for financial spillovers is then a VAR in levels with subsequent Granger-causality tests. We concentrate on the period that followed the introduction of the euro as spillovers should emerge more clearly once exchange-rate risk is eliminated; we exploit a dataset comprising daily observations on 10-year bond yields from January 2001 to June 2004. Results (not presented and available upon request) show that Granger-causality is never rejected for all variables and all equations and suggest that there is in fact co-determination of bond yields.

This being established, we are left with the main part of the problem yet unsolved: we need to determine the source of such interactions among government securities. The negative financial spillover hypothesis suggests that at least part of the co-movements is due to externalities stemming from the fiscal position of EMU member states. Theory therefore provides us with some guidance and directs our analysis towards the potential impact of domestic fiscal imbalances on foreign interest rates.

8.6.2 The role of fiscal policy

In order to analyse the impact of fiscal variables on bond yields, it is necessary to move to lower frequencies. In what follows we will once again exploit both quarterly and monthly data. These are still rather high frequencies in terms of fiscal indicators and we are going to pay a cost in terms of available series (and may be their reliability). On the other hand, the time span on which we can concentrate is not very large and these data allow us to maximize the number of observations.

Our empirical specification draws from recent works on the topic, especially Afonso and Strauch (2004); Ardagna *et al.* (2004); and Bernoth *et al.* (2004). The latter is especially interesting as it develops a very simple framework for analysing the relation between fiscal variables and bond yields. We have explored a number of different specifications, but decided to concentrate here on one similar to that used in section 8.5 in order to be consistent throughout the exposition. The estimating equation thus reads:

$$
ras_t^i = \beta_0 + \beta_1 t + \beta_2 int3m_t + \beta_3 infl_t + \beta_4 \left[\frac{surplus_t}{GDP_t} \right]^i
$$
$$
+ \beta_5 \left[\frac{debt_t}{GDP_t} \right]^i + \beta_6 \left[\frac{surplus_t}{GDP_t} \right]^{EMU-i} + \beta_7 \left[\frac{debt_t}{GDP_t} \right]^{EMU-i} + \varepsilon_t.
$$

$$(8.7)$$

On the left-hand side we have the 10-year relative asset swap with respect to Switzerland. Investigating the presence of financial spillovers among EMU member countries, we are forced to look for a reference country that is not part of the monetary union: we have opted for Switzerland as it is small enough not to exert particular influences on the international bond market, and its historical record is one of remarkable stability and sound fiscal position (the return on Swiss bonds is always lower than that paid on other European securities). In addition, Switzerland has not experienced any significant change in its budgetary position (contrary, for instance, to the United States, which would represent another natural point of reference) and this is another reason that makes it an excellent benchmark country. Moreover, we can feel sufficiently safe in assuming that the fiscal position of any EMU member state will not influence the yield on Swiss bond as the traditional neutrality of the latter country results in looser linkages with neighbouring nations.

The list of controls included in equation (8.7) comprises the three-month interest rate, inflation, domestic and foreign primary surplus and debt/GDP ratios.[23] The superscript i stands for the object countries of our study, namely France, Germany, Italy and the Netherlands, while the label *EMU-i* indicates the aggregated fiscal position of the other 11 EMU member countries. We have chosen to aggregate foreign fiscal variables in order to avoid potential collinearity problems. All variables are measured as deviation from the relevant Swiss figure. Data are taken from the OECD *Economic Outlook* except for swap rates which come from *Datastream*. Given that available fiscal indicators are at quarterly frequency, we are left with less than 60 observations.[24]

All variables (apart from the three-month interest rate) display a unit root, so we cannot simply proceed with estimation of the SUR in levels. We first tackle the problem by differencing all non-stationary variables: odd columns in Table 8.7 display results for such specification for each country. Unfortunately, none of the controls is significant, nor does the inclusion of the squares of the fiscal variables help to improve the situation much. Even columns present the results for an augmented specification in which the foreign fiscal variables are interacted with a dummy for EMU: in this way we can directly test the hypothesis that with the introduction of the single currency the fiscal position of other EMU member countries has gained importance. Relevant coefficients are significant in some cases (above all Italy), though the surplus coefficients display the wrong sign (so that a larger primary balance would result in a higher interest rate).

Alternatively, we test the hypothesis that equation (8.7) represents a long-run equilibrium relation and therefore test I(1) variables for cointegration. Residual-based tests on the four equations of the SUR give conflicting results: it is possible to reject the null of unit root (equivalent to no cointegration) for Italy, France and the Netherlands at 5%, 10% and 12.5% respectively, while this hypothesis cannot be rejected in the case of Germany. Nonetheless, we have decided to keep the four equations together and estimate the whole SUR by dynamic GLS (DGLS), as suggested by Stock and Watson (1993). Results are reported in Table 8.7: many coefficients are now significantly different from zero, but signs often change when

Table 8.7 Impact of domestic and foreign fiscal variables on yields

	France		Germany		Italy		Netherlands	
	(1)	(2)	(3)	(4)	(5)	(6)	(7)	(8)
3-month rate	−0.034	−0.039	−0.024	−0.040	−0.006	−0.020	−0.047	−0.054
	(2.57)*	(2.86)**	(1.33)	(2.02)*	(0.33)	(1.15)	(2.33)*	(2.59)*
Δ inflation	0.013	0.008	0.017	0.010	−0.107	−0.091	−0.005	−0.009
	(0.55)	(0.31)	(1.46)	(0.85)	(1.62)	(1.40)	(0.37)	(0.62)
Δ (surplus/GDP)$_{dom}$	−0.011	0.014	0.013	0.080	0.009	0.118	−0.004	−0.011
	(0.36)	(0.37)	(0.47)	(1.91)	(0.28)	(2.51)*	(0.19)	(0.51)
Δ (debt/GDP)$_{dom}$	−0.012	−0.009	0.010	0.019	−0.009	−0.017	−0.004	−0.005
	(0.38)	(0.27)	(0.61)	(1.06)	(0.43)	(0.88)	(0.32)	(0.35)
Δ (surplus/GDP)$_{for}$	−0.002	−0.032	0.005	−0.061	−0.098	−0.331	0.016	0.008
	(0.04)	(0.61)	(0.16)	(1.19)	(1.13)	(2.99)**	(0.37)	(0.18)
Δ (debt/GDP)$_{for}$	0.028	0.023	−0.018	−0.020	−0.079	−0.080	−0.019	−0.022
	(0.94)	(0.78)	(0.86)	(0.94)	(1.59)	(1.74)	(0.70)	(0.85)
Δ (surplus/GDP)$_{for}$ •EMU		0.157		0.250		0.813		0.216
		(1.27)		(1.94)		(3.12)**		(1.72)
Δ (debt/GDP)$_{for}$ •EMU		−0.003		−0.007		−0.019		−0.004
		(0.73)		(1.36)		(2.89)**		(0.89)
Observations	50	50	55	55	52	52	51	51
Adjusted R^2	−0.08	−0.05	−0.12	−0.06	0.03	0.11	−0.11	−0.06

Notes
SUR on 1st difference of dependent variable; monthly data; absolute value of HAC robust t-statistics in parenthesis; * significant at 5%; ** significant at 1%; constant and time trend not shown.

Table 8.8 DGLS estimates of the cointegrating relation

	France	Germany	Italy	Netherlands
	(1)	*(2)*	*(3)*	*(4)*
3-month rate	−0.051	−0.077	0.011	−0.121
	(4.70)**	(3.21)**	(0.43)	(3.53)**
inflation	0.044	−0.098	0.038	−0.096
	(2.28)*	(5.21)**	(0.48)	(5.33)**
(surplus/GDP)$_{dom}$	0.037	−0.138	0.111	−0.145
	(1.05)	(6.28)**	(1.41)	(4.14)**
(debt/GDP)$_{dom}$	0.209	0.016	−0.066	−0.130
	(5.36)**	(1.14)	(3.51)**	(8.28)**
(surplus/GDP)$_{for}$	−0.083	0.171	−0.249	0.119
	(1.97)*	(7.51)**	(1.64)	(3.05)**
(debt/GDP)$_{for}$	−0.178	−0.034	−0.046	0.081
	(4.71)**	(3.90)**	(3.16)**	(6.43)**
Observations	49	52	51	49
Adjusted R^2	0.76	0.94	0.92	0.82

Notes
1st difference of dependent variable; monthly data; absolute value of HAC robust t-statistics in parentheses; * significant at 5%; ** significant at 1%; constant and time trend not shown.

we move from one country to another and it is frankly difficult to tell a clear pattern in the results.

The fact that every country reacts differently to changes in its own fiscal position and in that of other countries may be read as a clue that financial markets can efficiently discriminate among different borrowers. This implies that each country faces a cost of borrowing that depends on the status it enjoys on financial markets and on other characteristics of its economic system and that financial spillovers are not particularly relevant.

In order to test for the absorption effect mentioned by Kenen (1995), we shift our attention to bond issues rather than primary balance/GDP ratios. Stock variables continue to appear in our analysis as they proxy for market depth and hence for liquidity.

In what follows we restrict our attention to Italy and Germany, as their Central Banks publish monthly series for the amount of securities issued by the central government and their total outstanding stock. Data are taken from the statistical annexes of the monthly publications of the Banca d'Italia and the Bundesbank. The estimating equation is not very different from the previous one, although it is now refined and adapted to the new dataset:

$$\Delta ras_t^i = \alpha_0 + \alpha_1 t + \alpha_2 \Delta ras_{t-1}^i + \alpha_3 \left[\frac{issue_t}{GDP_t} \right]^i + \alpha_4 \Delta \left[\frac{debt_t}{GDP_t} \right]^i$$

$$+ \alpha_5 \left[\frac{issue_t}{GDP_t} \right]^j + \alpha_6 \Delta \left[\frac{debt_t}{GDP_t} \right]^j + \varepsilon_t$$

(8.8)

We continue to use the RAS with respect to Switzerland as our dependent variable in order to be able to clean our data from exchange-rate risk. Superscripts i and j represent Italy or Germany: now we have a bidimensional system, which we again estimate by means of a SUR. Despite the fact that we have to focus on only two countries, we believe that they represent a significant sample in our search for financial spillovers. Germany is the leading economy in the euro area and its securities have long served as a benchmark in the bond market; Italy, on the other hand, is a large country (with respect to EMU), is characterized by a very large stock of debt and is traditionally viewed as a 'non-virtuous' country. The RAS and the total stock of debt to GDP are non-stationary and therefore enter equation (8.8) in first differences. Columns (1) and (3) of Table 8.9 report results derived from estimation using both 10-year (top panel) and 3-year bonds (bottom panel), in order to see whether different maturities display different behaviours.

Once again, coefficients on bond issues and outstanding stocks are barely significant, so that data offer not much support to the idea that, by absorbing a larger share of European saving, each government can raise the overall cost of borrowing.

The signs of the coefficients suggest that while Germany may suffer a limited degree of spillover stemming from the Italian issuing activity, the opposite does not hold. On the contrary, an increase in the stock of Italian debt has a negative impact on both the Italian and the German yield, signalling the presence of liquidity effects.

The finding that only Italian variables appear to matter (albeit marginally) lends credit to the view that financial markets are indeed able to discriminate among different issuers, so that the same action has dissimilar results depending on the identity of the debtor. Hence, the privileged status enjoyed by its securities would grant less stringent limits to the public finances of Germany, while the fact that Italy has one of the world's largest public debts implies closer surveillance by market participants.

This is reminiscent of the results by Flandreau *et al.* (1998), according to whom financial markets behave in non-linear ways and only beyond a given threshold do borrowers start feeling the bite of market discipline.[25]

Another attempt to improve the fit of the equation (and the results) consists of augmenting equation (8.8) along the line of Afonso and Strauch (2004). Table 8.9 displays on even columns the outcome of the empirical analysis when we include among the regressors the slope of the yield curve and a measure of stock market volatility. The former, which is measured by the difference between the yield on 10-year government bonds and the 3-month Euribor, captures future growth expectations: a steeper slope reduces the risk of private relative to government securities, and therefore pushes up the cost of borrowing for the government. On the contrary, the standard deviation of daily return on the S&P500 index proxies for stock market risk and is supposed to reduce the return required to hold safer assets (government bonds). Both panels of Table 8.9 highlight that such modifications do not produce any alteration in the results and give us some confidence in the fact that our findings are not driven by the particular specification chosen.

Table 8.9 Impact of bond issues on yields

	Italy		Germany	
	(1)	*(2)*	*(3)*	*(4)*
	panel A: 10-year rate			
Δ ras$_{t-1}$	−0.131	−0.140	−0.187	−0.184
	(1.93)	(2.06)*	(2.98)**	(2.94)**
Δ slp$_t$		0.024		0.053
		(0.39)		(1.25)
S&P500 volatility		4.922		0.989
		(1.40)		(0.41)
(issue/GDP)$_{ita}$	0.02	0.02	0.016	0.016
	(1.55)	(1.58)	(1.79)	(1.75)
Δ (stock/GDP)$_{ita}$	−0.008	−0.008	−0.011	−0.011
	(0.90)	(0.92)	(1.76)	(1.70)
(issue/GDP)$_{ger}$	−0.015	−0.015	−0.011	−0.01
	(0.67)	(0.67)	(0.74)	(0.64)
Δ (stock/GDP)$_{ger}$	0.015	0.016	0.017	0.016
	(0.82)	(0.89)	(1.43)	(1.26)
Observations	159	159	170	170
Adjusted R^2	0.01	0.05	0.16	0.16
	panel B: 3-year rate			
Δ ras$_{t-1}$	−0.311	−0.314	−0.352	−0.354
	(4.13)**	(4.14)**	(5.52)**	(5.56)**
Δ slp$_t$		0.008		0.085
		(0.11)		(1.50)
S&P500 volatility		1.892		0.869
		(0.48)		(0.26)
(issue/GDP)$_{ita}$	0.024	0.024	0.018	0.017
	(1.54)	(1.52)	(1.49)	(1.41)
Δ (stock/GDP)$_{ita}$	−0.016	−0.015	−0.017	−0.016
	(1.43)	(1.41)	(1.98)*	(1.89)
(issue/GDP)$_{ger}$	−0.003	−0.002	−0.004	−0.002
	(0.10)	(0.07)	(0.21)	(0.09)
Δ (stock/GDP)$_{ger}$	−0.002	−0.002	0.009	0.006
	(0.11)	(0.10)	(0.53)	(0.34)
Observations	136	136	170	170
Adjusted R^2	0.06	0.05	0.16	0.16

Notes
1st difference of dependent variable; monthly data; absolute value of HAC robust t-statistics in parentheses; * significant at 5%; ** significant at 1%; constant and time trend not shown.

8.7   Conclusions

The paper has investigated the presence of negative financial spillovers among euro area government bond yields and their relations with fiscal imbalances. While returns on assets issued by different European governments do show a large degree of co-movements, little evidence emerges to relate this common dynamics to the fiscal positions of EMU members.

We have reviewed a number of open economy models, focusing in particular on the predictions about the effect of a fiscal expansion on the international rate of interest. Theory does not provide clear-cut indications: different models give different outcomes; hence, the issue of fiscal spillovers remains an empirical question.

We have analysed the impact of German unification on European interest rates. Since this represented a large shift in the fiscal and external position of the leading European economy, one would expect it to result in a sensible movement in the cost of borrowing faced by other countries as capital started flowing into Germany to finance unification. Contrary to these predictions, evidence offers little support to the spillover hypothesis and shows that the fiscal deterioration affected only domestic interest rates.

The negative financial spillover hypothesis takes for granted that a relation exists linking domestic fiscal variables and interest rates. To gather some evidence on the topic, we have investigated whether the fiscal position of the euro area as a whole has any impact on the average yield of European government bonds. Econometric analysis does not highlight any significant relation between the two variables and therefore adds to the number of studies that postulates the neutrality of fiscal variables with respect to the cost of borrowing.

In the last part of the paper we have directly examined the behaviour of bonds issued by some EMU member governments. We have used a number of different specifications and considered both fiscal variables and bond issues in order to directly test the absorption hypothesis. Results are less clear-cut, but overall it appears that neither fiscal imbalances nor issuance activity have the direct negative impact on interest rates postulated in the SGP.

Notes

1 I am grateful to Roberto Tamborini, Axel Leijonhufvud, Gabriella Berloffa, Christopher Gilbert, Giuliana Passamani, seminar participants at Università di Trento and at the workshops Lectures on Macroeconomic Governance in the EMU, and The Architecture of Financial System Stability: from Market Micro Structure to Monetary Policy for helpful comments. Flavio Bazzana, Giorgio Cipriani, Gabriella Mazzalai and Enrico Salvetta helped me with the data. All remaining mistakes are only mine.
2 The experience of New York State default in 1975 may have made American financial markets efficient in controlling public borrowers.
3 In practice only large enough countries are likely to produce this result.
4 See Mundell (1963), Mundell (1964) and Fleming (1962).
5 For a comprehensive analysis of the role of fiscal policy in the neoclassical model see Barro (1989).
6 Relaxing any of the basic assumptions, the predictions of the model change: 'Ricardian equivalence' between debt and taxes ceases to hold and 'Keynesian' outcomes on the interest rate emerge. For instance, by assuming finite horizons for households, one obtains that higher future taxes will be levied partly after the death of currently living agents, so that government spending has a wealth effect that increases present consumption, reduces saving and bids up the interest rate (the Ricardian result continues to hold in presence of intergenerational altruism: hence, more than finite horizons themselves, what matters is the degree of linkage across generations). Other extensions

account for imperfect credit markets where different groups face different interest rates, uncertainty about future taxes and income streams and the presence of distortionary taxation.

7   The reason is that output is demand determined: therefore an unanticipated temporary rise in G_t results in a temporary rise in world output, with no effect on the amount of resource available to the private sector (see Obstfeld and Rogoff, 1996, chapter 10 for details).

8   See for instance Flandreau *et al.* (1998).

9   Empirically, Cottarelli and Mecagni (1991) find that, during the 1970s and 1980s, supply factors seem more relevant than risk indicators in pushing up the interest rate on Italian public debt. On the other hand, Codogno *et al.* (2003) conclude that international risk factors dominate liquidity in determining the yield spreads among EMU bonds.

10 In terms of debt/GDP ratio Germany is not the worst performer among European countries: in the same period, in fact, France and Italy display an even faster growth of debt relative to GDP. The economic expansion triggered by unification, together with the poor economic performances suffered by many European countries in the beginning of the 1990s can explain this apparent oddity.

11 A different measures of the flow impact of German unification can be found in Tamborini (1997, table 8.3). It is given by the ratio of government net borrowing (GNB) to the sum of gross private saving in the EU12 countries (GPS12) and measures the absorption of EU saving due to each national borrowing needs. German figures jump from 1.8% (1986–90) to 4.2% (1991–95).

12 Rose and Svensson (1994) quote the behavior of interest rates –which did not jump up until the onset of the crisis – to corroborate this view.

13 An alternative explanation for the lack of financial spillovers is that the latter were 'compressed' by accommodating monetary policies in European countries, unsustainable in light of the anti-inflationary stance pursued by the Bundesbank. While it is certainly true that a conflict between Germany and other countries emerged as the former economy was heating up under the stimulus of unification while Europe was sliding towards a recession, there is little evidence supporting the view that the British and Italian authorities pursued a particularly loose monetary policy in the period between German unification and the EMS crisis.

14 Yet one has to recognize that it is possible to observe no correlation between fiscal variables and interest rates for reasons that have little to do with Ricardian equivalence.

15 Seater (1993) is often regarded as the main reference on the topic, though it is somehow dated.

16 Preliminary analysis has been conducted also on nominal yields and, following Kormendi and Protopapadakis (2004), on the impact of fiscal imbalances on the current account: results gave a similar qualitative picture but were of a lesser statistical quality and are therefore not reported.

17 Hence we expect the coefficient on this variable to be negative as an increase in the primary balance should lower the borrowing cost faced by the government.

18 ADF, Phillips-Perron and KPSS tests.

19 Coefficients remains not statistically different from zero also when (8.2) is augmented with the squares of fiscal variables (primary balance and debt to GDP) to capture non-linear effects. Also, using the difference between long- and short-term yields as the dependent variable does not alter the results.

20 Data are taken from the ECB *Monthly Bulletin*, which is the reference for more information on the data.

21 See among others Lemmen and Goodhart (1999); Lønning (2000); Camarero *et al.* (2003); Codogno *et al.* (2003); Dunne *et al.* (2003); Hartman *et al.* (2003); Afonso and Strauch (2004); Bernoth *et al.* (2004); Piga and Valente (2004).

22 If the interest rate faced by a country depends on all other EMU countries' behaviour it is not possible to assess whether a lower yield spread between, say Italian and German

bonds depends on the strengthening of the Italian fiscal fundamentals, or rather on the effect of a weak Italian position on German yields (or on a mixture of the two effects).

23 We have chosen not to use the indicator of discretionary fiscal stance à la Blanchard (1990) because the first stage fit needed to compute the sensitivity of the primary balance to GDP growth (from which the Blanchard indicator is then constructed) is extremely poor and therefore our estimates very imprecise.

24 Previous versions of the work used both disaggregated fiscal variables for the four countries and monthly series obtained by interpolation. Results were dominated by noise and very poor and therefore are not reported.

25 To explore this intuition in more detail we have added the squares of bond issues and debt stocks to the estimating equation, but the picture does not change. Also, we have interacted them with a dummy for EMU, but again these new controls were not significant and results are not shown.

References

Afonso, A. and Strauch, R. (2004), 'Fiscal policy events and interest rate swap spreads: evidence from the EU', Working Paper 303, European Central Bank.

Aoki, M. and Leijonhufvud, A. (1987), 'The stock-flow analysis of investment', Working Paper 445, UCLA.

Ardagna, S., Caselli, F. and Lane, T. (2004), 'Fiscal discipline and the cost of public debt service: some estimates for OECD countries', Working Paper 10788, NBER.

Artis, M. and Winkler, B. (1999), 'The Stability Pact: trading off flexibility for credibility?', in M. Hughes Hallett, M. Hutchinson and S. Hougaard Jensen (eds), *Fiscal Aspects of European Monetary Integration*, Cambridge: Cambridge University Press. 157–88.

Baele, L., Ferrando, A., Hördahl, P., Krylova, E. and Monnet, C. (2004), 'Measuring financial integration in the euro area', Occasional Paper 14, ECB.

Barro, R. (1989), 'The neoclassical approach to fiscal policy', in R. Barro (ed.), *Modern Business Cycle Theory*, Cambridge: Harvard University Press. 178–235.

Bayoumi, T., Goldstein, M. and Woglom, G. (1993), 'Do credit markets discipline sovereign borrowers? Evidence from U.S. states', *Journal of Money Credit and Banking*, 27: 1045–59.

Beetsma, R. and Vermeylen, K. (2005), 'The effect of monetary unification on public debt and its real return', Working Paper 1400, CESifo.

Bernoth, K., von Hagen, J. and Schuknecht, L. (2004), 'Sovereign risk premia in the European bond market', Discussion Paper 4465, CEPR.

Blanchard, O. (1985), 'Debt, deficits and finite horizons', *Journal of Political Economy*, 93: 223–47.

——— (1990), 'Suggestions for a new set of fiscal indicators', Working Paper 79, OECD Economics Department.

Branson, W. (1988), 'International adjustment and the dollar: policy illusions and economic constraints', in W. Guth (ed.), *Economic Policy Coordination*, IMF. 44–84.

Breedon, F., Henry, B. and Williams, G. (1999), 'Long–term interest rates: evidence on the global capital market', *Oxford Review of Economic Policy*, 15: 128–42.

Brunila, A., Hukkinen, J. and Tujula, M. (1999), 'Indicators of the cyclically adjusted budget balance: the Bank of Finland's experience', Discussion Paper 1, Bank of Finland.

Buiter, W., Corsetti, G. and Roubini, N. (1993), 'Disavanzo eccessivo, ragionevolezza e nonsenso nel Trattato di Maastricht', *Rivista di Politica Economica*, VI: 3–82.

Bundesbank (1997), 'Trends in public sector debt since German unification', *Deutsche Bundesbank Monthly Report*, March: 17–31.

Camarero, M., Ordoñez, J. and Tamarit, C. (2003), 'Tests for interest rate convergence and structural break in the EMS: further analysis', *Applied Financial Economics*, 12: 447–56.

Cheung, S. (1996), 'Provincial credit ratings in Canada: an ordered probit analysis', Working Paper 96-6, Bank of Canada.

Chinn, M. and Frankel, J. (2003), 'The euro area and world interest rates', Working Paper 03-17, Santa Cruz Center for International Economics.

Codogno, L., Favero, C. and Missale, A. (2003), 'Governement bond spreads', *Economic Policy*, 18: 503–32.

Corsetti, G. and Pesenti, P. (2001), 'Welfare and macroeconomic interdependence', *Quarterly Journal of Economics*, 116: 421–45.

Cottarelli, C. and Mecagni, M. (1991), 'The risk premium over Italian government debt, 1976–88', in T. Mayer and F. Spinelli (eds), *Macroeconomics and Macroeconomic Policy Issues*, Vol. 11/91 of *Quaderni di Economia e Banca*, Trento: Banca di Trento e Bolzano. 33–72.

Diamond, P. (1965), 'National debt in a neoclassic growth model', *American Economic Review*, 55: 1126–50.

Dornbusch, R. and Wolf, H. (1992), 'Economic transition in Eastern Germany', *Brookings Papers on Economic Activity*, 1: 235–72.

Dunne, P., Moore, M. and Portes, R. (2003), 'Defining benchmark status: an application using euro-area bonds', Working Paper 9087, NBER.

Eichengreen, B. and Wyplosz, C. (1993), 'The unstable EMS', *Brookings Papers on Economic Activity*, 1: 51–143.

Farina, F. and Tamborini, R. (2002), 'Le politiche di stabilizzazione in Europa nel nuovo regime di unione monetaria', in F. Farina and R. Tamborini (eds), *Da Nazioni a Regioni. Mutamenti Strutturali e Istituzionali dopo l'Ingresso nella Unione Monetaria Europea*, Bologna: Il Mulino. 15–126.

Favero, C. (2001), *Applied Macroeconometrics*, Oxford: Oxford University Press.

Flandreau, M., Le Cacheaux, J. and Zumer, F. (1998), 'Stability without a pact? Lessons form the European gold standard, 1880–1914', *Economic Policy*, 13: 115–62.

Fleming, M. (1962), 'Domestic financial policies under fixed and under floating exchange rates', IMF Staff Papers, 9: 369–79.

Ford, R. and Laxton, D. (1999), 'World public debt and real interest rates', *Oxford Review of Economic Policy*, 15: 77–94.

Frenkel, J. and Razin, A. (1992), *Fiscal Policies and the World Economy*, 2nd edn, Cambridge: The MIT Press.

Giavazzi, F. and Pagano, M. (1988), 'The advantage of tying one's hands: EMS discipline and central bank credibility', *European Economic Review*, 32: 1055–82.

Gravelle, T. (1999), 'Liquidity of the government of Canada securities market: stylized facts and some market microstructure comparisons to the United States treasury market', Working Paper 11, Bank of Canada.

Hartman, P., Maddaloni, A. and Manganelli, S. (2003), 'The euro area financial system: structure, integration and policy initiatives', Working Paper 230, ECB.

Kenen, P. (1995), *Economic and Monetary Union in Europe*, Cambridge: Cambridge University Press.

Kormendi, R. and Protopapadakis, A. (2004), 'Budget deficits, current account deficits and interest rates: the systematic evidence on Ricardian equivalence', Macroeconomics

0403010, EconWPA. Online. Available HTTP: <http://ideas.repec.org/p/wpa/wuwpma/0403010.html> (accessed 18 October 2006).

Lamfalussy, A. (1989), 'Macro-coordination of fiscal policies in an economic and monetary union in Europe', in Committee for the Study of Economic and Monetary Union (ed.), *Report on Economic and Monetary Union in the European Community*, Office for the Official Publications of the European Communities. 91–125.

Leith, C. and Wren-Lewis, S. (2001), 'Compatibility between monetary and fiscal policy under EMU', Discussion paper in Economics 01-15, University of Glasgow.

Lemmen, J. and Goodhart, C. (1999), 'Credit risk and European government bond markets: a panel data econometric analysis', *Eastern Economic Journal*, 25: 77–107.

Lønning, I. (2000), 'Default premia on European government debt', *Weltwirtschaftliches Archiv*, 136: 259–83.

Mundell, R. (1963), 'Capital mobility and stabilization policy under fixed and flexible exchange rates', *Canadian Journal of Economics and Political Science*, 29: 475–85.

—— (1964), 'A reply: capital mobility and size', *Canadian Journal of Economics and Political Science*, 30: 421–31.

Obstfeld, M. and Rogoff, K. (1996), *Foundations of International Macroeconomics*, Cambridge: The MIT Press.

Perée, E. and Steinherr, A. (2001), 'The euro and capital markets: a new era', *World Economy*, 24: 1295–308.

Piga, G. and Valente, G. (2004), 'The term structure of interest rates and the public debt issuance policy: a note', *Finance Letters*, 2.

Restoy, F. (1996), 'Interest rates and fiscal discipline in monetary unions', *European Economic Review*, 40: 1629–46.

Rose, A. and Svensson, L. (1994), 'European exchange rate credibility before the fall', *European Economic Review*, 38: 1185–216.

Seater, J. (1993), 'Ricardian equivalence', *Journal of Economic Literature*, 31: 142–90.

Sinn, H.-W. (1996), 'International implication of German unification', Working Paper 5839, NBER.

Stock, J. and Watson, M. (1993), 'A simple estimator of cointegrating vectors in higher order integrated systems', *Econometrica*, 61: 783–820.

Tamborini, R. (1997), 'Living in the EMU. The dynamics of the Maastricht Treaty's fiscal rules', *Rivista Italiana degli Economisti*, II: 335–59.

—— (2002), 'One monetary giant with many fiscal dwarfs: the efficiency of macroeconomic stabilization policies in the EMU', Discussion paper 4.02, Dipartimento di Economia, Università di Trento.

Thygesen, N. (1999), 'Fiscal institutions in EMU and the Stability Pact', in A. Hughes Hallett, M. Hutchinson and S. Hougaard Jensen (eds), *Fiscal Aspects of European Monetary Integration*, Cambridge: Cambridge University Press. 15–36.

9 Inflation divergence and public deficits in a monetary union[*]

J. Creel and J. Le Cacheux

9.1 Introduction

The relationship between public deficits (or fiscal policy), inflation and interest rates has long given rise to an abundant literature. Two distinct seminal works can be emphasized. On the one hand, the Hicksian IS-LM model (see Hicks, 1937) reveals the positive short-term effect of public deficits on nominal interest rate. The ensuing 'crowding-out' effect would be detrimental to GDP. On the other hand, Diamond (1965)[1] showed that, in the long run, higher public deficits and debt may enhance social welfare when the capital stock exceeds the golden rule level (e.g. when the interest rate is below its natural level). In both cases, higher deficits and debts push interest rates up and private investment down.

This line of reasoning has been used as an argument for restricting fiscal policies in a monetary union: an expansionary fiscal policy would produce 'beggar-thy-neighbour' effects, since higher interest rates would be undergone not only by the country implementing the policy but also by the other monetary union member states. Although not the single argument,[2] it had strong influence on the adoption of fiscal convergence criteria in the Maastricht Treaty and on the enactment of the Stability and Growth Pact.

Despite strong theoretical support, the crowding-out effect remains disputable (see the seminal paper of B. Friedman, 1978, and a recent survey by Ducoudré, 2005). In a monetary union, for instance, wider financial markets after the monetary union was constituted reduce the sensitiveness of long-term interest rates to a domestic deficit.

The controversy between those arguing about crowding-out effects and those arguing about crowding-in effects remains important in the euro area. According to the former, higher deficits would produce higher interest rates, whereas, for the others, the reverse could be true. In empirical terms, since 1999, the discrepancy in fiscal deficits among euro area's member states has been large, while divergent inflation rates and divergent real interest rates have persisted. Is one responsible for the other? In this paper, we wish to analyse precisely the interrelationships between these variables and wish to study the determinants of inflation divergence and fiscal policies' divergence.

To do so, we take as a point of departure a recent model elaborated by R. Beetsma and K. Vermeylen (2005). Their model is an elegant framework which links real rates of return, public debts and inflation rates in a monetary union made up of a multiplicity of countries. They concluded that within a monetary union, 'the expected real interest rate paid on public debt exceeds its pre-unification level'. This result is explained as follows: 'a (public) debt increase in one country exerts a direct positive effect on the required rate of return on other countries' (public) debt when these countries all form a monetary union, while this effect is absent when the countries do not form a union.' They conclude that: 'monetary unification may cause worries in low-debt countries about the fiscal discipline of highly-indebted countries'.

This would suggest that crowding-out effects are larger after unification than before. However, their model is unable to fit the evidence on the two above-mentioned divergent patterns in the euro area: Beetsma and Vermeylen assume that inflation is perfectly correlated across countries participating in a monetary union and, by construction, real interest rates are also perfectly correlated.

We decided to use their model, but to relax the assumption of perfectly correlated inflation and real interest rates in a monetary union and to introduce inflation divergence instead. This led us to an inconsistency in the conclusion of the model. To solve the inconsistency, we introduce a distinction between two categories of public expenditures, productive and unproductive ones. The resulting model is admittedly rather different in spirit from Beetsma and Vermeylen's, but it seems more in line with reality in the euro area; and also to produce new results.

With this new framework, we demonstrate that the causation between inflation rates (and interest rates) and public deficits is reversed in comparison with Beetsma and Vermeylen's earlier statement. Our model then explains public deficits' divergence within the euro area by inflation divergence. Finally, an empirical investigation gives some support to this theoretical conclusion.

9.2 The stylized facts

The relationship between public deficits and long-term interest rates has a long history which goes beyond the scope of this paper.[3] Simple statistics may be used to shed light on this relationship within the euro area.

The early years of the Stability and Growth Pact have been rather turbulent: despite general improvements of public finances in 1999 and 2000, public deficits have started increasing in 2001 in all euro area countries, except Belgium and France, where the starting point was 2002, and Spain, whose starting point was 2004 (see Figure 9.1). Four countries among the ten euro area member states[4] have even exceeded the deficit threshold: France and Germany since 2002, Portugal in 2001 and the Netherlands in 2003.

Although the Stability and Growth Pact was meant as a mechanism fostering fiscal discipline, it has been poorly enforced. The rationale behind the discipline embedded in the Pact is to prevent inflationary pressures that the independent

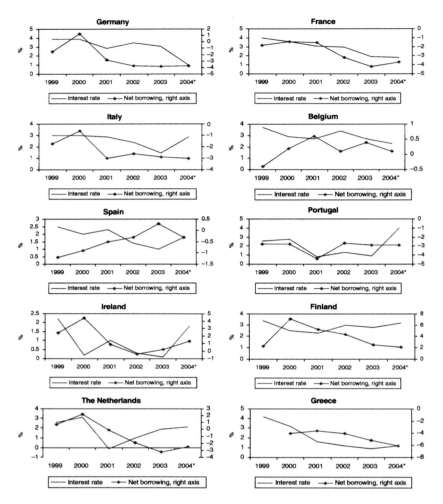

Figure 9.1 Public deficits and interest rates in Euro area countries.

Source: European Commission, Spring Forecasts 2005.

Notes
Interest rate means "real long-term interest rate", i.e. nominal long-term interest rate deflated by the yearly variation of the harmonized index of consumer prices. *Net borrowing* is net borrowing of general government expressed in percent of GDP.

European Central Bank would have to curb ultimately. With binding fiscal constraints, the ECB was meant to be able to focus on private inflation determinants and to improve the overall price competitiveness of the euro area.[5]

So, has the indiscipline of some major euro area countries led to higher inflation or to higher real interest rates on public bonds?

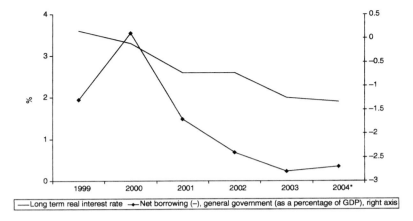

Figure 9.2 Public deficit and the real long-term interest rate in the Euro area.
Source: European Commission, Spring Forecasts 2005.

Figure 9.2 displays the evolution of public finances and that of real long-term interest rates in the euro area; it appears that a sensible decrease in the long-term real interest rate has occurred despite a sharp increase in public deficits.

Except in Belgium, Spain and Finland, a positive relationship between public surpluses and real interest rates is also found in most of the euro area countries (*cf.* Figure 9.1).

9.3 The euro area's puzzle

Of course, basic empirical evidence that poorly disciplined fiscal policies do not seem to have increased real interest rates is not a necessary or sufficient proof for rejection of the theory of crowding-out effects. The above-presented data do not permit discrimination between different determinants of long-term interest rates. Indeed, the fiscal part of these determinants may have been compensated by an appropriate monetary policy, a dramatic change in the liquidity preference of households and so on.

If macroeconomic data are useless in this respect, we propose to turn towards a micro-founded theoretical model to investigate the real long-term interest rates' determinants. Beetsma and Vermeylen (2005) have developed a nice micro-founded framework in which they model the link between public debt and the interest rate in a general equilibrium setting. They make use of two strong assumptions: the correlations among inflation rates and among real long-term interest rates are increasing and finally perfect when countries form a monetary union, to be compared with the pre-union situation. These two assumptions are crucial for their final conclusion, according to which an extended union-wide crowding-out effect is expected when one country in the monetary union increases its public debt.

Nevertheless, diverging monetary conditions within the euro area can be identified in the covariance matrices, respectively for the real long-term interest rates (Table 9.1) and for the inflation rates (Table 9.2) between 1999 and 2004. In these tables, we have set in bold the values of the covariance which were at least superior to 0.5. In the first case, only Greece and to a lesser extent Germany seem to have converging long-run real interest rates vis-à-vis their euro area partners. In the second case, only the Netherlands seems to generate a covariance of their inflation rate with that of other countries superior to 0.5. Convergent inflation rates occur among 'small countries' (Austria, Greece and Portugal vis-à-vis the Netherlands), but still remain a scarce situation.

Data in Figure 9.3 also show that the convergence of long-term real interest rates within the euro area is far from complete. The same applies to the inflation rates

Table 9.1 Covariance matrix for the long term real interest rates in the Euro area, 1999–2004

	Bel	Dnk	Grc	Spa	Fra	Ire	Ita	Nld	Aus	Por
Bel										
Dnk	0.4									
Grc	0.4	0.6								
Spa	0.1	0.1	0.5							
Fra	0.4	0.6	0.8	0.3						
Ire	0.1	−0.2	0.7	0.4	0.3					
Ita	0.0	−0.1	0.4	0.3	0.2	0.4				
Nld	0.1	−0.1	0.5	0.0	0.0	0.4	0.0			
Aus	0.4	0.8	0.7	0.1	0.6	0.1	0.0	0.1		
Por	−0.1	−0.8	0.4	0.2	−0.2	0.8	0.4	0.7	−0.3	
Fin	0.1	0.0	0.2	0.0	0.0	0.2	0.0	0.3	0.1	0.3

Sources: European Commission, authors' computations.

Table 9.2 Covariance matrix for the inflation rates in the Euro area, 1999–2004

	Bel	Dnk	Grc	Spa	Fra	Ire	Ita	Nld	Aus	Por
Bel										
Dnk	0.2									
Grc	0.1	0.2								
Spa	0.1	0.1	0.2							
Fra	0.1	0.1	0.3	0.2						
Ire	0.4	0.2	0.4	0.5	0.4					
Ita	0.1	0.1	0.2	0.2	0.2	0.3				
Nld	0.3	0.4	0.6	0.1	0.2	0.2	0.0			
Aus	0.3	0.3	0.3	0.2	0.2	0.5	0.1	0.5		
Por	0.2	0.3	0.4	0.1	0.3	0.3	0.1	0.8	0.4	
Fin	0.4	0.2	0.1	0.2	0.1	0.5	0.1	0.4	0.4	0.2

Source: European Commission, authors' computations.

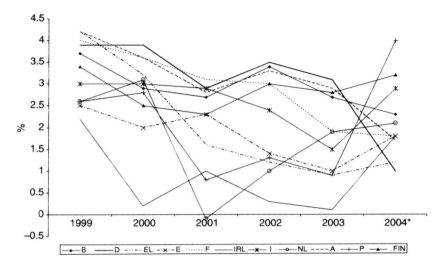

Figure 9.3 Domestic real long term interest rates in the Euro area.

Source: European Commission, Spring Forecasts 2005.

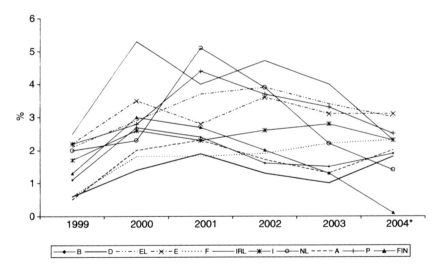

Figure 9.4 Domestic HICP-based inflation rates in the Euro area.

Source: European Commission, Spring Forecasts 2005.

(*cf.* Figure 9.4); although convergence has improved since 1999, except the recent experiences of the Netherlands and Finland, the range of domestic inflation rates is still large and explains the discrepancy of real interest rates: nominal interest rates have already converged, but insofar as inflation divergence within the euro area persists, so does real interest rate spreads. Identifying the sources of inflation divergence is crucial in this respect.

The convergence of nominal long-term interest rates reveals that financial markets do not discriminate among euro area's governments despite the *no-bail-out* clause. For those who argue that inflation trends impinge on long-run nominal interest rates along the Fisher equation, for instance, the present situation in the euro area, with divergent inflation rates and highly convergent nominal interest rates, is a *puzzle*.

In fact, the usual links between inflation and long-run nominal interest rates can be at least twofold. First, present inflation may fuel expectations of future inflation and, hence, may have a direct positive impact on nominal interest rates (the Fisher effect). Second, nominal interest rates and inflation rates may have a common determinant: fiscal policy. Via the goods and the capital markets, public deficits may produce inflationary pressures and may increase the nominal interest rates, hence provoking the so-called crowding-out effect. Basing upon the stylized fact that the nominal interest rate in the euro area has generally been higher the higher net [? SENSE ?] *lending* by general governments (see Figure 9.2), the crowding-out effect does not seem to be validated, and we have to turn towards the direct link between inflation and public deficits to gather the pieces of the European puzzle.

9.4   The model by Beetsma and Vermeylen

Thanks to the convergence criteria established in the Maastricht Treaty, and in a context of full liberalization of markets for goods and services (European capital markets had already been liberalized since 1990), inflation convergence in the euro area has indeed occurred in the pre-unification period; it was therefore considered likely to go on after the launching of the single currency in January 1999. Since 1999, however, inflation divergence within the euro area has been a major and early concern for the ECB[6] and has been precisely documented (Duarte, 2003; Honohan and Lane, 2003; Angeloni and Ehrmann, 2004). Most contributions endeavour to characterize the determinants of inflation divergence and they fail to conclude that public deficits have had an impact. Since Beetsma and Vermeylen's normative conclusion is exactly the opposite, it has been appealing to extend their model to make it fit the empirical literature.

Most of the assumptions that will be introduced in the model hinge extensively on the modelling choices made by Beetsma and Vermeylen. Although some are quite strong and are related to a monetarist framework, which empirical reliability is, at best, questionable, we have decided to take Beetsma and Vermeylen's model as our theoretical point of departure; their model is the most recent one trying to link public debt, inflation and real interest rates in a monetary union.

9.4.1   The model

In a world made up of N countries, where countries $1, \ldots, N^U$ form a monetary union ($N > 1$ and $1 < N^U \le N$), countries are constituted of two-period overlapping generations of a constant size (normalized to one). The representative agent in each country i maximizes an expected lifetime quadratic utility subject to the budget constraint:

$$U_t^i = C_{1,t}^i - \frac{1}{2}\gamma \left(C_{1,t}^i\right)^2 + \frac{1}{1+\rho}E_t\left[C_{2,t+1}^i - \frac{1}{2}\gamma \left(C_{2,t+1}^i\right)^2\right] \qquad (9.1)$$

$$C_{2,t+1}^i = (Y - T_{i,t} - C_{1,t}^i)\left[\sum_{j=1}^{N}\omega_{j,t}^i(1 + r_{j,t+1}) + \left(1 - \sum_{j=1}^{N}\omega_{j,t}^i\right)(1 + r^*)\right],$$
$$(9.2)$$

where $C_{1,t}^i$ and $C_{2,t+1}^i$ are the representative agent's consumption in periods t and $t+1$, respectively, ρ is the agent's discount rate, E_t is the expectations operator conditional on the available information, γ a positive parameter, Y the agent's endowment, $T_{i,t}$ the taxes paid by the representative agent, $\omega_{j,t}^i$ the share of this agent's savings in period t invested in public debt (or bonds) of country j, $r_{j,t+1}$ is the real interest rate paid in period $t+1$ on public debt and r^* the real, risk-free, interest rate on private savings.

Each government is able to spend an amount $G_{i,t}$ at period t and finance it by raising taxes $T_{i,t}$ and/or by issuing public debt $B_{i,t}$, following the usual dynamic budget constraint:

$$B_{i,t} = G_{i,t} + B_{i,t-1}(1 + r_{i,t}) - T_{i,t}. \qquad (9.3)$$

Beetsma and Vermeylen argue that fiscal policy is described as a trade-off faced by governments between the cost of raising taxes and the cost of deferring them, hence

$$L_{i,t}^{gov} = T_{i,t} + \frac{1}{1+\beta_i}E_t\left[B_{i,t}(1 + r_{i,t+1})\right], \qquad (9.4)$$

where parameter β_i 'captures the relative importance that government i attaches to the interests of the taxpayers'.

As for central banks, Beetsma and Vermeylen assume that: first, the central bank determines at period t the growth rate of the money supply $m_{i,t}$ from period t to $t+1$; second, the inflation rate is closely, although stochastically, related to the growth rate of the money supply:

$$\pi_{i,t} = m_{i,t}(1 + \varepsilon_{i,t}), \qquad (9.5)$$

with $\pi_{i,t}$ the inflation rate in country i between periods t and $t+1$, and the stochastic term $\varepsilon_{i,t} \sim N(0,\sigma^2)$ is $i.i.d.$ over time and across countries; and, third, central banks' loss function incorporates two objectives: maintaining price stability and stabilizing public debt. The parameter λ in equation (9.6) below, in the case of monetary union, can be interpreted as the degree of central bank's dependence on the government:

$$L_t^{cb,u} = \frac{1}{2} E_t \left(\pi_{t+1}^u\right)^2 + \lambda^u E_t \left[\frac{1}{N^u} \sum_{i=1}^{N^u} B_{i,t}(1 + r_{i,t+1})\right], \tag{9.6}$$

with $\lambda^u > 0$ and N^U is the number of countries (out of N) forming a monetary union.

Under perfect foresight, the expected *nominal* interest rate is equal to the actual future *nominal* interest rate, hence

$$r_{i,t+1} = r_{i,t+1}^e + \pi_{i,t}^e - \pi_{i,t}, \tag{9.5b}$$

and as uncertainty in the model only stems from the inflation rate (equation (9.5)), the variance of the domestic real debt return follows:

$$Var_t(r_{i,t+1}) = Var_t(\pi_{i,t+1}) = m_{i,t+1}^2 \sigma^2. \tag{9.7}$$

Unlike Beetsma and Vermeylen, we disregard the assumption that inflation rates and, thus here, real debt returns would be perfectly correlated across countries in the monetary union. On the contrary, and as discussed in the preceding section, these correlations are low and we assume in the following that they are very close to zero, hence

$$\begin{aligned} \text{cov}_t(r_{i,t+1}; r_{j,t+1}) &= 0 \quad \forall i \neq j \\ \text{cov}_t(\pi_{i,t}; \pi_{j,t}) &= 0 \quad \forall i \neq j. \end{aligned} \tag{9.8}$$

These assumptions do introduce inflation divergence in the framework. Note that they will have a strong consequence on the inconsistency we have found in Beetsma and Vermeylen's conclusions. This we interpret as a weakness of their framework: they can demonstrate a close relationship between public debt, inflation rate and real interest rates, but only insofar as inflation divergence is understated.

9.4.2 An inconsistent result under EMU

Incorporating the budget constraint of the representative young agent of country i in her first-order conditions with respect to her decisions to hold country j's public debt and to invest in the risk-free technology, and aggregating across the representative agents of the different countries, taking into account the equilibrium conditions and assuming that $r^* = \rho$, where ρ is the agent's discount rate, the 'mean-variance'-expression for the demand for country i's debt as a function of the expected real interest rate is

$$r_{i,t+1}^e = r^* + \mu_t \left[B_{i,t} Var_t(r_{i,t+1})\right] \tag{9.9}$$

with $\mu_t = \frac{\gamma}{N(1-\gamma\bar{C}_{1,t})}$; and $\bar{C}_{1,t} = \frac{C_{1,t}}{N}$.

The intuition is as follows: representative agents demand public debt until its real return equals the real return on private assets plus a risk premium proportional to public debt's holdings and the variability of the real interest rate. Thanks to diversification opportunities, the risk premium is lower, the higher the number of the countries in the world. Moreover, a growing debt might reduce the real rate of return but only insofar as the variance of this rate is also sharply reduced.

In a Nash situation, each government minimizes its loss function (9.4) subject to its budget constraint (9.3). Full information incorporated in (9.9) is given, so that

$$r^e_{i,t+1} = \beta_i - \mu_t \left[B_{i,t} Var_t(r_{i,t+1}) \right].$$ (9.10)

For countries participating in a monetary union, the common central bank sets m^u_t to minimize equation (9.6) subject to

$$\pi_{u,t} = m_{u,t}(1 + \varepsilon_{u,t}),$$ (9.5b)

taking domestic debts, expected real rates of return and expected inflation rates as given, yielding

$$m^u_{t+1} = \pi^{e,u}_{t+1} = \frac{\lambda^u \bar{B}^u_t}{1 + \sigma^2},$$ (9.11)

with $\bar{B}^u_t = \frac{1}{N^u} \sum_{i=1}^{N^u} B^u_{i,t}$, the average level of public debt in the monetary union.

Substituting equation (9.11) into equation (9.7) gives

$$Var_t(r_{u,t+1}) = \left(\frac{\lambda^u \bar{B}^u_t}{1 + \sigma^2} \right)^2 \sigma^2 \equiv \hat{\sigma}^2 \quad \forall i \in [1, N^u].$$ (9.12)

The variability of the average public debt real return depends on the uncertainty of the relationship between money and average inflation, and on the average level of public debt in the monetary union.

At equilibrium eqns. (9.9) and (9.10) give the steady state level of public debt for country i:

$$B^*_{i,t} = \frac{\beta_i - r^*}{2\mu_t Var(r_{i,t+1})}.$$ (9.13)

Substituting (9.12) into (9.13) yields

$$B^*_{i,t} = \frac{(\beta_i - r^*)(1 + \sigma^2)^2}{2\mu_t \left(\lambda^u \bar{B}^u_t \right)^2 \sigma^2}.$$ (9.14)

Eqn (9.14) states that the steady state level of debt in country i is lower the higher the average of public debts in the monetary union. Unfortunately, this statement is supposed to hold for any country participating in the union, hence for all countries of the union, and, of course, if all countries decrease their respective debt level, the monetary union average will also decrease, not increase!

This specification of the model incorporating inflation divergence thus leads to an inconsistency. The model by Beetsma and Vermeylen without inflation divergence is therefore highly specific. No general conclusion on the relationship between public debt and real returns can be drawn from their framework.

9.5   A variant to the model by Beetsma and Vermeylen

9.5.1 Doing without inflation divergence

Disregarding inflation divergence, a very typical situation within a monetary union arises: any country that's debt is growing, all else equal in the other countries of the monetary union, will provoke higher uncertainty in the whole union that will feed inflationary pressures. Average inflation in the monetary union can be rewritten as a function of the average public debt level, substituting equation (9.11) into equation (9.5b):

$$\pi_{u,t} = \frac{1}{N^u} \sum_{i=1}^{N^u} \pi_{i,t}^u = \frac{\lambda^u (1 + \varepsilon_{u,t})}{(1 + \sigma^2)} \bar{B}_t^u . \tag{9.15}$$

Average inflation rate in the monetary union also depends on the average level of public debt, so that a country implementing a *lax* fiscal policy will make its partner countries suffer from a higher average inflation rate which will trigger a restrictive monetary policy by the common central bank. This kind of argument is very usual in the macroeconomic literature. The story that one poorly behaving country can adversely affect the entire union is exactly the argument that led the governments of future EMU to legislate, in the Maastricht Treaty, that each country was responsible for its own debt and that other countries would not be bound by solidarity.

9.5.2 Taking inflation divergence seriously

However, acknowledging the presence of inflation divergence in the monetary union, the conclusion of the model is no longer satisfactory. The inconsistency has to be solved. To succeed in this task, we modified the fiscal policy part of the model. In Beetsma and Vermeylen, fiscal policy is described as a trade-off faced by governments between the cost of raising taxes and the cost of deferring them (their equation (4)). In a rational expectations framework and since public expenditures are not productive, Ricardian equivalence must hold, so that private agents are indifferent between higher taxes today and higher taxes in the future. However, the trade-off as it stands in

Beetsma and Vermeylen's model is not the only choice facing fiscal policy in contemporary economies; rather, we assume that the trade-off may be between the cost of raising taxes and the cost of deferring them *only insofar as* public expenditures *are not* productive. Ricardian equivalence does not hold in this setting.

On the one hand, our assumption entails that governments have their loss *lowered* if they are able to finance *productive* expenditures via public debt issuance. On the other hand, financing such expenditures via taxation is costly. Higher taxes in period *t* thus reduce the lifetime welfare of the present generation, which has to pay the taxes in period *t* but does not benefit from the productive expenditures whose positive externalities will occur only in the future.

Public expenditures hence split in two main categories: some are productive $(G_{i,t}^p)$ and can be associated with high-productivity (investment) expenditures; while others are not $(G_{i,t}^{np})$ and can be associated with low-productivity (consumption) expenditures. Of course, $G_{i,t} = G_{i,t}^p + G_{i,t}^{np}$. If public expenditures are productive, issuing public debt is beneficial to the governments (as it is presumably for the whole domestic economy), that is, the government's loss is reduced, all else equal.

Because the general model does not incorporate economic growth, the distinction between productive and unproductive expenditures has to rely on a specific mechanism. This mechanism is related to the 'crowding-in vs. crowding-out effects' debate (Friedman, 1978): productive expenditures have an *ex post* rate of return superior to that of unproductive expenditures; within a perfect foresight framework, they hence reduce the present financial cost of public debt, here represented by $r_{i,t+1}$, in comparison with the financing of unproductive expenditures. Productive expenditures impinge positively on welfare in that they provoke a crowding-in effect, while unproductive expenditures produce a crowding-out effect.

On theoretical grounds, we thus depart from Beetsma and Vermeylen in terms of the specification of governments' loss functions: the government of country *i* minimizes a loss function of the form:

$$L_{i,t}^{gov} = T_{i,t} + \frac{1}{1 + \beta_i} E_t \left[B_{i,t}(r_{i,t+1} - r^*) \right],$$
(9.4b)

where β_i is now the rate at which government of country *i* discounts the real debt burden for the future generations.

We also interpret the presence of public debt in central banks' loss functions differently from Beetsma and Vermeylen: public debt may be inflationary in the future if it *does not* finance a productive public investment. Hence, we assume that central banks can possibly accept a higher current inflation rate insofar as it eases the financing process of a *productive* capital asset. However, this monetary policy is inefficient (or costly) if this real public debt finances unproductive public consumption. The central bank hence faces an uncertainty as regards the productive or unproductive nature of public expenditures, a reason why the inflation rate is stochastic. The parameter λ in eqn (9.8) can be interpreted as the degree of *indirect* participation of the central bank in the implementation of public investment.

In this new setting, the government's problem is somewhat different from what it was in Beetsma and Vermeylen's framework. If public investment (or *productive* public spending) becomes the key variable of the government, the latter will control the financing of this spending. In the logic of the Golden Rule of Public Finance, which is implicit in our fiscal framework, taxes pay for current expenditures, and public debt 'pays' for public investment: the government will hence choose public debt so that it maximizes its welfare.

In a Nash situation, each government minimizes its loss function (9.4b) subject to its budget constraint (9.3):

$$-\left(\frac{1}{1+\beta_i}\right)\left[E_t\left(r_{i,t+1}-r^*\right)-E_{t+1}\left(r_{i,t+2}-r^*\right)\left(1+r_{i,t+1}\right)\right]=0. \quad (9.16)$$

Under the assumptions that $r_{i,t}^2 \to 0$ and $r_{i,t}.r^* \to 0$, one obtains

$$E_t(r_{i,t+1}) = E_t(r_{i,t+2}). \quad (9.17)$$

Proposition 1

In equilibrium, under perfect foresight, the path of the real return on public debt is constant over time; thus, an optimal level of public debt exists in each economy and it is designed by this steady state rate of return.

Proof

(directly ensuing from equation (9.17)).

Applying equation (9.5b) forward, substituting into (9.9), also stated forward, and using equation (9.17), the general solution for the real return on public debt is

$$Var_t(r_{i,t+1}) = \frac{E_t\pi_{i,t+1}^e - \pi_{i,t}^e - (E_t\pi_{i,t+1} - \pi_{i,t})}{\mu_t B_{i,t} - \mu_{t+1}E_t B_{i,t+1}}. \quad (9.18)$$

Uncertainty on public debt's return depends on three distinct, though related, dynamics: first, the dynamics of expectations for the inflation path; second, the dynamics of future effective inflation; and the prospective evolution of public debt. The higher expected acceleration of inflation or the lower effective acceleration of inflation, the higher uncertainty; and the higher future fiscal surplus, the lower uncertainty.

As, in this framework, it is assumed that uncertainty only stems from the monetary aggregate which is set by the ECB, the variance of average inflation is the same as the variance of domestic inflation rates,[7] so that

$$Var_t(r_{u,t+1}) = Var_t(r_{i,t+1}) = (m_t^u)^2\sigma^2. \quad (9.19)$$

Substituting equations (9.12) and (9.19) in equation (9.18) yields the average public debt level:

$$(\bar{B}_t^u)^2 = \frac{(1+\sigma^2)^2}{\sigma^2(\lambda^u)^2} \left[\frac{E_t\pi_{i,t+1}^e - \pi_{i,t}^e - (E_t\pi_{i,t+1} - \pi_{i,t})}{-E_t d_{gov_i,t+1}} \right] \quad \forall i \in [1, N^U]$$

(9.20)

with $d_{gov,t+1} = E_t G_{i,t+1} + B_{i,t} E_t r_{i,t+1} - E_t T_{i,t+1}$, the fiscal deficit inclusive of net interest payments.

Equation (9.20) holds for every country in the monetary union and there is actually a close relationship between domestic inflation dynamics, future domestic fiscal policies and the *average* public debt level. Moreover, the inconsistency has disappeared: all else equal, eqn (9.20) states that the average level of debt in the monetary union decreases if the public surplus increases in one member state. QED.

Now, rewriting equation (9.20) for two countries i and j which are member states of the monetary union gives

$$\frac{E_t\left[\pi_{i,t+1} - \pi_{i,t+1}^e\right]}{E_t d_{gov_i,t+1}} = \frac{E_t\left[\pi_{j,t+1} - \pi_{j,t+1}^e\right]}{E_t d_{gov_j,t+1}} \quad \forall i \neq j \text{ with } (i,j) \in [1, N^u]^2.$$

(9.21)

Proposition 2

The general solution of the model implies that monetary uncertainty in a monetary union may necessitate the implementation of heterogeneous domestic fiscal policies by the member states.

Proof

If, for any reason, both countries do expect the same future inflation rate, but the realized inflation rates differ, future fiscal policies *must* be different according to equation (9.21).

The intuition is as follows. In equilibrium, each domestic market for public debt in the monetary union must be balanced and the optimal level of real public debt is given by equation (9.17) and is fixed. Since monetary policy is common to all member states, the variances of the domestic inflation rates and real interest rates must converge, that is, their divergence is stabilized (equation (9.19)), so that, *in fine*, the divergence among domestic public debts is also stabilized. This also means that the levels of public debts in the monetary union *(can) differ*. Moreover, if one country in the monetary union has a higher inflation rate than expected, in comparison with its other partners, this country has to implement a more expansionary fiscal policy than its partners', in order for its *real* public debt not to diverge too much from its optimal initial level. Thus, *overall* public debt in the monetary union does not diverge from its initial level. Equilibrium is satisfied on all markets, domestic and union-wide.

Stated shortly, as inflation tends to reduce *real* public debt, a country can satisfy its present value budget constraint with a growing fiscal deficit. This mechanism can be related to the 'real-balance-Pigouvian effect' of the FTPL (Woodford, 2001): if one can demonstrate the existence of a given optimal level of public debt, economic behaviours as expressed in equations (9.18), (9.12) and (9.19) should always tend to make actual debt converge to this optimum. QED.

9.5.3 Discussing inflation determinants

Of course, the model does not say much on the determinants of inflation; within this modified Beetsma and Vermeylen's framework, inflation remains a pure monetary phenomenon. Although this is a very disputable issue, the current framework for the ECB monetary policy strategy still hinges extensively on the Quantity theory: reliance of the first pillar on M3 growth rate is one important example. The conclusion of our model is thus that, even if one were to believe in the Quantity theory, fiscal policy would matter, but not in the usual sense: the causality does not go from deficits to inflation like in Sargent and Wallace (1981), but from inflation to deficits.

In light of proposition 2, the relevance of the SGP adopted in 1997 can be questioned. The SGP – that is, the adoption of an homogeneous limit on public deficit among countries in the EU[8] and an homogenous mid-term target for the cyclically adjusted deficit – leads automatically to some standardization of the European economies as they should have the same actual and expected inflation rates, according to equations (9.20) and (9.21). This, however, seems quite at odds with the present situation in the EU. Though nominal convergence has been largely increased, in part due to the Maastricht Treaty criteria which were the prerequisites to the adoption of the euro, discrepancies between European countries still provoke persistent real divergence.

Real divergence is not only related to the usual 'GDP-per-capita' divergence – it has been following a converging path between EU countries well before the transition process towards adopting the euro – but also to some important domestic economic structures. Different international specialization and different trade partners, with Germany and Austria relatively more open towards the Central and Eastern European countries (CEECs) and Russia than France, for instance; different situations as regards the labour market, with France and Germany still facing mass unemployment while the Netherlands had almost reached full employment a few years ago and Spain has steeply decreased its unemployment rate; different situations as regards labour productivity, hence a different pace for supply-driven inflation; all these elements may continue to provoke some de-synchronization of European business cycles and different paths for domestic inflation rates. Though this de-synchronization has been reduced in the years preceding the adoption of the euro (see Bentoglio *et al.*, 2001 and Fidrmuc and Korhonen, 2001), the occurrence of asymmetric shocks as well as different economic structures still remain a prominent issue in the euro area (seminal work on this topic is due to Bayoumi and Eichengreen, 1993). Real and inflation divergence must be taken seriously.

9.6 An application to Euro area member states

9.6.1 The empirical model

From the above theoretical model, inflation divergence can be an explaining variable in the equation of public deficits divergence, whereas inflation may not be determined by public finances.

Public deficits, exclusive of interest payments, are usually explained by the output gap and the level of public debt (see Barro, 1986; Bohn, 1998). In the following, we use the public deficit inclusive of interest payments as the dependent variable accordingly with the theoretical model.

We also compute the whole data set in difference vis-à-vis the average-weighted value in the euro area. All data come from the OECD dataset. Descriptive statistics are given in Table 9.3 below. The standard deviation of public deficits' difference is quite high, amounting to 3.7% of GDP, while inflation divergence has a standard deviation of 4.5%. Not reported in Table 9.3, the mean of inflation divergence in the euro area has decreased over the transition period towards euro's adoption, but it has increased again since its adoption: over the 1992–2003 period, the mean of inflation divergence was 0.4%, but was slightly above at 0.5% between 1999 and 2004.

The general specification for public deficits' divergence can be written as

$$\text{ps}_t = c + \alpha_{\text{gap}} \, \text{gap}_t + \alpha_{\text{debt}} \, \text{debt}_t + \alpha_{inf} \, inf_t + \varepsilon_t,$$

where ps_t is public surplus, gap_t is the output gap, debt_t is the net public debt and inf_t is the inflation rate based upon the Harmonized Index of Consumer Prices (HICP). Surpluses and debts are expressed in per cent of GDP; output gaps and inflation rates are expressed in per cent.

To correct for endogeneity between explained and explanatory variables, we have performed multivariate panel regressions using the general method of moments (GMM). One-lag explaining variables have been used as instruments.

Table 9.3 Descriptive statistics, pooled series, 1980–2004

	CPI (%)	Public debt (% of GDP)	Output gap (%)	Public deficit (% of GDP)
Mean	1.1	7.6	−0.2	−0.2
Median	0.1	−1.5	−0.1	0.1
Maximum	23.2	82.0	7.2	10.6
Minimum	−7.7	−115.4	−9.5	−11.1
Std. Dev.	4.50	38.82	2.21	3.72
Observations	264	264	264	264
Cross sections	11	11	11	11

Source: OECD.

9.6.2 Estimation results

Estimation results are reported in Table 9.4. Results for multivariate panel regressions establish the relative contributions of the output gap, net public debt and the inflation rate, all stated in difference vis-à-vis the euro area average, in driving euro area public surplus' differentials, also stated in difference vis-à-vis the euro area average.

The pooled GMM estimate for the inflation differential is not significant over the 1999–2004 sample (equations (9.1) and (9.4) in Table 9.4). The public debt differential is the only explanatory variable of the discrepancy in public surpluses within the constituted euro area, although not with fixed effects: a higher-than-average level of public debt is logically correlated with a higher-than-average public *deficit*. The GMM estimate testifies for causation from debts to deficits: high debt levels reduce fiscal margins for manoeuvre.

Increasing the sample to the period beginning with the Maastricht Treaty (1992–2004), hence taking into account the convergence process,[9] the inflation differential has a statistically significant impact on public deficits' differentials: a higher-than-average inflation rate provokes a higher-than-average public *deficit*. This result is robust to the introduction of fixed effects and to sample change provided the full sample is chosen. This confirms the theoretical result.

This may seem at odds with the specific situation of Germany since 2000, where inflation has been dramatically reduced whereas public deficits were set above the SGP threshold. On a longer time-horizon, however, the result is no longer surprising: higher deficit countries, like Italy, have long had higher inflation rates than the EU average; whereas low deficit countries, like Germany, have long had lower inflation rates than the EU average. We interpret the situation of Germany since 2000 as a transitory change in its own history (see also Creel and Le Cacheux, 2006).

Table 9.4 Panel public surplus regressions, pooled GMM estimates

	Without fixed effects			With fixed effects		
	(1) 1999–2004	(2) 1992–2004	(3) 1980–2004	(4) 1999–2004	(5) 1992–2004	(6) 1980–2004
gap	0.42	0.44	0.29	0.23	0.03	0.26
	(1.3)	(5.5)***	(3.4)***	(0.4)	(0.1)	(2.5)**
debt	−0.03	−0.03	−0.06	−0.23	−0.12	−0.07
	(4.3)***	(6.1)***	(14.6)***	(1.4)	(3.6)***	(4.7)***
inf	−0.21	−0.47	−0.27	0.39	−0.82	−0.35
	(0.2)	(4.9)***	(6.3)***	(0.4)	(5.2)***	(4.3)***
R^2	0.35	0.45	0.54	0.54	0.62	0.59
see	1.96	1.84	2.57	1.91	1.59	2.53
Obs.	66	143	275	66	143	275

Notes
Standard errors are White-corrected for heteroscedasticity. *, **, *** denote significance at the 10, 5 and 1% levels respectively.

Moreover, although public deficits cannot reasonably be attributed exclusively to inflation rates – they are not in our regressions which incorporate other explanatory variables like the output gap and public debt – we have argued in the theoretical framework and we argue in the empirical part of the paper that the convergence towards, and the constitution of, a monetary union in Europe have exacerbated the incidental power of inflation divergence on public deficits' divergence.

Also noteworthy in our estimation results, the explanatory power of public debts' differential is high on the two longer samples, with or without fixed effects. Finally, a higher-than-average output gap tends to induce a higher-than-euro-area-average fiscal surplus. This latter statement is true without fixed effects over the two following periods: 1992–2004 and 1980–2004, and true on the larger one provided fixed effects are introduced. In this respect, reliance on cyclically adjusted deficits in the SGP seems reasonable.[10]

9.7 Conclusions

This chapter analysed a possible explanation for the interrelationships between inflation divergence and public deficits' divergence in a monetary union. Although inflation convergence was expected, thanks to higher competition and higher transparency, inflation divergence has remained an important issue. As such, it has incidence on trade balances among euro area member states – highly competitive countries gain trade market shares at the expense of their low-competitive EU partners – it has also had incidence on the efficiency of the ECB monetary policy: a single short-run interest rate like the repo rate cannot handle heterogeneity of situations.

In this context, it has sometimes been argued that diverging situations of public finances were responsible for diverging inflation trends: higher inflation and higher long-term interest rates were supposed to occur in those countries implementing expansionary or lax fiscal policies. The existence of crowding-out effects was considered crucial in this respect.

Data from the first years of existence of the euro do not confirm the argument. Despite high deficits in some euro area member states, long-term interest rates in Europe have continued to decrease, and then to remain at low levels, since the beginning of the new millennium.

Reversing the causation between inflation, long-term interest rates, and public deficits may be considered as an option. In a theoretical model including some monetarist properties, which should have given some strength to the crowding-out effect argument, but also including a mechanism discriminating between productive and unproductive public expenditures, which has given some realism to the overall setting, we have demonstrated that inflation divergence, resulting from shocks unrelated to public finances, can explain public deficits' divergence in a monetary union. To ensure fiscal solvency at their country level, but also at the monetary union level for which a shadow market for public debts does exist, countries with higher-than-average inflation rates, hence lower-than-average real public debt, have to implement higher-than-average public deficits. The latter are a stabilizing device in a general equilibrium framework like the one described in the theoretical part of the paper.

To escape general equilibrium issues, empirical tests have been performed: public deficits' divergence has been explained not only by inflation divergence, but also by divergence in the output gap and in ratios of public debts on GDP. Empirical tests do not invalidate our main theoretical result, though they may suggest that other forces have also been at work since the launching of the euro.

We conclude that inflation divergence in Europe may have been responsible for the diverging patterns of public finances in the same area, some countries having had to let their public deficits go adrift to cope with high inflation pressures. Despite the constitution of the euro area, the issue remains and must be accommodated by different fiscal strategies. Homogeneous fiscal rules, like in the SGP, are not optimal in this respect, at least insofar as inflation convergence has not been achieved.

Notes

* Helpful comments by Michele Fratianni, Henri Sterdyniak and Koen Vermeylen on a preliminary draft are gratefully acknowledged. We do also thank participants at Journées AFSE 2003 in Lille, at Third Journées internationales d'études Jean Monnet 2003 in Bordeaux, and Third Lectures on macroeconomic governance in the EMU 2006 in Siena for their remarks on this draft. The usual disclaimer applies.
1 Other important contributions are Modigliani (1961) and Tobin (1965). See also Elmendorf and Mankiw (1999) for a survey.
2 See Fitoussi and Padoa-Schioppa (2005) for a comprehensive investigation on why European countries adopted fiscal rules with a ceiling on public deficits and why they urged fiscal consolidations. See also Le Cacheux (2006).
3 See Laubach (2004) for a recent review of the literature.
4 Luxemburg is not documented here. The case of Greece is specific: Eurostat has discovered rather late (in 2004!) that public finances data for this country were heavily biased. In 2001, when Greece joined the euro area, her public deficit was in fact well above the 3%-of-GDP limit.
5 See Fitoussi and Padoa-Schioppa (2005) for a comprehensive analysis.
6 See former ECB President W. Duisenberg's 6 September 2000 speech 'Are Different Price Developments in the Euro Area a Cause for Concern?', or 'Inflation Differentials in a Monetary Union', in the Monthly Bulletin of the ECB, October 1999.
7 Note that it does not mean that inflation rates *per se* do not differ among countries forming a monetary union.
8 The SGP applies to all EU members. Nevertheless, only euro area members may incur fines if they do not fulfil the dispositions of the Pact.
9 At that time, most future euro area members had already begun mimicking the German monetary policy, thus reducing the discrepancy of nominal short-run interest rates to levels that made these countries behave somewhat on the monetary side, as if they were already in a monetary union.
10 The critical appraisal of cyclically adjusted deficits is beyond the scope of this chapter. See Farina and Ricciuti (2006) for a comprehensive discussion and the elaboration of an alternative computation method.

References

Angeloni, I. and Ehrmann, M. (2004), 'Euro area inflation differentials', ECB Working Paper no. 388.

Barro, R. J. (1986), 'US deficits since WW I', *Scandinavian Journal of Economics*, 88: 195–222.

Barro, R. J. and Gordon, D. B. (1983), 'A positive theory of monetary policy in a natural-rate model', *Journal of Political Economy*, 91: 589–610.

Bayoumi, T. and Eichengreen, B. (1993), 'Shocking aspects of European unification', in F. Torres and F. Giavazzi (eds), *Adjustment and Growth in the EMU*, Cambridge: Cambridge University Press.

Beetsma, R. and Vermeylen, K. (2005), 'The effect of monetary unification on public debt and its real return', CESifo Working Paper no. 1400 (also CEPR Discussion Paper no. 3491, 2002).

Bentoglio, G., Fayolle, J. and Lemoine, M. (2002), 'Unity and plurality of the European cycle', OFCE Working Paper, 2002–03.

Bergin, P. R. (2000), 'Fiscal solvency and price level determination in a monetary union', *Journal of Monetary Economics*, 45: 37–53.

Bohn, H. (1998), 'The behavior of US public debt and deficits', *Quarterly Journal of Economics*, 113: 949–63.

Creel, J. and Le Cacheux, J. (2006), 'La nouvelle désinflation compétitive européenne', *Revue de l'OFCE*, 98: 9–36.

Diamond, P. A. (1965), 'National debt in a neoclassical growth model', *American Economic Review*, 55: 1126–50.

Duarte, M. (2003), 'The Euro and inflation divergence in Europe', *FRB of Richmond Economic Quarterly*, 89: 53–70.

Ducoudré, B. (2005), 'Fiscal policy and interest rates', OFCE Working Paper no. 7, July.

Elmendorf, D. W. and Mankiw, N. G. (1999), 'Government debt', in J. B. Taylor and M. Woodford (eds), *Handbook of Macroeconomics*, Volume IC, chapter 25, Amsterdam: Elsevier.

Farina, F. and Ricciuti, R. (2006), 'L'évaluation des politiques budgétaires en Europe: règles budgétaires et marges de manoeuvre des gouvernements', *Revue de l'OFCE*, 99: 275–301.

Fidrmuc, J. and Korhonen, I. (2001), 'Similarity of supply and demand shocks between the euro area and the CEECs', Bank of Finland, BOFIT Discussion Paper, no. 14.

Fitoussi, J.-P. and Padoa-Schioppa, F. (eds) (2005), *Report on the State of the European Union*, Basingstoke: Palgrave MacMillan.

Friedman, B. M (1978), 'Crowding out or crowding in? the economic consequences of financing government deficits', *Brookings Papers on Economic Activity*, 3: 593–641.

Gros, D. and Thygesen, N. (1992), *European Monetary Integration*, London and NY: Longman and St Martin's Press.

Hicks, J. R. (1937), 'Mr Keynes and the "Classics": a suggested interpretation', *Econometrica*, 5: 147–59.

Honohan, P. and Lane, P. R. (2003), 'Divergent inflation rates in EMU', *Economic Policy*, 37: 357–94.

Laubach, T. (2004), 'The effects of budget deficits on interest rates: a review of empirical results', Paper presented at the Sixth Banca d'Italia Workshop on Public Finances, Perugia, Italy, April.

Le Cacheux, J. (2006), 'To co-ordinate or not to co-ordinate', in I. Linsenmann, C. O. Meyer and W. Wessels (eds), *Economic Government of the EU, a Balance Sheet of New Modes of Policy Coordination*, Basingstoke: Palgrave MacMillan.

Leeper, E. (1991), 'Equilibria under "Active" and "Passive" monetary policies', *Journal of Monetary Economics*, 27: 129–47.

Modigliani, F. (1961), 'Long-run implications of alternative fiscal policies and the burden of the national debt', *Economic Journal*, 71: 730–55.

Modigliani, F. and Sutch, R. (1966), 'Innovations in interest rate policy', *American Economic Review*, 56: 178–97.

Sargent, T. J. and Wallace, N. (1981), 'Some unpleasant monetarist arithmetic', Federal Reserve Bank of Minneapolis, *Quarterly Review*, 5: 1–17.

Tobin, J. (1965), 'The burden of the public debt: a review article', *Journal of Finance*, 20: 679–82.

Woodford, M. (1996), 'Control of the public debt: a requirement for price stability?', NBER Working Paper no. 5684.

—— (2001) 'Fiscal requirement for price stability', *Journal of Money, Credit, and Banking*, 33: 669–728.

Index